AF541822

# CORPORATE LAW
# AND
# GOVERNANCE

# CORPORATE LAW AND GOVERNANCE

*Edited by*

Dr. Arun Kumar Singh

**REGAL PUBLICATIONS**

New Delhi - 110 027

CORPORATE LAW AND GOVERNANCE

ISBN 978-81-8484-373-6



*Typeset by*
THE LASER PRINTERS
8/15, 3rd Floor, Subhash Nagar, New Delhi-110027

*Printed in India at*
MAYUR ENTERPRISES,
WZ Plot No. 3, Gujjar Market, Tihar Village, New Delhi-110018

*Published by*
REGAL PUBLICATIONS
F-159, Rajouri Garden, New Delhi-110027
Phones : 45546396, 25435369
E-mail : regalbookspub@yahoo.com,
regaldeepbooks@yahoo.com

# Contents

## PART IV
## Corporate Social Responsibility



## PART V
## Money and the Corporate Law



## PART VI
## Corporate Governance

# Preface

We are living in the 21st century which is an era of globalization. In the present situation despite economic reforms we are facing economic crises. To improve this condition international economic independence has become common phrase describing the present day condition of economic relations and laws. In present day nations are so interlinked that no nation can take independent decision for their business. That is why, it is tried to regulate international market by international provisions in the form of WTO. In this challenging situation Indian law has also been changed to open the Indian market for foreigners to run their business with limited liability. Another reason to open the market for all is making countries economically sound. This is because the country will not develop unless economically sound. But simultaneously we should consider this factor that the development does not adversely affect the environment as well as the human rights of the people. This is a fact that threat perceptions relating to corporate management in the form of social cause such as standards of labors and their security measures, environmental standards, deployments of manpowers are really there. This book is the edited version of the papers written from the various legal fraternities. It contains Six Parts. The First Part is Commercial Transaction and the Corporate Law, it contains three papers. The first paper is concerned about the problems related to sale of description. The second article highlights the relevance of standard form of contract in globalized word. The third paper is related with comparative study of the traditional partnership and limited liability partnership. The Second Part is Corporate Law and Environment. It deals with Environmental Crime *vis-a-vis* Corporate Criminal responsibility and environmental protection through global partnership.

Part Third discusses consumers and the corporate sectors, it highlights Protection of Consumers considering Human Rights aspects. Part Four deals with Corporate Social Responsibility and the role of these sectors for protection of human rights. The Fifth Part is related to Money and the Corporate Law. It throws light on Money Laundering and Plastic Money. The Sixth Part emphasize on Corporate Governance. It deals with Oppression and Mismanagement, Restructuring Corporate Governance in Fraudsters' Regime, Control Mechanism in Corporate Governance and Corporate e-Governance.

DR. ARUN KUMAR SINGH

# About Contributors

**Dr. S.K. Singh**, Senior Lecturer, Department of Law, T.D.P.G. Law College, Jaunpur, U.P.

**Dr. P.K. Pandey**, Assistant Professor, Centre for Juridical Studies, Dibrugarh University, Dibrugarh, Assam.

**Dr. Arun Kumar Singh**, Assistant Professor, Department of Law, North-Eastern Hill University, Shillong, Meghalaya.

**Dr. Ranjit Sil**, Assistant Professor, Department of Law, North-Eastern Hill University, Shillong, Meghalaya.

**Dr. Rakesh Kumar**, Assistant Professor in Law, Agra College, Agra, U.P.

**Dr. C.P. Upadhyay**, Associate Professor of Law, Faculty of Law, Banaras Hindu University, Varanasi, U.P.

**Dr. Pradip Kumar Das**, Assistant Professor of Law, Haldia Law College, Haldia, West Bengal.

**Rajib Hassan**, Assistant Professor of Law, Haldia Law College, Haldia, West Bengal.

**Dr. Sukanta Sarkar**, Assistant Professor, Faculty of Management Studies, ICFAI University, Agartala, Tripura.

**Dr. Uday Shankar**, Assistant Professor of Law, Rajiv Gandhi School of Intellectual Property Law, Indian Institute of Technology, Kharagpur, West Bengal.

**Mr. Divya Tyagi**, Assistant Professor of Law, KIITS Law School, Cuttack, Orissa.

**Dr. R.D. Dubey**, Assistant Professor, Department of Law, University of North Bengal, Darjeeling, West Bengal.

**Priya Roy**, Research Scholar, Department of Law, University of North Bengal, Darjeeling.

**Dr. Ravinder Kumar**, Assistant Professor, University School of Law and Legal Studies, Guru Gobind Singh Indraprastha University, Delhi.

**Dr. Lily Srivastava**, Associate Professor in Law, SJNPG College, Associated College of Lucknow University, Lucknow, U.P.

**Dr. Naveen Kumar**, Assistant Professor, Department of Law, North-Eastern Hill University, Shillong, Meghalaya.

**Sukanya Acharya**, B.A., LL.B. (Hons.), LL.M. (Business Laws).

**Dr. Dipak Das**, Associate Professor (Law), Hidayatullah National Law University, Raipur (C.G.).

**Rakesh Gupta**, LLM, Vth Semester, 2008, Faculty of Law, University of Delhi.

# Table of Cases

# PART I

# COMMERCIAL TRANSACTION AND THE CORPORATE LAW

CHAPTER 1

# The Problem of Implied Conditions in Case of Sale by Description

*Dr. S.K. Singh*

## PROLOGUE

The social customs, morals and human behaviour are ever-changing. The success to every legal system depends upon how much it is adaptable to such situations and alive to such changes in society. The Judiciary being administrator of Justice and interpreter of law, does the same in manner to make it more purposeful and useful according to the need of the time. Any legal framework which is not so equipped is found to be branded as orthodox and may lose its efficacy. With the passage of time, the lacuna of legislation comes to surface and requires reform for mitigation of its vigour. This paper deals with some of the problems relating to Implied Conditions in Sales by description under the (Indian) Sale of Goods Act, 1930, and the English Sale of Goods Act, 1893.

It is controversial as to what amounts to sale of specific goods and goods sold by description. It has also become controversial as to what constitutes description.[1]

The provision relating to the sale of specific goods and goods sold by description as contained in the Indian Sale of Goods Act, 1930 as well as the Sale of Goods Act, 1893 of U.K. and the problems arising therefore have been discussed in the paper.

1. *Ashington Piggeries v. Christopher Hill Ltd.* (1971) 1 All. E.R. 847.

### (A) Meaning and Criteria of Sale by Description

The Act does not define the term 'description'. The ordinary principles of law should be applied in interpreting it. The term description usually means a particular class, kind, variety or species of goods. Halsbury[2] states it thus:

> "Goods are sold by description where the buyer enters into the contract of sale in reliance on the description of the goods given by or on behalf of the seller." It seems, however, the term should be confined to cases where the identification of the goods which are the subject matter of the bargain depends upon the description.[3] This seems to have been the opinion of Judge (Chalmers, the draftsman of the English Statute, as to the meaning of the term as used in that Act. In this, annotated reprint of the statute, the learned draftsman says with reference to Sec. 13 of the English Act, "Where the parties are agreed on the thing sold, a misdescription of it in the contract may be immaterial for *falsa demonstration non nocet*."[4]

In *Varley v. Whipp*[5], it is shown that a less rigid interpretation may perhaps be put upon the term 'description' as applicable to specific goods under the Act, than would have been placed upon it at Common Law.

At common Law, the most usual instance of a contract of sale of goods "by description" was an agreement to sell unascertained or future goods a certain description, i.e. kind or class. In *Heyworth v. Hutchinson*[6] a case where specific bales of wool were sold "guaranteed about similar to samples", and the question was as to the right of the buyer to reject them for inferiority, Blackburn J. said: "Generally speaking, when the contract is to any goods, such a clause is a condition going to the essence of the contract, but when the contract is as to specific goods, the clause is only collateral to the contract."

The distinction is artificial between such a case and a case where the buyer sees the goods and agrees to buy what he sees,

2. Halsbury's Laws of England, (3rd Ed.), Vol. 34, pp. 47-48.
3. Samuel Williston, "On Sales" (Revised Ed.), Vol. 1, Section 224, p. 573.
4. *Ibid.*
5. (1900) 1 Q.B. 513.
6. (1867) L.R. 2 Q.B. 451.

relying on a description given by the seller the truth of which inspection can not determine. Whether the buyer sees the goods or not, it is the description which includes him to buy, but it is not the description which identifies the goods. It seems not improbably in view of this that the English Courts may extend the definition of sale by description to every case where the buyer relies upon descriptive words.[7]

In *Sorabji Hormusha Joshi and Co. v. M. Ismail and another*[8] the Madras High Court held that where the description of the goods is the basis of the contract the case is one of sale of goods by description.

What sort of criteria have been offered by the courts for deciding whether specific goods have been sold by description? An important statement is that of Dixon J. in *Australian Knitting Mills Ltd. v. Grant*[9].

> "When identified goods are sold, it is obvious that they remain the subject of the sale whether they do, or do not, correspond with the description which the parties have given them. But, however certainly the identity of the goods may be established, the parties must, since the intention is expressed or communicated, refer in some way to the goods. They must use some 'description' to refer to them. A difficulty; therefore, cannot but arise in determining when the sale is 'by' the description and when not. Apparently the distinction is between sales of things of which the physical identity is all important. When the ground upon which the goods are selected or identified is between sales of things sought or chosen by the buyer because of their description and of things of which the goods are selected or identified is their correspondence to a description and when, therefore, it may be said that the buyer primarily relies upon their classification or possession of attributes, then, notwithstanding that they are bought by description."

In ordinary case of a sale over the counter by a shopkeeper to a customer, who calls for an article of a given description, inspects the specimens produced, and buys one, the transaction

7. *Supra* note 2, p. 574.
8. AIR 1960 Mad. 520.
9. (1933) 50 C.L.R. 387 at pp. 417-18.

is sale by description. The Judicial Committee in *Grant v. Australian Knitting Mills Ltd.*,[10] observed:

> "It may also be pointed out that there is a sale by description even though the buyer is buying something displayed before him on the counter: a thing is sold by description, though it is specific, so long as it is sold not merely as the specific thing but as a thing corresponding to a description, e.g. woollen under-garments, hot-water bottle a second hand reaping machine, to select a few obvious illustrations."
>
> It is submitted that it appear from these statements that the fact that language descriptive of the subject-matter is incorporated in a contract of sale of specific goods does not mean that the sale is automatically a sale by description. As Dixon J. pointed out:
>
> "..... however certainly the identity of the goods may be established, the parties must, since the intention is expressed or communicated, refer in some way to the goods. They must use some 'description' to refer to them."

Otherwise the only type of case in which a contract of sale of specific goods is not a sale by description would be where the buyer points to something and says: "Sell me this" and the seller says "yes". Some judicial statements might be construed as going almost this, e.g., "All sales are by description unless they are sales of specific goods sold as such, and neither expressly nor impliedly held out as having any particular description.[11] But it is submitted that where the contract is for the sale of an identified subject-matter, then the buyer must show not only that language descriptive of it was incorporated in the contract but also that it is apparent from the words used by the parties in contracting or is to be implied from the circumstances that he really and ultimately relied upon the description, before there is a sale by description.[12]

10. (1936) A.C. 100.
11. *Sargood Gardiner Pty. Ltd. v. Carmichael*, (1941) 42 S.R. (N.S.W.) 85-87.
12. Feltham, J.D., "The Sale by Description of Specific goods" (1969), Vol. 16, J.B.L., pp. 20-21.

### (B) Non-conformity with Description and Redresses of the Buyer

Ordinarily, if there is non-compliance with the terms, the buyer is entitled to reject the goods. However, it is controversial as to when goods are said to be not in conformity with the description. It is an accepted principle that trivial inconformity gives no ground for rejection. However, rejection has been allowed in a number of cases, where the goods did not correspond with their description, even though such non-confirmity was no cause of loss or damage to the buyer.[13]

In *Jormal Kastur Chand v. Hassanali Khanbhai*[14] 76 lbs, of a particular commodity were packed in a case against 80 lbs stipulated in the contract, even though the marking on the cases corresponded with the marking mentioned in the contract. It was held that the buyer was entitled to reject. The markings of cases were immaterial and the nature of contract even though the buyer suffered no loss for such packing, still he was allowed to reject the goods on the ground of non-conformity with description. The law should take into account the conflicting claims of parties and bring about justice in a way which may not operate harshly upon the seller. The proof of loss or damage by the buyer must be demanded and the convenience to the seller may also be taken into consideration.

In *Mohindra Supply Co. v. G.G. in Council*[15] where the contract related to supply of solidified fuel in containers of certain specification, a full bench of the Punjab High Court held that the inspector rejecting the goods on the ground of improper packing was not entitled to do so for the reason that the instrument of authority did not empower him to reject. From the terms of contract, it was construed that the packing in suitable container did not form part of contract—description of the goods even though in the case of solidified fuel, packing must be a very important factor in a contract for supplying that commodity.

It was the duty of the court to draw an inference from the nature of the contract, under the particular circumstances of the case that packing formed description of the contract. In this

13. *Acros Ltd. v. Ronaasen* (1933) A.C. 470; *Re Moore & Co. Ltd. v. Landauer & Co.* (121) 2 K.B. 519; *Ballantine v. Craman & Bosman* (1923) 129 L.T. 502.
14. AIR (1954) Saurashtra 79.
15. AIR (1954) Punjab 211.

connection it would be relevant to note *Justice Ameer Ali's* following observations in the case of *Andrew Yule & Co.*[16]

> "Smell is undoubtedly a quality which can form part of the description of the goods. Obviously if there was a contract for odourless paraffin oil, goods carrying smell would not conform to the description. In the above case where the contract was for the supply of hessian cloth it was held that as the hessian cloth gave a bad smell, though otherwise perfectly in order it did not conform to the description."

There is no provision in the Indian Act with regard to a situation where the buyer rejects the goods after having accepted them because they do not correspond with the description. The question is: can the seller still fulfil his contractual obligation by supplying the goods of right type to the buyer within the time stipulated for delivery or face the suit for damages? Further, if the seller is intending to supply goods of right type after they have been rejected what should he do? Also, what should the buyer do if he finds, subsequent to his acceptance that non-conformity of description of any unit or item is subsequentially impairing its value? The answer to all these problems could be found in Uniform Commercial Code.[17]

The provision of the Code relating to cure by seller by improper tender or delivery provides that: (1) where any tender or delivery by the seller is rejected because of non-conformity with description and the time for performance has not yet expired, the seller may reasonably notify the buyer of his intention to cure and may then within the contract time make a conforming delivery; and (2) where the buyer rejects a non-conforming tender which the seller had reasonable grounds to believe would be acceptable with or without money allowance, the seller may, if he reasonably notifies the buyer, have further reasonable time to substitute a conforming tender.

Section 2-608 of the Code dealing with revocation of acceptance in whole or in part says that the buyer may revoke his acceptance of a lot or commercial unit whose non-conformity substantially impairs its value to him, if he accepted it (a) on the reasonable assumption that is non-conformity would be cured and it has not been reasonably cured, or (b) without discovery or

16. AIR (1932) Cal. 879 at 879-81.
17. Uniform Commercial Code, Sections 2-508; and 2-608.

such non-conformity, if his acceptance was reasonably induced either by the difficulty of discovery before acceptance or by the seller's assurance. Clause (2) of section 2-608 says that revocation of acceptance should be made within a reasonable time.

It is submitted that the law as it exits in U.C.C. seems to be more sound that the Indian Law and, therefore, the provisions of U.C.C. if incorporated in the Indian Sale of Goods Act, 1930, would serve more useful purpose.

There are two views regarding sale by description. The first is a narrow view not going beyond the classification of goods i.e., the seller must supply peas not beans, chalk not cheese and that quality and fines do not form part of description. The second view is a broader one and it regards details of measurement, time of delivery, shipment, fitness, quality, etc. as part of contract description.

An *Ashington Piggenies v. Christopher Hill Ltd.*,[18] herring meal was contaminated with a substance, known as D.M.N.A. the addition of which rendered the goods harmful and as a result thereof, the minks died. The House of Lords observed that the description only concerned with identifying the goods contracted and would not include "fair average quality of the season" under description.[19]

It is submitted that the decision is open to objection, in so far as it affirms that (1) the goods correspond with their description and the addition of D.M.N.A. in small quantity did not change the description, and (2) "the fair average quality" did not form the description but it related to quality of the goods. It may be recollected that in *Pinnock Bross v. Lewis and Peat Ltd.*,[20] one person purchased from another person a quantity of copra cake under terms "the goods are not warranted free from any defect rendering them unmerchantable which would not be apparent on reasonable examination." It was discovered later on that the copra cake was adulterated with castor beans which rendered it poisonous. Roche J. held that the exemption clause did not protect the sellers as the goods did not correspond with their description.

18. *Supra* note 1.
19. For a criticism of this view, refer Annual Survey of Commonwealth Law (1971); Ingrid Patient, "More Lore on Section 14" (1970) 33 Mod. L. Rev. 565 and "Ruminating on Mink Food", 34 Mod. L. Rev. 557 at pp. 557-59.
20. (1923) 1, K.B. 690.

In *Assington Piggeries case,* the compounders suggested certain changes in the formula provided by the buyers. One was that herring meal, instead of Rice meal should be used. It may be pointed out that D.M.N.A. was used as a substitute to a salt which was obviously a new substance, though used in very small quantities in preparation of mink food. If the addition of a substance in small quantity changes the quality of goods, it could well be said that it amounts to supplying the goods of different description. It is not the quantity that matters but the potential danger inherent in that. In *Wilson v. Rickett Co. Ltd.*[21], an explosion was caused in a consignment of coal, when placed on fire by the buyer. This happened due to the presence of an explosive substance in the coal. The buyer would have succeeded on this ground, had he pleaded that the addition of an explosive, even in small quantities rendered it a thing of a different description. Lord Abinger observed in *Chanter v. Hopkins*[22], that if a man orders copper for sheathing ships, which is a specific type of material, the seller will not be supplying the goods as per description if he applies the copper of a different type.

In *Tehran-Europe Company Ltd. v. Balton Tractor Ltd.*[23], Diplock J. remarked that the description of the goods which is dealt within section 13 (corresponding to section 15 of the Indian Act) may will be with reference to the particular purpose for which the buyer requires them. But Davies L.J. reading the judgment of the Court, in Ashington Piggeries case, remarked that in the opinion of the court it would have made no difference if the word 'mink food' were used as contract-description for this would mean that the food was intended for mink, but not that it was suitable for mink.

It is submitted that if such were the interpretation then the very purpose of description is defeated. The seller's obligation to supply the goods of right quality should be classified under more than one section.

In *Shiv Lingappa Shankarappa v. Balakrishna Chettair & Sons*[24] the subject matter of sale was demangan tur dal which was recognised as of best quality. The dal was loaded in rain and after having soaked water, it could not be described as best quality. It

21. (1954) 1, Q.B. 598.
22. (1938) 4, M&W 399.
23. (1968) 2, Q.B. 545.
24. AIR 1962 Mad. 426.

was held that the dal supplied did not conform to the description. Also in the case of *Bihari Lal v. Baldeo Prasad,*[25] it was observed that the sale of goods by description may have reference to the quality of goods. Where food stuffs were purchased by description, an implied condition to their fitness and quality would also arise. The seller was bound to supply goods in conformity with the contract and of merchantable quality.

In *Mali & Co. v. V.A.R. Firm*[26] it was observed that in order that goods are immediately saleable in the market, they should conform to the description laid about their quality. In the case of *Bombay Burmah Trading Corporation v. Agha Mohd. Khaleel Shirazi,*[27] it was held that the goods supplied were not as per the contract description (specification) and hence they were unmerchantable and not fit for particular purpose as railway sleepers. In *Agha Mirza Naser Ali Khoyee Co. v. Cordon Woodroffe,*[28] the same High Court observed that the term that the goods shall be of merchantable quality, was fulfilled, when they did not differ from the normal quality of the described goods, including under the term "quality" that state or condition, as required by the contract. There are a number of cases decided in India to the same effect.[29] P.S. Atiyah also conceded that if the contract calls for goods of a certain quality, this may itself become a part of contract-description.[30]

In the light of the above discussion, it is suggested that 'description' being an important term under the law relating to sale of goods should be defined in such manner so as to include "the statement which may be essential to the identity of the goods as contracted e.g. as to quality or fitness, place of origin or of shipment, time of despatch or delivery-mode of packing, etc."[31] The case involved the sale of two ships with an exception of 'errors of description'. Their dead weight capacity was 360 tons, instead of 460 tons stated in the written particulars. Bailhache J.

25. AIR 1955 Mad. 271.
26. AIR 1923 Mad. 252.
27. AIR 1934 Mad. 453.
28. AIR 1937 Mad. 40.
29. *Bansilal Ramnath v. Ram Chand Tolaram,* AIR 1930, Lahore 843 (N); *Peer Mohammad v. Dallo Ram,* AIR 1919 Mad. 728.
30. Atiyah, P.S., The Sale of Goods, 4th Ed., p. 34.
31. *National Traders v. Hindustan Soap Works,* AIR 1959, Mad. 112.

held the sellers not liable on the ground that they were protected by the exception clause. The steps in his reasoning were:

(i) An exception of "errors of description" does not apply to conditions of the contract.

(ii) On the sale of a specific existing chattel, a statement as to some quality of the chattel is a warranty, and not a condition unless the absence of the quality makes the thing sold different in kind from the thing described in the contract.

(iii) The difference of 100 tons deadweight was a matter of degree, not of kind and was therefore a matter of warranty.

(iv) It bring a matter of warranty, the misdescription of the deadweight capacity was covered by the exception clause.

It is of course true that an exception of 'errors of description' does not apply to conditions, to the extent that any description not affected by the exception applies in full force and, therefore, operates as condition, but Bilhache J. was, with respect, begging the question of issue when he suggested that the exception did not apply to the descriptive words to the extent that they constituted a condition. His test was approved by Salmond J., again in respect of specific goods only, in *Taylor v. Combined Buyers.*"[32]

*THE ASHINGTON PIGGERIES CASE*[33]

Two contracts were involved in that case.

**(1) The First Contract**

The problem under the first contract was whether herring meal contaminated with DMNA (dimethinitrosamine) compiled with the description of "herring meal". All their Lordships except Lord Dilhorne held that it did so comply. However, with respect, it is submitted that the conclusion reached by Lord Dilhorne is the one which might have been expected on earlier authority. This was a sale by description of future goods, so that the words 'herring meal' defined the goods to be supplied. The buyer ought

32. (1917) 2 K.B. 606.

33. *Supra* note 1.

to have been entitled to receive goods which possess additional attributes implied by the expression 'herring meal', and which did not access additional attribute not normally incidental to such meal. As was said by Milno J. at first instance, "herring meal does not normally contain a poison".

The crucial part of the reasoning is, of course, the matter of identification. In adopting the identification test, their Lordship appear to have accepted the submission of counsel for the plaintiff and for the third party. It appear from the summary in the Law Reports that counsel argued that S. 13 related identity, while quality was dealt with in Sec. 15. However, the cases reported as being cited in support of the identity analysis dealt with the sale of existing goods or involved exception clause, or both and two of them, are *Varley v. Whipp*[34] and *Macpherson Trains & Co. Ltd. v. Howard Ross & Co. Ltd.*[35] In the former, the description by which a specific reaper had been sold was held to include it being a self-binder, at Upton, nearly new and as having been used to cut only about fifty or sixty acres. In the later case, a reference to goods as 'due London approximately 8th June' was held to the part of the contract description. But, clearly, the effects of exception clauses in the cases relief on, and the distinction between existing and future goods, appear to have been overlooked. Moreover, it also seems not unlikely that in minds of those concerned, non-compliance with description under section 13, a matter of 'fundamental breach' in the sense of discharge for breach, was identified with the 'difference in kind' type of 'fundamental breach' which was said to be unexcludable in *Smeaton Hanscomb & Co. Ltd. v. Sassoon L. Setty Son & Co.*[36] and *Karsales v. Wallis.*[37] Yet, as has already been explained, the two types of 'fundamental breach' are quite different, as the Smeaton Hancomb case itself illustrates. In that case, Devlin J. was at paints to show that 'fundamental breach' in the sense of a 'different in kind' was something narrower than a breach of condition, which is what non-compliance with S.13 amounts to.

To treat, S. 13 as requiring only that goods delivered be on the same 'kind' or 'identity' as those described is in effect to take a test devised to shelter buyers from the effect of exception

34. *Supra* note 4.
35. (1990) 1 Q.B. 513.
36. (1955) 1 W.L.R. 640.
37. (1953) 2 All E.G. 1471.

clauses, and use it to diminish the rights given to buyers by the Sale of Goods Act.

**(2) The Second Contract**

Like the first contract, the contract between the plaintiffs and the Norwegian third party was for the sale of future goods. But it differed in that it contained on exception clause, the object of which was to prevent rejection for faults and defects, or if the goods were damaged or inferior. Moreover, to the description 'Norwegian herring meal' were appended the words 'fair average quality of the season' and 'expected to analyse not less than 70 percent protein, not more than 12 percent fat and not more than 4 percent salt.' Along side this clause was the marginal note 'quantity and description'. The contract also contained a clause providing for an allowance for any excess of fat and salt upto one percent of the whole in each case, at which point the buyer would be entitled to reject.

On general principles the words "fair avérage quality of the season and the expected analysis provision" ought, had they, stood alone to have been treated as part of the description by which the mean had been sold, because they helped to define the goods which were to be delivered, but under this second contract there was, again on general principles, two reasons for restricting the contractual description. One was typographical. The words 'Norwegian herring meal' were alone, set out in capitals. This was hardly decisive and might be said to have been affect by the marginal reference to 'quantity and description'.

On general principles, then, the Norwegian herring meal was not sold by description to the extent that it had faults, defects, or was damaged or inferior.

In the event, of course, the majority of their Lordships, applying their identify test, concluded that the contaminated meal was 'Norwegian herring meal', and therefore complied with description. However, in the context of the second contract, their reference to identity' might also be justified as the application of an objective test or a stenotypes to the problem of finding the residually binding description in a contract containing exception clauses.

### (3) Sale by Description of Specific Goods and Exemption Clauses

The term 'specific goods' has also not been differentiated from goods sold by 'description', at common Law, the most usual instance of sale of goods by description was sale of unascertained or future goods of a certain description, i.e. class or kind. In ancient England, the maxim of caveat emptor was a dominant feature of sales of horses in market overt. The result was that if a buyer purchased a horse after duly examining it in the market, he could not repudiate the contract later. The reason was that such goods were known as 'specific goods' for which the said rule applied. In order to protect himself from the rigours of this rule, a buyer usually obtained warranties from the seller to the effect that he would accept the horse back if it was found to be unsound. Such warranty being subsequent and separate from the seller's promise to sell made the whole transaction look like two separate contracts, one of sale of specific goods and the other a special contract of warranty (they mostly appeared to be collateral in form). Since, the contract of sale of specific goods was executed (i.e. payment of price for delivery of horse) the other part of the contract namely (express warranty) always appeared to be executory. This distinction, is artificial and inefficient though it became the cornerstone upon which, in the nineteenth century, the whole conceptual framework of the law of sale of goods was built.[38] At common law specific goods could also be sold by description. But the intention had to be ascertained from the terms of contract and other surrounding circumstances. As a general rule, a contract for that article as such.[39]

In two earlier cases,[40] the courts had declared that where the goods were specific and the property therein had passed to the buyer after acceptance, he could not reject the goods and unilaterally revest the title in the seller.[41] These decisions were

---

38. *Supra* note 6 at 447.
39. Market overt means an open, public, legally constituted market. See Atiyah, P.S., The Sale of Goods Forth ed. pp. 194-95 for a discussion on this rule. For its history refer Hamilton, The Ancient Maxim of Caveat Emptor, (1931), Vol. 40 (Yale L.J.), p. 1133 at 1166-9.
40. *Street v. Blay* (1831) 2 B. & Ad. 456, *Dawson v. Collis* (1851) 10 CB 523.
41. See Uniform Commercial Code, S. 2-401(4), it reads : "A rejection or other refusal by the buyer to receive or retain the goods whether or not justified, or a justified revocation of acceptance revests of title to the

rather unhappy. If a buyer purchases a horse of unsound mind, warranted as sound, it will be little satisfaction to him if he gets the horse at half the price and damages for breach of warranty of its unsoundness.[42] It is noteworthy that this anomaly has been removed in India[43] as well as in England.[44]

At common law, a statement as to quality of goods sold by description amounted to 'condition' and in case of specific goods, amounted to 'warranty'.[45] In a case it was held that the transaction was sale by description and sale being conditional, the property in the goods had not passed, and hence the buyer could reject the machine.[46] But, in a later case[47] where certain ships, each with a dead weight capacity of 360 tons were sold with particulars that they were, *inter alia* of 460 tons each and that the sellers were 'not accountable for efforts in description', it was held that there was only a breach of warranty and not condition. Thus, these two cases stand in contrast—in the former, the existing goods were construed as goods 'sold by description' and in the latter, similarly situated goods were held to be 'specific'. It is, therefore, clear that, the line of demarcation between 'condition' and 'warranty' or between 'specific goods' and 'goods sold by description' is not very sharp.

---

goods in the seller. Such revesting occurs by operation of law and is not a sale.

42. See Williston, 'Rescission for Breach of Warranty', Vol. 16 H.L.R. 465 at 472.
43. Section 3 of the Amendment Act, 1963 omitted the words "or where the contract is for specific good, the property in which he has passed to the buyer" from Section 13(2) of the Sale of Goods Act, 1930. The effect of this omission is that the buyer shall have a right to reject the goods even though the property in them has passed to him.
44. Section 4(1) of the Misrepresentation Act, 1967 repealed the words "or where the contract is for specific goods the property in which has passed to the buyer" in Section 11(1)(C) of the Sale of Goods Act, 1893. Section 4(2) inserted the words "except where section 34 of this Act otherwise provides" before Section 35.
45. See *Street v. Blay* (1831) 2 B & Ad. 456; *Harrison v. Knowles & Foster* (1917) 2 K.B. 606. Also see *Nichol v. Godts* (1854) 10 ex. 191 at 193 where Park, C.B. remarked that "Warranty affects quality and not the nature of article itself."
46. *Willer v. Schillizzi* (1856) 17 C.B. 619 (where the Sale was of a machine, stated to be new which the buyer had not seen).
47. *Jones v. Just* (1867) L.R. 3 Q.B. 197.

The essential difference between a contract of sale of unascertained goods and a contract of sale of specific goods is also relevant to the construction of exemption clauses as to matters of description. In the case of contracts of sale of unascertained goods such clauses may be narrowly construed so as to avoid the result that the seller's promises are devoid of all contractual effect.[48] Where a contract is for the sale of an identified subject, matter, there is less scope for such an agreement. The seller is in any event bound to deliver the identified article regardless of whether or not it corresponds with descriptive language. The fact that the article does not so correspond, will not strip the seller is promise of all contractual effect. Nonetheless, even in the case of contract of sale of specific goods exemption clauses are normally narrowly construed so as not entirely to eliminate all necessity of correspondence with the contract description.[49] On the other hand, in the case of a contract of sale of specific goods an exemption clause may modify the scope of the description with which the goods must correspond, may have the effect of putting language which would otherwise be treated as part of the description outside the scope of Section 15 of Sale of Goods Act, 1930.[50] It may be that in an appropriate case the language of the exemption clause might show that the contract was for the purchase of the article as it stood and that the buyer bought without reliance on any descriptive language used, thus totally excluding the concept of a sale by description.

48. *Supra* note 11, p. 24.
49. *Shepherd v. Kain* (1821) 5 B. & Alld. 290; Compare *Taylor v. Bullen* (1850) 5 Ex. 779.
50. Compare *Taylor v. Bullen* (1850) 5 Ex. 779.

# CHAPTER 2

# Relevance of Standard Form Contracts in Globalised Commercial World: An Analytical Study

*Dr. P.K. Pandey*

## INTRODUCTION

In globalised commercial world, the traditional concept of contract that both parties must be agreed, there must be *consensus ad idem* and so on could not survive for a long time. Now, where everything is going very fast, no one has time for such type of transactions. Under such circumstances, the concept of Standard Form Contract (SFC) came into being. SFCs are not a new method of conducting business. 'In the fifteenth century, such contracts were already in use in parts of Europe, when standard insurance policies had been issued; as well as worldwide in the seventeenth century, when charter-parties and bills of lading were drafted in a standard form.'[1] The general use of standard form contracts became widespread in the industrial revolution era of the nineteenth century.[2] Since then, the use of standard form contracts has become the main method of doing business wherever there is legal-commercial activity. Furthermore, the development of Internet transactions has given standard term

1. W.S. Holdsworth, History of English Law, 7th ed. (London: Methuen 1956), 255-256 and 290-295.
2. P. Aronstam, Consumer Protection, Freedom of Contract and the Law. (Cape Town: Juta & Company Limited, 1979) at 17.

contracts an increased importance.[3] In this chapter, the concept, relevance and protective measures evolved by Judiciary has been dealt.

## WHAT IS STANDARD FORM CONTRACT?

Those contracts, in which one party proposes to other party with pre-determined fixed conditions or terms for contract and other party has to accept or refuse but cannot alter any term or condition, are called SFC. *New Jersey Law Revision Commission* defines SFC as:

> "Standard form contract" is a written or other record of legal terms used by a seller offering to sell a product to a buyer in an open market for the purpose of specifying the rights and obligations of buyer and seller in a sale.[4]

*Australian Securities and Investments Management* defines SFC as:

> In broad terms, a standard form contract will typically be one that has been prepared by one party to the contract (the supplier) and is not subject to negotiation between the parties—that is, it is offered on a 'take it or leave it' basis.[5]

The characteristics of SFCs are as:

- It is an agreement between two parties that contains pre - drawn terms and is used by a business entity or firm in transactions with consumers.
- Generally, the will of the user of such contracts' terms dominates the transaction.
- The consumer is required to accept contractual terms without negotiations notwithstanding some particulars.
- Often the consumer accepts such terms without knowing or understanding such.

In general terms, standardized printed forms of contracts with blank spaces to be filled in by each individual are offered by one party and second party has to fill in and sign on, after that a

3. Available at http://lawspace.law.uct.ac.za/dspace/bitstream/2165/242/1/BraunJ_2005.pdf
4. Final Report relating to Standard Form Contracts, 2008 available at http://www.lawrev.state.nj.us/rpts/contract.pdf
5. http://www.asic.gov.au/asic/asic.nsf/byHeadline/Unfair-contract-terms-law?opendocument

completed contract comes into existence between the parties. SFC is a better option for smooth running of business as well as for society. The practice of entering into contract through SFC has become very common and need of hour. The main cause for the introduction of SFC is the enormous increase in the number of contracts. For instance, Indian Railway is entering into variety of contracts daily with huge numbers. It is not possible for Indian Railway to negotiate separately with each and every person in every case. If the Railway will start to draft separate contract with each person, the business will be closed.

## NEED AND IMPORTANCE

As **Kessler** has observed that 'in so far as the reduction of costs of production and distribution thus achieved is reflected in reduced prices, society as a whole ultimately benefits from the use of standard contracts.'[6] Further, there are a lot of advantages of SFCs like:

- Certainty of terms
- Time Saving
- Uniformity
- Reduction in transactions costs

*Cheshire's Law of Contract* mentions that the process of mass production and distribution, which has largely supplemented if it has not supplemented individual effort, has introduced the mass contract—uniform documents which must be accepted by all who deal with large-scale organizations. Such documents are not in themselves novelties: the classical lawyer of the mid-Victorian years found himself struggling to adjust his simple conceptions of contract to the demands of such powerful bodies as the railway companies. But in the present century, many corporations, both public and private, have found it useful to adopt, as the basis of their transactions, a series of standard forms with which their customers can do little but comply.

But, taking the recourse of helplessness of individuals, the businessmen or the financially stronger party started to put such type of terms in contract which are of escaping nature. Generally, the stronger party mentions such terms which may be

6. Contracts of Adhesion—Some Thoughts about Freedom of Contract, 1943, *Columbia Law Review*, 629.

interpreted for his benefit and as the weaker party has not any option so, generally, no one cares about the terms of contract. As **Lord Denning** observed in *Thornton v. Shoe Lane Parking Ltd.*[7] that 'no customer in thousand ever read the conditions if he had stopped to do so, he would have missed the train or the boat.'

The SFCs have various names, the French call them "Contracts d'adhesion", and the Americans call them "adhesion contracts" or "contracts of adhesion". In Black's Law Dictionary[8], 'Adhesion contracts' are defined as follows:

> A standard-form contract prepared by one party, to be signed by the party in a weaker position, usually a consumer, who has little choice about the terms. Also termed Contract of adhesion; adhesory contract; adhesionary contract; take it or leave it contract; leonire contract.

*New Jersey Law Revision Commission* observed that 'the use of standard form contracts eliminates the need to negotiate contracts individually for transactions taking place in the marketplace and may reduce the costs of goods and services. However, since the seller alone drafts standard form contracts, they may contain one-sided and unfair terms.'[9]

In *Indian Contract Act, 1872*, there is no any provision relating to SFC. To protect the weaker party of contract, the Judiciary has played a vital role and in this connection judiciary evolved various principles also. But, in those circumstances where the party has accepted the terms knowingly or unknowingly, it is very tough to provide relief as 'it is the established position of law in India and UK that the courts interfere with the provisions of standard form contracts only in instances where it appears that a party may have exercised undue influence over the weaker counterparty.'[10] Protective measures evolved by Judiciary are as—

**Adequate and Reasonable Notice**: Where a party is offering SFC, he must provide adequate, reasonable and proper notice regarding terms/conditions of proposal. The person to whom the offer is made must have opportunity to take decision to enter

7. (1971) 1 All ER 686 CA.
8. 7th Ed. at 38.
9. Final Report relating to Standard Form Contracts, 2008 available at http://www.lawrev.state.nj.us/rpts/contract.pdf
10. *Surinder Singh Barmi v. IPL and another* decided on February 08, 2013 available at http://indiankanoon.org/doc/24381926/

into such contract or not; after taking into account the all facts and matters relating to offer. The offeror must take all steps to drag the attention of other party concerned. When one party is offering as SFC and there are some exemption clauses also, it is his responsibility to bring those exemptions in knowledge of other party otherwise those exemptions will not be binding on other party.

There is a leading case on this point *Henderson v. Stevenson*[11] in which the plaintiff purchased a steamer ticket. On back side of ticket, there were some exemption clauses under which company was exempted from liability in case of loss or injury to passengers or luggage but, to indicate those exemption clauses, there was no any mark on the face of ticket. Due to the fault caused by company's servants, the plaintiff lost his luggage and claimed for damage. The House of Lords held that the plaintiff is entitled to recover the loss and the exemption clause is not binding on plaintiff due to lack of reasonable notice.

But, if the offeror has done what he could do reasonably to attract the other party's attention but other party does not read or see those terms, it will be presumed that there was adequate and reasonable notice about those conditions. In *Parker v. South Eastern Railway Co.*[12] the plaintiff deposited his bag in defendant's cloakroom. On depositing, he got receipt on which an indication was mentioned as 'see back' where there were various printed conditions including a condition in which liability for any package was limited only for £10. Plaintiff's bag was lost in defendant's cloakroom and plaintiff claimed for bag's value which was more than £10. Plaintiff admitted that there were printed matter on ticket but denied having read them. The court held that the conditions mentioned on ticket were binding on plaintiff.

In India, the law laid down in Parker's case has been followed.

**Notice must be Contemporaneous**: It means the terms of contract by intended parties must be given to other party before the contract or at least at the time of contract so that the other party can take decision to enter into contract or not. If the party who is offering standard form does not provide terms and

11. (1875) 2 HL (SC) App. 470.
12. (1877) 2 CPD 416.

conditions contemporaneous the other party will not be bound by those terms or conditions. For instance in *Olley v. Marborough Court Ltd.*[13], a couple hired a room in a hotel. They paid the amount and received the receipt for the money paid. When they entered in the room, they saw a board inside the room on which a statement was written, as 'the proprietors will not be held responsible for articles lost or stolen'. The couple lost their articles. It was held that they were entitled to recover the loss. It was observed that the hotel manager could not seek the protection of the exemption clause present on the board in the room, because it was a subsequent notice and not the notice given at the time of taking the room for hire. Therefore, notice must be always contemporaneous with the contract.

## UNREASONABLE TERMS

To protect the weaker party of contract, the Judiciary has evolved the principle of exclusion of unreasonable terms. If the terms of contract are unreasonable, they will be treated as unenforceable. Unreasonable terms are those which can defeat the very purpose of contract or they are inconsistent with public policy. For example, a laundry receipt containing conditions that customer can claim only 15% of the market price of value of article if lost[14], only 8% of the cost of a garment would be payable in case of loss[15].

## EXCLUSION CLAUSE FOR TORT

Though a party can take the plea of exclusion clause, but that exclusion clause will protect only in respect of contractual obligation and not in Tort. If the SFC offeror exempts himself from any liability under contract, those exemptions will be available only for contract. For example, A, a service provider delivered his goods as bailment for consideration and there are various exemption clauses where he is free from any liability under contract of bailment. He can take plea of exclusion clause but if there is ground of any tortuous liability he cannot escape from this and will be liable.

13. (1949) 1 All ER 127 CA.
14. *Lilly White v. Mannuswami*, AIR 1966 Madras 13.
15. *M. Siddalingappa v. T. Nataraj*, AIR 1970 Mysore 154.

## STRICT CONSTRUCTION

The terms of exclusion from contractual liability are constructed strictly. An ambiguity in respect of meaning of terms of contract will be constructed in favour of weaker party. The term *'contra proferentem'* is applicable in such cases which means that 'if there is any doubt as to the meaning and scope of excluding or limiting term, the ambiguity will be resolved against the party who has inserted it.

## THEORY OF FUNDAMENTAL BREACH

This theory has been evolved by Judiciary to control unreasonable consequences of wide and sweeping exemption clauses. *Davies v. Collins*[16] is a well-known leading case on this point where the plaintiff gave his dress to the defendant for cleaning and received a receipt for the amount paid. The receipt contained a statement that 'every care is exercised in cleaning and all orders are accepted at owner's risk'. The sub-contractor of the defendant lost the dress. It was held the defendant was liable because he committed fundamental breach in giving dress to the sub-contractor for washing and he did not take personal care as it was in the receipt given to the plaintiff.

**Exemption Clause and Third Party**: As it is clear that the contract is enforceable and binding only between parties so any third party can not avail any benefit under any contract. If there is any exemption clause in contract, that will be binding only on parties concerned of that contract and not on third parties. If any third party is injured and there is exemption clause, the exemption clause cannot protect the pleading party. Such types of provisions are intended for the protection of life and security of people at mass level who are not parties of a contract otherwise two persons can enter into contract and can provide a lot of exemptions and in this way they can injure to anyone. For instance, if 'A', a courier and 'B', a businessman, entered into contract and 'B' is under duty to send goods from Allahabad to Varanasi 'A' is exempted from any loss caused by goods to anyone. But, due to explosion in goods, 'D', a passenger, is injured. Here 'A' cannot plea that he was exempted rather he is liable for injury caused by his goods.

16. (1945) 1 All ER 247.

In *Haseldine v. C.A. Daw & Son Ltd.*[17], the owners of a block of flats employed the defendants' engineers to repair a lift in the building. Owing to their negligence, the lift was badly repaired and the plaintiff, a visitor to the premises was injured when the lift fell to the bottom of the lift-shaft. The defendant was held liable in tort for negligence. It was also held that the duty to the third party does not arise out of the contract, but independently of it.

In *M.K. Abraham and Co. v. State of Kerala and another*[18], decided on 7 July 2009 the Supreme Court held that if a contract consists of a printed form with cyclostyled amendments, typed additions and deletions and handwritten corrections, an endeavour shall be made to give effect to all the provisions. However, in the event of apparent or irreconcilable inconsistency, the following rules of construction will normally apply:

(i) The cyclostyled amendments will prevail over the printed terms;
(ii) The type-written additions will prevail over the printed terms and cyclostyled amendments; and
(iii) Hand written corrections will prevail over the printed terms, cyclostyled amendments and typed written additions.

In *Surinder Singh Barmi v. IPL and another*[19], decided on February 8, 2013 the Competition Commission of India held that the Commission may interfere with the provisions of standard form contracts only in instances where it appears that a party may have exercised undue influence over the weaker counterparty in contravention of the provisions of the Act.

Law Commission of India[20] observed that SFCs are really pretended contracts that have only the name of contract. In these, a single will is exclusively predominant, acting as unilateral will, which dictates its terms not to an individual but to an indeterminate collectively. The individual's participation consists of a mere adherence, often unknowing, to the document drafted unilaterally and insisted upon by the powerful enterprise, the

17. (1941) 2 KB 343.
18. http://164.100.9.38/judis/handle/123456789/25994.
19. http://indiankanoon.org/doc/24381926/
20. 103rd Report on Unfair Terms in Contract, 1984.

conditions imposed by the document upon the customer, are not open to discussion, nor are they subject to negotiation between the parties, but the contract has to be accepted or rejected as a whole. The pen of the individual signing on the dotted line does not really represent his substantial agreement with the terms in it, but creates a fiction that he has agreed to such terms. The characteristics, usually and traditionally associated with a contract, such as freedom to contract and consensus, are absent from these so-called contracts. Further, the Law Commission recommended to insert a new Chapter IV-A as:

> **Section 67-A.** (1) Where the Court, on the terms of the contract or on the evidence adduced by the parties, comes to the conclusion that the contract or any part of it is unconscionable, it may refuse to enforce the contract or the part that it holds to be unconscionable.
> (2) Without prejudice to the generality of the provisions of this section, a contract or part of it is deemed to be unconscionable if it exempts any party thereto from—(a) the liability for wilful breach of the contract, or (b) the consequences of negligence.

**Law Commission of India** in its 199$^{th}$ Report on 'Unfair (Procedural & Substantive) Terms in Contract', 2006 observed that the recommendation made by the Law Commission in its 103$^{rd}$ Report (1984), was wide, and did not restrict itself to any particular type of contract. The Commission recommended *'Unfair (Procedural and Substantive) Terms in Contract Bill, 2006'* to declare certain provisions of the laws relating to contracts and specific performance, as procedural and substantive, to further define unfairness in contracts, as procedural and substantive, to determine impact of unfairness on contracts, to provide guidelines for such determination and to enable Courts to grant certain reliefs to relieve parties from the effect of unfairness in contracts. The Bill provides in detail on unfair terms in contracts. Relating to unfairness, it divides in two parts—procedural and substantive. In procedural, there are few sections of Indian Contract Act, 1872 as Secs. 15, 16 and 19-A, 17, 18, 19. A contract or a term thereof is procedurally unfair if it has resulted in an unjust advantage or unjust disadvantage to one party on account of the conduct of the other party or the manner in which or circumstances under which the contract has been entered into or the term thereof has been arrived at by the parties.[21] A contract or a term thereof is substantively unfair if such contract or the term thereof is in itself harsh, oppressive or unconscionable to one of the parties.[22] Sec. 9 says that 'a contract or a term thereof shall be deemed to be substantively unfair if it:

(a) excludes or restricts liability for negligence;
(b) excludes or restricts liability for breach of express or implied terms of a contract without adequate justification therefor.'

Sec. 17 provides that when a contract or a term is unfair, the Court may grant any one or more of the following reliefs:

(a) refusing to enforce the contract or the term thereof;
(b) declaring the contract or the term is unenforceable or void;
(c) varying the terms of contract so as to remove the unfairness;
(d) refund of the consideration or price paid;
(e) compensation or damages;
(f) permanent injunction;
(g) mandatory injunction; or
(h) any other relief which the interests of justice require as a consequence of the non-enforcement of the contract or the term thereof which is unfair:

Provided that where the contract or its term is procedurally unfair as stated in section 5, the person who suffers the disadvantage may, at his option, insist that the contract or term shall be performed, and that he shall be put in the position in which he would have been if the conduct, manner or circumstances referred to in that section did not permit the disadvantageous term to form part of the contract.

For the purpose of granting the reliefs under above-mentioned, the Court may determine if any of the terms of the contract which are unfair are severable and thereafter whether and to what extent and in what manner, the remaining terms of the contract can be enforced or given effect to.

21. Sec. 5.
22. Sec. 12.

## CONCLUDING OBSERVATIONS

The device of a new type of contract, i.e. standard form contract is common in today's complex structure of giant corporations with vast infrastructural organization. The use of standard terms and conditions is confined not only to contracts in commercial transactions, but contracts with public authorities, multinational corporations, or in banking and insurance business, etc. Standard form contracts have become common place in the trade practices of the 20th and 21st century. They are found in almost every branch of industry and commerce, consumer contracts, employment, hire purchase, insurance, administration, any form of travel, or the courier services, or while downloading software contracts from the internet, etc.[23] In this scenario, such questions that what are the protective measures available in case of SFC are of utmost importance. To protect the weaker party of contract, undoubtedly the Judiciary has played a crucial role but, in fact, Judiciary also felt helplessness in those cases where the reasonable and adequate notice is given but the weaker party has not seen or has seen but accepted that condition only due to some circumstances.

23. Law Commission of India, 199th Report on 'Unfair (Procedural & Substantive) Terms in Contract'.

CHAPTER 3

# Partnership and Limited Liability: A Comparative Analysis of Indian Partnership Act, 1932 and Limited Liability Partnership Act, 2008

*Dr. Arun Kumar Singh*

## INTRODUCTION

The moment we start talking about partnership a notion appears in the mind that two or more persons are agreed to run a business for getting some benefit. It is true that when a business is run by two or more persons it will provide more benefits rather than a sole trade business. This fact appears correct mathematically. For example, A and B were friends. They started their business separately. A invested Rs. X in his business and B invested Rs. Y in his business. After one year the amount of A became X times more and B's amount became Y times more. After one year from the date of starting the business A and B decided to merge their business as well as amounts. The mixed invested amount of A and B will be $X^2+Y^2$. The sons of A and B decided to run their business jointly. A's son invested Rs. X and B's son invested Rs Y. their total amount is X+Y. Suppose after one year the invested money became X+Y times more because of profit in their business. It will be $(X+Y)^2$, i.e. $X^2+ Y^2 + 2XY$. If we compare the amount of the business of fathers and the amount of the business of sons it is found that the amount of sons is 2XY more. However, the investments in both businesses are same. From the above facts it appears that business run in partnership provide more benefit in comparison of sole trade business because it is an improvement of sole trade business where one single individual with his own resources, skill and efforts carries on his own business. That is why the Indian legislatures decided to make provisions for the business run in the partnership. Firstly, it was provided under the Indian Contract Act, 1872.[1] But it was repealed in 1932 and new legislation known as The Indian Partnership Act, 1932 came into force.[2] Under the Partnership Act the liability of partners is unlimited because it is based on mutual agency. The concept of mutual agency is that all are principles and all are agents. But in 2008 a new legislation came into existence known as Limited Liability Partnership, 2008 which provides that liability of partners in a partnership business will be limited. But this Act is other than the Indian Partnership Act, 1932 and will not affect the provisions of the Act of 1932. Although Limited Liability Partnership and Company both have legal entity as well as limited liability for the partners and stakeholders respectively, but limited liability partnership is different from the company. The objective of this paper is to make the comparative study of the Indian Partnership Act, 1932 and the Limited Liability Partnership Act, 2008. And also it is attempted to point out the pros and cons of both Acts. Apart from this it is also tried to highlight the role of judiciary wherever felt necessary.

## MEANING AND CONCEPT OF PARTNERSHIP

Partnership is a form of organization where any two or more people can join together for carrying on some business jointly. First time it was defined in the Indian Contract Act, 1872 as "partnership is the relation which subsists between the persons who have agreed to combine their property, labour or skill in some business and to share the profits thereof between them".[3]

According to Pollock, "partnership is the relation which subsists between persons who have agreed to share the profits of

1. Sections 239-266 of the Indian Contract Act, 1872 provided about the partnership.
2. The Act came into force on 1st October 1932 except section 69 which came into force on 1st October, 1933.
3. Section 239 of the Indian Contract Act, 1872.

a business carried on by all or any of them on behalf of all of them."[4]

The Indian Partnership Act, 1932 adopted the definition of Pollock with slight modification. It provides "partnership is the relation between the persons who have agreed to share the profits of business carried on by all or any of them acting for all."[5]

The definition given under section 4 of the Indian Partnership Act, 1932 replaced the definition given in section 239 of the Indian Contract Act, 1872. The definition of partnership given in the Indian Partnership Act is wider than the definition of Indian Contract Act because it includes the important element of 'mutual agency' which was absent in the definition of the Indian Contract Act, 1872. From the above definitions it appears that minimum number of persons to create partnership is two. But about the maximum number of partners in a business the Act of 1932 is silent. That is why to determine the maximum number of partners in a firm we have to consider the Companies Act, 1956 which imposes limitation to the maximum number of partners in a partnership firm. In a partnership for the purpose of carrying on banking business the maximum number of partners will be 10 whereas incase of other businesses the maximum number of the partners will be of 20.[6] If the number of the partners exceeds above limit it must be registered under the Companies Act, 1956. Otherwise the association will be considered as illegal association.[7] So far as the liability is concerned, in the Indian Partnership Act, 1932 the liability of partners are unlimited because it is based on mutual agency.[8] But the only thing absent in the traditional partnership is legal entity because the moment all the partners or all but one partner leave the firm the partnership is dissolved.[9] This is because a traditional firm is nothing but collective name of the

4. Pollock's DIGEST OF THE LAW OF PARTNERSHIP in Avtar Singh, Law of Partnership, Principles, Practice and Taxation, 2003, Eastern Book Company, Lucknow, p. 9.
5. Section 4 of the Indian Partnership Act, 1932.
6. Section 11 of the Companies Act, 1956.
7. Section 11(2) of the Companies Act, 1956, See also *Badri Prasad v. Nagarmal*, 1959 Supp (1) SCR 749.
8. Section 4 of the Act.
9. Section 39 of the Indian Partnership Act, 1932.

partnership.[10] But for the tax purposes it is considered to have legal entity. The word person as used in the Income Tax Act, 1969 includes a firm under the category of assesses.[11] If a traditional partnership is compared with a company it is found that the company has legal entity in all senses but the liability of its stakeholders is limited up to their shares and a stakeholder can transfer his share to anyone he likes, whereas a partner cannot substitute anyone on his place unless all other partners are agreed to the same.

## INTRODUCTION OF LIMITED LIABILITY PARTNERSHIPS IN INDIA

So far as limited liability partnership is concerned it is a new concept. Limited liability partnership (herein after LLP) concept was introduced in order to adopt a corporate form, which combines the organizational flexibility and tax status of partnership with advantage of limited liability for its partners. In India, businesses mainly operate as companies, sole proprietorships and partnerships. Introducing LLPs, as a new business structure would be helpful to solve the problems regarding sole proprietorship which is generally unregulated, the partnership which is regulated by the Indian Partnership Act, 1932, and Limited Liability Companies, governed by the Companies Act, 1956.

First time the introduction of limited liability partnership was thought in 1957 which was rejected by the 7th Law Commission of India. Thereafter in 1997 Abid Hussain Committee recommended the introduction of Limited Liability Partnerships in India. Again in 2003 Naresh Chandra Committee was constituted for the above purpose. Naresh Chandra Committee submitted its report on 23rd July 2005 and made the following observations: "In increasing litigious market environment, prospect of being a member of a partnership firm with unlimited liability is, to say the least, risky and unattractive. Indeed the chief reason why the firms of professionals, such as accountants, have not grown in size to successfully meet the challenge of the international competition. This makes LLPs a most attractive vehicle for partnership among professionals such

10. *Supra* note 8.
11. Section 2(31) of the Income Tax Act.

as lawyers and accountants." In the Committee's view, the scope of LLP should be made available to firms providing professional services, as opposed to trading firms and/or manufacturing firms for the reason it will help evaluate its advantage and risks; and based on such evaluation and experience. The LLP form could be considered for extension to small-scale Industries.[12] The LLP Act, 2008 came into existence after the recommendation of Irani Committee. In 2007 LLP Bill was referred to the Parliamentary Committee for Examination. The Committee submitted its report to the Parliament on 27th November 2007 with certain changes. So, on 1st May 2008 new Bill was approved by the Union Cabinet. On 21st October 2008, the LLP Bill, 2008 was introduced in the Parliament. The LLP Bill was passed by Rajya Sabha on 24th October 2008 and by Lok Sabha on 12th December, 2008. The President gave his assent on the Bill on 7th January 2009. The LLP Act, 2008 was published in the Official Gazette on 9th January 2009 and notified on 31st March 2009. The Act came into force on 1st April 2009.

## PROVISIONS OF LIMITED LIABILITY PARTNERSHIP IN OTHER COUNTRIES

The concept of limited partnership prevails in many countries, especially developed countries. Under this provision, "general partners", including those in actual control of operations of a partnership business, alone would be exposed to unlimited liability to debtors of the business, while the enterprise would be able access capital from other partners whose liability would be limited to their contribution of capital. The LLPs are very popular form of business in United States and United Kingdom.

### (A) United States of America

In the United States of America, the limited partnerships emerged in the early 1990s; while only two states allowed LLPs in 1992, over forty had adopted LLP statutes by the time LLPs were added to the Uniform Partnership Act (UPA) in 1996. In the United States, each individual state has its own law governing

12. Dr. Pradeep Kumar Singh, 'Limited Liability Partnership (LLPs) & Taxation Issues', http//www.indiamba.com visited on 7 September 2009.

their formation.[13] Although found in many business fields, the LLP is an especially popular form of organization among professionals, particularly lawyers, accountants and architects. In Texas (LLP statute was enacted in 1991 which provided response to the liability that had been imposed on partners of firms by government agencies in relation to massive savings and loan failures in the 1980s.[14] Another reason for the introduction of LLPs was the increasing number of malpractice suits that were being filed against larger general partnerships. The statute protected partners from personal liability for claims related to a co-partner's negligence, omission, in competency, errors or malfeasance. In 1994 the Revised Uniform Partnership Act (RUPA) was promulgated to reinforce the changes occurring in partnership law generally. A number of states permitted formation of LLPs. In 1997, the success of LLPs in various states triggered the adoption of comprehensive LLP provisions into the RUPA. By 2001 the concept of LLPs spread rapidly from 2 states in 1992 to all 51 states.[15]

**(B) United Kingdom**

The Limited Liability Partnership is a recent development in UK. It has been introduced by the Limited Liability Partnerships Act, 2000. The Act became law on 1st April 2001. In an LLP, all partners have a form of limited liability, similar to that of the shareholders of a corporation. However, the partners have the right to manage the business directly, and different level of tax liability than in a corporation. Under UK law, the LLP is a "fiscal transparency". In other words, it is not subject to taxation. Only the members are liable to taxation. Since the middle of the 19th century, there has been a continuing pressure to relax the provisions surrounding the limited company form and to introduce a new corporate structure for small and medium sized business organisations. In pursuance of that, major accountancy firms organised in the form of partnerships with unlimited liability, wanting to limit the liability of an individual partner to act specifically related to that partner, launched a campaign for

13. Ashish Ahuja, 'Limited Liability Partnership Act, 2009: Some issues' on http://www.bcasonline.org/webadmin/res_material/resfiles last visited on 11th November, 2010.
14. *Ibid.*
15. *Ibid.*

the creation of the LLPs in the UK in between 1980-1990.[16] The UK Companies Act, 1989 was amended to allow accountancy firms to work as limited liability companies.[17] The joint and several liabilities of general partners, however, remained. In the 1990s, the accountancy firms in the UK again campaigned to secure proportional liability in Partnership firms. This finally led to the passing of the Limited Liability Partnership Act, 2000. The UK Limited Liability Partnership Act, 2000 came into effect in April 2001 and introduced an idea for international business. The essential features of the UK's LLP are that, it is a body corporate and has a separate legal personality.[18] An LLP can own any property and undertake any contract. The liability of members is normally limited to the extent of their contribution.

## COMPARATIVE ANALYSIS OF INDIAN PARTNERSHIP ACT, 1932 AND LIMITED LIABILITY PARTNERSHIP ACT, 2008

LLP is a body incorporates formed and incorporated under the Limited Liability Partnership Act, 2008 which is a distinct legal entity separate from that of its partners. It has perpetual succession. Any change in the partners will not affect the existence, rights or liabilities of the LLP. This in term is heard once in a way in this country as a concept that is worthy of consideration for introduction. In India, the businesses operate mainly as companies, sole proprietorship and partnerships. Different laws of the country govern these. However, there is a gap in the business structure, which needs to be filled so as to enable high growth in the service sector especially that related to the professionals. This gap is sought to be bridged by introduce-ing a Limited Liability Partnership Law.[19] So far as a comparison between limited liability partnership and traditional partnership is concerned the LLP is a separate legal entity but the liability of their partners limited to their agreed contribution.[20] A traditional

16. *Ibid.*
17. *Ibid.*
18. *Ibid.*
19. Garima, 'The Concept of Limited Liability Partnership: Application of the LLP Regime in India and its feasibility' on http://www.legalserviceindia.com/article/l122-Limited-Liability-Partnership.html' visited on 1st September 2010.
20. Section 3 of the Limited Liability Partnership Act, 2008.

partnership firm is not a legal entity. The limited liability partnership is not liable for the acts done by the partners outside the scope of their authority and the partners are also not responsible for the wrongful acts of any other partner.[21] Similarly, any obligation of the Limited Liability Partnership is the sole obligation of the Limited Liability Partnership and not of its partners personally. So they are protected from the act of other partners which is different from the traditional partnership. In the traditional partnership every partner is jointly and severally liable and the firm is also liable for the wrongful acts or omissions of any partner.[22]

In *Hamlyn v. John Huston & Co.*,[23] one of the partners of a firm bribed the clerk of the other firm to get some secret documents due to which it suffered loss. He sued the defendant firm and the firm was held liable.

As far as taxation is concerned a partnership shall be treated as a separate legal entity. For the purposes of taxation the LLP's will also be treated as a "firm" as defined in the Partnership Act, 1932. But the problem is that, in case of traditional partnership the rate is 30%+Surcharge+Cess, while it is not clear in case of Limited Liability Partnership. In traditional partnership the registration of a partnership firm is not compulsory as the law is silent on it but registration and incorporation of a LLP is compulsory as per the LLP Act, 2008 itself.[24] There is certain advantage of limited Liability Partnership. It is organized and operate on the basis of agreement. In case of traditional partnership although a minor cannot be the partner of a firm but with the consent of other partners he can be inducted for his benefit.[25] He has freedom to be or not to be the partner of the firm after attaining the age of majority. But after attaining the majority he is bound to exercise this option. If he opts negative, he and his property will not be liable for the former act of the firm. But, if he exercises his option in positive sense then he will be personally liable for the former acts done by firm and partners (during the period when he was minor).[26] Not only this, even if he did not

21. Section 27 of the LLP Act, 2008.
22. Sections 25 and 26 of the Indian Partnership Act, 1932.
23. (1903) 1 KB 81.
24. Section 34 of the LLP Act, 2008.
25. Section 30 of the Indian Partnership Act, 1932.
26. Section 30(7) (a) of the Indian Partnership Act, 1932.

exercise this option after attaining the age of majority and six months passed he shall be deemed to be partner of the firm.[27]

One more thing of Limited Liability partnership is that, it is mandatory to file disclosures by Limited Liability Partnership as per the LLP Act, 2008 itself. The law being silent on traditional partnership firms is not mandatory to file disclosures. Apart from the foregoing in Limited Liability Partnership registration is compulsory[28] but it is optional in case of traditional partnership.

In case of traditional partnership audit is compulsory, whereas in case of limited liability partnership the audit is required if the contribution is 25 lakhs or annual turnover is 40 lakhs or above. It may be that bankers have more creditworthy in the Limited Liability Partnership rather than a traditional partnership because LLP has legal entity. Not only has this it had perpetual succession also.[29]

One more important thing is in case of traditional partnership foreigners cannot be the partner of the firm but in a Limited Liability Partnership a foreigner can be the partner of the firm. So the limited liability partnership provides opportunity to invest foreigners in India without having joint liability with other partners. But one debatable point is, if a foreigner partner of the limited liability partnership commits some wrong against creditors or some other persons and leaves the partnership as well as India other partners will not be liable for the act of the outgoing partner. This will lose the credibility of the partnership in the eye of creditors and other businessmen who want to establish relationship with such firm.

From the above discussion it appears that Limited Liability Partnership has more similarities to a company. But there is difference between the company and Limited Liability Partnership. In the company internal governance structure is regulated by the Companies Act, 1956, whereas in the Limited Liability Partnership it is based on the contractual agreement between the partners. Besides this the management-ownership divides in the company but it does not lie in the limited liability partnership.

Now the question is if there is little bit difference and very much resemblance between LLP and traditional partnership then why did not amendment take place in the Indian Partnership

27. *Ibid,* Section 30(5).
28. Section 34 of the LLP Act, 2008.
29. Section 30(2) of the LLP Act, 2008.

Act, 1932. What was the requirement to bring new legislation? The answer may be that the traditional partnership was based on joint and several liabilities, therefore, much knowledge-based sectors found it unsuitable. It was also felt that a flexible working environment with limited liability could promote the business not only in India but abroad.

Apart from the above, there should not be any confusion whether LLP will have overriding effect on traditional partnership or not, because Section 3(4) of the LLP Act, 2008 provides that the provisions of this Acts are other than the Acts which are in existence.[30]

One more provision which make Limited Liability Partnership more reasonable is that any firm can be converted into Limited Liability Partnership.[31] Similarly, any private company can also be converted into LLP.[32] But these provisions are subject to the provisions of no security interest subsisting on its neither asset nor enforce at the time of application. But it is not easy to show that no security interest subsisting on any interest. Besides this, if a company or firm has been converted in to limited liability partnership can it be reconverted in its old status? The Act is silent about this matter.

## CONCLUDING OBSERVATIONS

Present situation is high significance of economic trends not only in India but across the world. Now it has become highly necessary to enable Indian entities also to have the requisite choice in corporate organizations to compete on international level because of the growing role of service and knowledge-based enterprises and emerging international competition.

As per the above discussion, it is best to say that a limited liability partnership not only renders protection to the partners but also retains all the benefits of a partnership. Although the traditional partnership holds one advantage that it is not compulsory for partnership to get registered before any statutory authority while on the other hand under the Limited Liability Act, 2008, the process of which may be cumbersome. Still in my opinion the balance is tilted in favour of the latter. The Liability

30. See also section 71 of LLP Act, 2008.
31. Section 55 of the LLP Act, 2008.
32. Section 56 of LLP Act, 2008.

of the partners incurred in the normal course of business is that of LLP and it does not extend to the personal assets of the partners. This is a great relief to the partners, particularly professionals like Company Secretaries, Chartered Accountants, Cost Accountants, Advocates and other professionals. The Government of India should create a facilitating environment for entrepreneurs, service providers and professionals to meet the global competition. The introduction of LLPs in India is a good beginning towards a long journey. The hybrid structure of LLP will facilitate entrepreneurs, service providers and professionals to organize and operate in an innovative and efficient manner for effectively competing in the global market. Neglected themes like limited partnership and small private companies should be given priority attention in the interest of small entrepreneurs in all sectors. One lacuna which is there in the LLP Act, 2008 is not to accept the suggestion of the Naresh Chandra Committee. The Committee had suggested making provision for compulsory insurance of the partners which is not appearing in the LLP Act, 2008.

# PART II

# CORPORATE LAW AND ENVIRONMENT

# CHAPTER 4

# Environmental Crime *vis-a-vis* Corporate Criminal Responsibility: Prospect and Problem in Defining and Determining

*Dr. Ranjit Sil*

## INTRODUCTION

Finding a place of the new term 'Environmental Crime' in the definition clause of the Environmental laws is a new quest for and approaches to the enforcement of environmental regulations. Though the development of Environmental Criminal law has been in slow pace and process and discrepancy as to the legal recognition of the concept are noticed in different laws relating to the environmental regulations the environmental issues in the recent years have become more important in the public eyes. With the rising trends of public interest in the environment and the understanding of the consequences of environmental harm, attempts to theorize the environmental offence or **green criminology** have been made by some western jurists[1]. Some of them are of the view that although the environmental crime on an apparent judgment generally viewed as a 'lesser' offence than 'real' crimes, indeed the environmental crime should find place with 'traditional' crimes in the criminal justice system. The only hurdle to the recognition of this claim from legislative view is the definitional aspects of crime. The moral foundation of real criminal law is that a crime requires both an unlawful act and the

1. M. Halsey (1997), Current issues in Criminology 217 as found in Environmental Law by Stuart Bell & Donald McGillivray, Sixth edition, Oxford University Press, at p. 277.

requisite mental responsibility or fault[2]. The traditional or real crimes are the acts which are evil in them and therefore, considered to be clearly unacceptable behaviour in society first and then prohibited by the law of the land. Unlike the real crime, the environmental crime is not thought to be inherently immoral and harm to the environment is, in many situations, considered to be acceptable. Tolerance of such harm caused to the environment and the permit to such activities is, first, conceived and rooted in the notion of developmental activities by the State itself and by the instrumentalities of State as well as the public corporate bodies and in some cases the private citizens too. In a mixed economy the government as well as the public bodies both are required to enter into venturing the developmental and economic activities, *prima facie* for the welfare of the citizens in a social welfare State. The presence of industrial operators in large number is required for the economic welfare of the country and to meet the national production demand. Consequent harm to the environment is inherent with many industrial activities and therefore, State was initially prepared to allow such industrial activities with the consequent harm to the environment under license or authorization scheme. Under the common law, the ownership denotes the right of the owner to possess, use and enjoy the thing he owns which even includes right to consuming, destroying or alienating the things. Under the doctrine of right to choose the uses to which an owner can put his land belongs exclusively to his choice. But in the recent past the law of ecology and environment has substantially curtailed this right of the owner to enjoy his peace of land granted under the common law doctrine of ownership. It is the collective jurisprudence of municipal administration that has made its first in road into the domain of the doctrine of ownership[3].

The aim of this paper is to trace the development of the concept of environmental crime through certain established incidences and to show how the environmental protection mechanism has grown from the potential of civil liability as a tool to act for that and demand of present day situation to place the environmental crime as a separate and independent study under the criminal administration of justice system and at the same

2. Definition of crime as in Indian Penal Code.
3. Divan Shyam and Armin Rosen Cranz, Environmental Law and Policy in India, Oxford University Press, at pp. 392-93.

time, the problem and prospects in defining the environmental crime before its inclusion.

## DEFINITION OF ENVIRONMENTAL CRIME

It is difficult to give any straight forward, precise, formulated definition of the environmental crime because of the basic differences between the moral and legal meaning of the term. In general, it may mean crime against environment. Some writers consider that environmental crime should cover activities which may be lawful or licensed but which cause significant environmental harm.

An environmental crime is an unauthorized act or omission that violates the law and is therefore, subject to criminal prosecution and criminal sanction. This offence harms or endangers people's physical safety or health as well as the environment itself. It serves the interests of either organizations—typically corporations or individuals[4].

An environmental crime is an act committed with the intent to harm or with a potential to cause harm to ecological or biological systems and for the purpose of securing business or personal advantage[5].

In the course of evolution of green criminology, it is the foremost requirement to define environmental crime because it will help setting a number of key aspects of criminal liability for environmental harm and in prosecuting the offenders. But a legal definition of environmental crime is uncertain because of the problematic and uncertain definition of environmental law. From a narrower point of view environmental crime primarily may mean or include those acts or omissions which directly or indirectly damage the environment and which are as such declared prohibitory in nature by statute. On the other hand, the broader aspect of environmental crime demands the incorporation of a wide range of activities and offenders having potential threat to the environment and ecological balance but

4. Y. Situ and D. Emmons, Environmental Crime; The Criminal Justice Systems Role in Protecting the Environment (Thousand Oaks: Sage, 2000), 3 found in, Environmental Law by Stuart Bell and Donald McGillivray, Sixth Edition, Oxfords at p. 277.
5. M. Clifford, Environmental Crime: Enforcement, Policy and Social Responsibility (Gaithersburg: Aspen, 1998), 26, *Ibid.*, at p. 277.

uncertainty in scientific knowledge is the problem for the broader definition of environmental crime. From a legalistic point of view defining environmental crime has jurisdictional and geographical limitations. The ground reality is that the emergence of this branch of law is very recent and mostly dependent upon the international agreements where under the signatories are obligatory to impose the standard criminal sanctions. In contrast to the municipal laws, the international laws are of weak enforceability and slow progress. The matters of sovereign immunity as well as the political interest in the world forum play vital role in formulating the international norms. Moreover, variance is there in the sense that an environmental crime in one country may not be the same in another country. In the national level, the attitude to environmental harm is generally a matter of decision and policy option, largely dependent upon the political set-up and administrative action of the government. Pollution is generally considered as a way of life by the people belonging to lower strata in the society and who are living within or in the vicinity of industrial areas and at the same time it is a matter of luxury for the high status people who are the contributory to the pollution. Therefore, it is required to determine or demarcate the boundaries wherein environmental crimes are located.

Until the second half of this twentieth century, environmentalism was seen as primarily of aesthetic interest and as a local health hazards. As science and industry gained more power to alter the environment, the awareness dawned that environmental deterioration affected not only the leisure of the rich and the health of the poor, but also the well-being of human race and of the planet itself. There has been progress in environmental protection.

Environmental justice has now become the most sensitive issue. The relationship between poverty and environmental pollution has gained priority to be studied on national and international level. It is broadly recognized that poor citizens are more likely to suffer the consequences of environmental pollution than other citizens, on both the national and international level. Internationally, less affluent nations tend to have more severe environmental problems than wealthier nations. On the other, on the national level, the urban poor, certain ethnic sectors of the society are the sufferer for environmentally undesirable activities. Many transnational corporations, mostly of the developed countries have chosen to move environmentally dangerous industrial activities to the developing world. Intellectual property right over plant genetic resources has now become one of the most controversial environmental justice issues. The privatization of bio-technology and plant genetic resources is primarily derived from the less developed countries and those are patented in developed countries. This is in gross violation of the right of access of the developing countries of origin of these plant genetic resources to humankind's common heritage. The export of environmental harm to the world's poorer nations is a serious threat to the world's poor. The most glaring example is the lethal 1984 Union Carbide gas leak in Bhopal. It became evident that the protective measures and redundant system usually put in place in the United States were not in place in India. The massive mortality, approximate 8000, and a massive morbidity of 50,000 people were the chilling testimony to the fact that by offering less protection indifferent value was placed on the lives in India than on the lives in the United States[6]. Therefore today it is widely accepted that many of the present day environmental problems were and still are, originated from corporate industrial activities. And with the new prospect in science and technological growth, especially bio-technological progress and newer innovation are continuously posing threat to the environmental degradation or ecology risk with the presence of corporate actors in the international economic order.

## POST-INDUSTRIAL RISK AND MODERN ENVIRONMENTAL LAW

The development of environmental law in India is the result of judicial response to the complaints of its citizens against environmental degradation starting in 1990s. In the initial stage there was little to distinguish the field of environmental law from the general body of law. The body of case law too was unremarkable. Most of the pre-1980 'environmental cases' were either actions in tort or standard agency prosecutions under an environmental statute. During this early period the environment

6. Bhattacharya, Jayanta, Global Corporate Environmentalism, Asian Books Private Limited, Daryaganj, N. Delhi, at p. 45.

enjoyed no special protection from the judiciary. Actually the transformation took place after the incidence of Bhopal Gas Leak disaster of December 1984. Another feature of new regime is the vesting of enormous administrative power in the enforcement agencies[7] and creation of new enforcement agencies or strengthening of the existing ones.[8] This shift from the judicial to administrative enforcement of environmental laws was intended to improve the compliances. In the course of time the concept of risk has become the activating concept of modern environmental law, and a dominant organizing principle in late 20th century societies. During the process of industrialization of society most of the environmental risks like discharge of contaminated and industrial waste into spring water, emissions of pollutants from the factories, deforestation, contamination of soils, were considered as first generation of risks. But more recently, particularly the post-industrial society has witnessed the ascendancy of a new generation of risks like climate change, loss of bio-diversity, ozone depletion, mass disaster from hazardous industrial emission including loss of lives, etc.

## CORPORATE CRIMINAL LIABILITY AND THE INDIAN JUDICIARY

It is well known fact that corporations today play an important role in the society not only in the sense that it creates business and contribute in economic development of the country but it influences the life of the common people. Corporate Criminal Liability is very difficult to determine because it would deviate then from the normal theoretical foundation of criminal law jurisprudence that crime involves an illegal act (actus reus) and a culpable mental act (mens rea), the principle underlain in the maxim-actus non facit reum nisi, mens sit rea which means

7. Pollution Control Board was empowered to direct a polluter to shut down an offending factory or order the withdrawal of its power supply, previously the Board had to approach a magistrate to enjoin the polluter.
8. The authorities constituted under the Environment Impact Assessment (EIA) Regulations of 1994. The Union Ministry of Environment and Forests is responsible for evaluating EIA reports submitted by Project Proponents. For large projects the review is carried out in consultation with a committee of experts.

that to make one liable it must be shown that act or omission has been done which was forbidden by law and has been done with guilty intent. But corporation is not a natural person and therefore, cannot be subjected to imprisonment which is one of the most important option of punishment in view of the deterrent effect of punishment theory. However, the criminal law jurisprudence has set one exception to this general principle in form of doctrine of strict liability and absolute liability in which one may be held liable in absence of any guilty intent. But the rules of interpretation is that unless the statute either clearly or by necessary implication rules out *mens rea* as a constituent part of a crime an accused should not be found guilty of an offence against the criminal law unless he has got a guilty mind. Absolute liability is not to be lightly presumed but has to be clearly established.[9] In *Vellipa Textile Ltd. case*[10] a three judge Bench of the Supreme Court has ruled that a company being a juristic person can neither be imprisoned nor be asked to pay fine for an offence that calls for only imprisonment or imprisonment plus fine under the relevant law. The Court said that the ruling, however, does not apply to a company's director and employees who can be punished with imprisonment or imprisonment and fine. The majority view was that corporate criminal liability can not be imposed without making corresponding legislative changes as for example, the imposition of fine in lieu of imprisonment. To bring such a legislative change in criminal jurisprudence is a legislative function which parliament can do only. Such legislative changes have taken place in Australia, France, the Netherlands, and Belgium. The United States, United Kingdom and Canada also have rules allowing punishment of corporate entities. The dissenting judge said that Court would be unfair in holding that a company could not be prosecuted.

*Standard Chartered Bank and others etc. v. Directorate of Enforcement and others etc.*,[11] is the landmark decision in this regard wherein the Supreme Court expressed its majority view that there is no immunity to the companies from prosecution merely because the prosecution is in respect of the offences for which the punishment prescribed is mandatory imprisonment. As the company cannot be sentenced to imprisonment, the Court

9. *State of Maharashtra v. Mayer Hans George*, AIR 1965 SC 722.
10. (2004) 1 C.L.J. 21.
11. AIR 2005 SC 2622.

cannot impose that punishment but when imprisonment and fine is the prescribed punishment the Court can impose the punishment of fine which could be enforced against the company. The Court observed that it is sheer violence to commonsense that the legislature intended to punish the corporate bodies for minor and silly offences and extended immunity of prosecution to major and grave economic crimes. So far as the juristic person is concerned as regard to the company the Court can always impose a sentence of fine. This appears to be the intention of the legislature. As per the scheme of various enactments and the Indian Penal Code mandatory custodial sentence is prescribed for grave offences. If the contrary view is accepted no corporate bodies could be prosecuted for the grave offences whereas they could be prosecuted for the minor offences as the sentence prescribed therein is custodial sentence or fine. The intention of the legislature is not to give complete immunity from prosecution to the corporate bodies for these grave offences.

The principle of strict interpretation of criminal statutes requires that the substantive offences created by the statute which does not exclude corporations should be enforced strictly and anyone rendering itself liable for actions under the said provision, be it corporation or a natural person, should face prosecution, conviction and sentence. There are many statutes[12] making corporation liable for conviction which prescribe punishment by way of imprisonment as well as fine. Furthermore even in relation to a penal statute any narrow and pedantic construction may not always be given effect to. The law would have to be interpreted having regard to the subject matter of the offence and the object of the law it seeks to achieve. The purpose of the law is not to allow the offender to sneak out of the meshes of law. Criminal jurisprudence does not say so.

The law is primarily based on the terms of the statutes. In the case of absolute liability where the legislature by the clearest intendment establishes an offence where liability arises instantly upon the breach of the statutory prohibition, no particular state of mind is a prerequisite to guilt. Corporation and individual persons stand on the same footing in the face of such a statutory offence. It is only in case requiring *mens rea*, a question arises

12. Section 48A of the MRTP Act, 1969 which specifically makes corporations liable for prosecution while at the same providing that in case of conviction they will be liable to imprisonment and also fine.

whether a corporation could be attracted with requisite *mens rea* to prove the guilt. The Indian Parliament was cognizant of the problem and had proposed an amendment of the IPC[13] which specifically was intended to take care of a situation where the offender is a company and the offence is mandatorily punishable with imprisonment in which case the option was given to the Court to sentence such a corporate offender to fine only.

The Court can not aid the legislative defective phrasing of an Act and can not add and mend, and by construction make up deficiencies which are left there. It is not open to the Court to read the words "imprisonment and fine" as "imprisonment or fine". Such a construction is impossible. While it may be permissible for the Court to read the word 'and' as 'or' or *vice-versa,* whatever the interpretation, it must be uniformly applied to all situations. If the conjunction 'and' is read disjunctively as 'or' then the intention of the parliament definitely be defeated as the mandatory form of imprisonment would not be available even in case of a natural person. It is trite principle that punishment must follow the conviction.

## RECOMMENDATION OF LAW COMMISSION OF INDIA

The legal difficulties arise out of the above situation were noticed by the law commission of India and in its **41st Report**, the commission suggested amendment to Section 62 of the Indian Penal Code by adding the following lines:

> "In every case in which the offence is only punishable with imprisonment or with imprisonment and fine and the offender is a company or other body corporate or an association of individual, it shall be competent to the Court to sentence such offender to fine only."

But this recommendation got no response from the parliament and again in its **47th Report**[14] the law commission made the following recommendation to be inserted in the Indian Penal Code as say Section 62:

(1) In every case in which the offence is punishable with imprisonment only or with imprisonment and fine, and

13. IPC (Amendment) Bill, 1972, Clause 72(a).
14. Paragraph 8(3) of the Report.

the offender is a corporation it shall be competent to the Court to sentence such offender to fine only,

(2) In every case in which the offence is punishable with imprisonment and any other punishment not being fine and the offender is a corporation it shall be competent to the Court to sentence such offender to fine, and

(3) In this section 'corporation' means an incorporated company or other body corporate and includes a firm and other association of individuals.

But the Bill prepared on the basis of this recommendation lapsed and it did not become law. However, few were accepted by the parliament and by Taxation Statute.

## CONCLUSION AND SUGGESTIONS

The corporate bodies today undertake series of activities that affect the life, liberty and property of the citizens. The corporate bodies now occupies such a large portion of the industrial, commercial and sociological sectors that amenability of the corporation to a criminal law is essential to have a peaceful society with stable economy. Therefore, it can not be said that there is blanket immunity for any company from any prosecution for serious offences merely because the prosecution would ultimately entail a sentence of mandatory imprisonment. Such an observation was held by the majority view in *Standard Chartered Bank and Others v. Directorate of Enforcement and Others.* The emergence of the concept of corporate criminal liability under the environmental laws has been taking shape over the decades deviating from the earlier belief that corporate bodies could not be held criminally liable due to the prevailing thought of the principles of criminal liability comprising the need to establish guilty intent and having capacity to receive the threat of imprisonment which is not practicable to be implemented on corporate bodies for its juristic fiction and legal entity different from natural one. According to the cardinal principles of criminal law corporate bodies are not possible to be brought before the court physically for prosecuting and therefore, having no scope of examining or cross-examining to prove and establish the *mens rea* which is requisite to sustain a criminal conviction which corporation lacks. On the other hand, the definition of the word 'person' as found in different statute[15] convey the same meaning attributing that the word 'person' includes any company or association or bodies of persons whether incorporated or not. This makes it clear that company or corporations can be subjected to penal liability. There is example of statute making corporation liable for conviction which prescribes punishment by way of imprisonment as well as fine.[16] The Supreme Court in *Standard Chartered Bank and Others v. Directorate of Enforcement and Others*, by majority view overruled the judgment of the Vellipa Textile Ltd. Case and decided that the mandatory sentence of imprisonment and fine is to be imposed, namely on persons coming under category (ii) and (iii) alone but where it can be imposed namely on a company fine will be the only punishment.

Recognizing corporate criminal liability is open to criticism and much debated topic. Several arguments are placed to counter its acceptability. The critics say that once such liability be recognized such may pose harm to businesses and it may confer too much discretion in prosecutor. Another argument is that it might have effect of over criminalization or may encourage the illegal activities. Some critics opined that imposing criminal liability over corporate bodies may hurt the innocent actors, say shareholders, bondholders or other creditors, employees and even the community in which the corporation is located who likely will have to pay higher prices because of penalties imposed on the corporate bodies. Advocates of corporate criminal liability suggest that corporate behavior can be alterled in two ways by criminal prosecutions. First, general deterrence of similar behavior by many is achieved through publicity about corporate prosecutions and secondly, options for sentencing convicted corporations such as probation which requires implementation of an effective corporate compliance plan.

The alternative to corporate criminal liability is the prosecution of culpable individuals within an organization but it is not always possible to identify the responsible individuals within a large organization. Therefore, adoption of a more appropriate standard for assessing such liability is urged by many critics. They viewed that problem underlies with the reliance on vicarious liability which is inconsistent with the

15. Section 11 of the Indian Penal Code as well as Section 3(42) in the General Clauses Act.
16. *Supra* note 12.

criminal laws focus on personal guilt through one's own conduct and intent.

The development of the law relating to corporate criminal liability is greatly influenced by the English law. The need for the proper law relating to corporate criminal liability in a legal system especially in the developing countries like India is felt due to the fact that Industrial development has led to the growth of a number of factories many of which are engaged in hazardous or inherently dangerous activities. In spite of having some specific laws to regulate the working of those factories there is no specific legislation providing for compensation and damages to outsiders who may suffer on account of any industrial accident. Normally the principle of corporate personality of a company is respected in most of the cases. The distinct personality of a company is the statutory privilege. But in case of any proven fact of illegality or irregularity the individuals behind the corporate shield can not be protected as the court is then competent to disregard this distinct identity by lifting or piercing the corporate veil. The company Act, 1956 has empowered the Court to lift the veil to reach the persons who are in fact responsible for the culpable or wrongful act. We should take lesson from Bhopal incidence which is one of the greatest industrial tragedies and industrial accidents in human history. The US parent company Union Carbide escaped from criminal liability and the sorry state of affairs that Warren Anderson, its chairman was allowed to go scot free. The Court has passed the sentence against the accused only with the charge of causing death by negligence which carries a maximum imprisonment of two years instead of trying the offenders for the charge of culpable homicide not amounting to murder which carries a maximum punishment of 10 years imprisonment. The question arises that does this verdict render any justice to the ill fated victims, those nameless and voiceless thousands who are no more? Therefore, in this context India as a developing country should think deeply to develop mechanism either through stringent administrative sanction or more comprehensive and effective legislation. Generally in Britain, where large companies commit environmental offences, prosecution is brought against that company rather than any one individual who might have responsibility within that company. This is in contrast to many civil law countries where the doctrine of corporate liability is not particularly developed.[17] Under British Law any director, manager, secretary, or other similar officer of a corporate body can be prosecuted personally if the offence is committed with their consent or connivance, or is attributable to their neglect as stated in Section 157 of EPA, Section 217 of Water Resources Act, 1991, Section 331 of Town and Country Planning Act, 1990 provided these sections are not applicable where the allegation is against an individual as principal in their own right. In *Standard Chartered Bank and Others v. Directorate of Enforcement and Others* the Supreme Court of India ultimately held that the corporation could be prosecuted and punished with fines, regardless of the mandatory punishment of imprisonment required under the respective statute. Where individual liability is difficult to determine, prosecution of the corporation is an attractive alternative. The prosecution of the company is the only way to allocate responsibility for white collar crime. The main object behind the attribution of an artificial personality to a company is the expectation from a company its contribution for the growth and development of the nation. As regard to the criminal liability of the corporation the approach has changed over the years from these being no concept of a liability for criminal acts of corporation to liability based on the identification of some persons as the alter ego of the company. The need of the hour is to have greater control, monitoring and accountability of the corporate activities in a globalised economy. A corporation deemed to be a state within the meaning of Article 12 of the Constitution and acting as agency of the government. Another aspect to be emphasized is that where the punishment is imprisonment and fine, even if the Court may impose penalty by way of fine, it can not go beyond the maximum prescribed fine in the relevant statutory provision. But to make the purpose of criminal sanction effective the imposition of fine should have the financial impact on the defendant so as to reflect the deterrent effect. Therefore, any imposition of financial penalty must be an effective sanction when viewed against the resources of the defendant. The fine must be at a level to make some impact on the company and overcome any suggestion that it is cheaper to pay the fine than to undertake the work that is necessary to

17. Bell Stuart & Donald McGillivray, Environmental Law, Sixth edition: Oxford University Press, Oxford at p. 289.

prevent the offence in the first place. On the other hand, the fine should not be so high that it would threaten the viability of the community itself and affect the community's economic benefit.

Lastly, in addition to the traditional kind of punishment i.e., imposition of fine some alternative mechanism to deter the corporate offender behavior has already been suggested in some developed nation like developing environmental management system; rectification of environmental damage; supervision of compliance by the regulator by placing a representative in the company's Board; by giving statement to be placed in the corporate offender's annual report; requiring money to be deposited by the erring corporate body into a trust or Court account which would be activated to address any environmental harm; requiring the placing of an advert in the national media explaining the circumstances; requiring the completion of an environmental improvement project and/or community education programmes at a cost of a specified sum equal to the benefit obtained by the offender. The Court may require giving the order to the offending corporations to supervise the upgrading of plant and equipment and proper training rather than paying a fine.

CHAPTER 5

# Environmental Protection through Global Partnership

*Dr. Rakesh Kumar*

The protection and improvement of the human environment is a major issue which affects the well-being of peoples and economic development throughout the world.[1] Today society's interaction with nature is so extensive that environmental question has assumed proportions affecting all humanity. Rapid industrializations, expanding urbanization, population explosion, over-exploitation of natural resources, depletion of traditional resources of energy and raw materials, disruption of natural ecological balance, lack of environmental education, unawareness of consequences of environmental degradation, destruction of multitude of animals and plants species for economic reason or for no good reason, changed agricultural practices, extremely neglected and filthy civic amenities and modern luxurious living are some of the factors which are mainly responsible for environmental degradation.[2]

Poverty is the fundamental cause which makes people to over-exploit the natural resources for meeting their basic needs. 'Poverty and Need' are indeed the greatest polluters.[3] In the developing countries most of the environmental problems are caused by under-development. Millions continue to live far below the minimum levels required for a decent human

1. Proclamation 2 of the Declaration the UN Conference on Human Environment, 1972.
2. *Sri Sachidanand Pandey v. State of West Bengal*, AIR 1987 SC 1109.
3. Brundtland Commission's Report, 1987.

existence, deprived of adequate food and clothing, shelter and education, health and sanitation. Indeed, the natural growth of population continuously presents problems for the preservation of the environment. Therefore, the developing countries must direct their efforts to development, bearing in mind their priorities and the need to safeguard and improve the environment. For the same purpose, the industrialized countries should make efforts to reduce the gap themselves and the developing countries. In the industrialized countries, environmental problems are generally related to industrialization and technological development.

During the past few decades numerous incredible and devastating events have focused the domestic and global to the impending danger of environmental devastation, and protecting the global environment has emerged as one of the major challenges in international relation. Many global environmental treaties and regional and bilateral agreements have been negotiated. Governments of States endorsed a number of comprehensive action plans for implementing sustainable development and resultantly there is an increase enriched body of international environmental law and policy. But, unfortunately, such enriched body of treaties, action plans, and other instruments have not reversed global environmental decline and today every major environmental indicator is worse than it was at the time "Earth Summit".[4] Due to climate change there is marked increase in temperature; gradual deterioration of ozone layer, extinction of plant and animal species at higher rate and accumulation of toxic chemicals in living organism.

**Stockholm Agreements**

The United Nations Conference on the Human Environment, also known as the Stockholm Conference, was convened under United Nations auspices held in Stockholm, Sweden from June 5-16, 1972. It was the UN's first major conference on international environmental issues, and marked a turning point in the development of international environmental politics.

When the UN General Assembly decided to convene the Stockholm Conference, at the initiative of the Government of Sweden, UN Secretary-General U. Thant invited Maurice Strong

4. *Ibid.*

to lead it as Secretary-General of the Conference. The conference was opened and addressed by the Swedish Prime Minister Olof Palme and secretary-general Kurt Waldheim to discuss the state of the global environment. Attended by the representatives of 113 countries, 19 inter-governmental agencies, and more than 400 inter-governmental and non-governmental organizations, it is widely recognized as the beginning of modern political and public awareness of global environmental problems. The meeting agreed upon a Declaration containing 26 principles concerning the environment and development; an Action Plan with 109 recommendations, and a Resolution. It was proclaimed that Man is both creature and molder of his environment, which gives him physical sustenance and affords him the opportunity for intellectual, moral, social and spiritual growth. In the long and tortuous evolution of the human race on this planet a stage has been reached when, through the rapid acceleration of science and technology, man has acquired the power to transform his environment in countless ways and on an unprecedented scale. Both aspects of man's environment, the natural and the man-made, are essential to his well-being and to the enjoyment of basic human rights the right to life itself.[5] In order to impose co-operative responsibility, it was asserted:

> Man has constantly to sum up experience and go on discovering, inventing, creating and advancing. In our time, man's capability to transform his surroundings, if used wisely, can bring to all peoples the benefits of development and the opportunity to enhance the quality of life.[6]... A point has been reached in history when we must shape our actions throughout the world with a more prudent care for their environmental consequences. Through ignorance or indifference we can do massive and irreversible harm to the earthly environment on which our life and well-being depend. Conversely, through fuller knowledge and wiser action, we can achieve for ourselves and our posterity a better life in an environment... What is needed is an enthusiastic but calm state of mind and intense but orderly work. For the purpose of attaining freedom in the world of

5. Proclamation 1 of the Declaration the UN Conference on Human Environment, 1972.
6. Proclamation 3, *ibid.*

nature, man must use knowledge to build, in collaboration with nature, a better environment....[7] To achieve this environmental goal will demand the acceptance of responsibility by citizens and communities and by enterprises and institutions at every level, all sharing equitably in common efforts. Individuals in all walks of life as well as organizations in many fields, by their values and the sum of their actions, will shape the world environment of the future. Local and national governments will bear the greatest burden for large-scale environmental policy and action within their jurisdictions. International cooperation is also needed in order to raise resources to support the developing countries in carrying out their responsibilities in this field. A growing class of environmental problems, because they are regional or global in extent or because they affect the common international realm, will require extensive cooperation among nations and action by international organizations in the common interest.[8]

United Nations Conference on the Human Environment, 1972 confirmed not only the emergence of environment protection as new focus of legal activity but also laid emphasis on close interrelationship between development and environment. The Conference called upon Governments and peoples to exert common efforts for the preservation and improvement of the human environment, for the benefit of all the people and for their posterity and imposed a special responsibility on human being to safeguard and wisely manage the heritage of wildlife and its habitat, which are now gravely imperiled by a combination of adverse factors. Nature conservation, including wildlife, must therefore receive importance in planning for economic development.[9] The capacity of the earth to produce vital renewable resources must be maintained and, wherever practicable, restored or improved.[10] The other important agreements for global partnership to protect the environment are:

(i) to safeguard the natural resources of the earth, including the air, water, land, flora and fauna and

7. Proclamation 6, *ibid.*
8. Proclaimation 7, *ibid.*
9. Principle 4, *ibid.*
10. Principle 3, *ibid.*

especially representative samples of natural ecosystems for the benefit of present and future generations,[11]

(ii) to develop the international law regarding liability and compensation for the victims of pollution and other environmental damage[12] and to handle international matters concerning the protection and improvement of the environment in a cooperative spirit by all countries,[13]

(iii) to guard against the danger of future exhaustion of the non-renewable resources of the earth for the benefits of all mankind,[14]

(iv) to prevent pollution of the seas by substances that are liable to create hazards to human health, to harm living resources and marine life, to damage amenities or to interfere with other legitimate uses of the sea,[15] and

(v) to apply Science and technology for the identification, avoidance and control of environmental risks and the solution of environmental problems and for the common good of mankind.[16]

## The Promise of Rio[17]

Environment has clearly emerged as one of the biggest contemporary issues we face today. Issues such as climate change, global warming trend, acid rain, ozone depletion, loss of biological diversity, etc. have resulted in creating awareness of the environmental problems. The foundation of global security is also threatened due to unprecedented

11. Principle 2, *ibid.*
12. Principle 22, *ibid.*
13. Principle 24, *ibid.*
14. Principle 5, *ibid.*
15. Principle 7, *ibid.*
16. Principle 18, *ibid.*
17. The United Nations Conference on Environment and Development (UNCED), also known as the Rio Summit, Rio Conference, Earth Summit was a major United Nations conference held in Rio de Janeiro from 3 June to 14 June 1992. 172 governments participated, with 108 sending their heads of state or government. Some 2,400 representatives of non-governmental organizations (NGOs) attended, with 17,000 people at the parallel NGO "Global Forum", who had Consultative Status.

increase in human population and changed living patterns. The global concern shall be marked from the preambular assertion made at the Earth Summit, 1992:

> Humanity stands at a defining moment in history. We are confronted with a perpetuation of disparities between and within nations, a worsening of poverty, hunger, ill-health and illiteracy, and the continuing deterioration of the ecosystems on which we depends for our well-being.[18]

The "Earth Summit" is the turning point for global environmental policy. More than one hundred countries deliberated at the Rio Summit, which sought to merge two critical international concerns—environmental protection and economic development. For developing countries, the merger of environment and development was a major improvement over earlier environmental conferences and provided hope for increased North-South cooperation. The issues addressed included:

(i) systematic scrutiny of patterns of production—particularly the production of toxic components, such as lead in gasoline, or poisonous waste including radioactive chemicals;
(ii) alternative sources of energy to replace the use of fossil fuels which are linked to global climate change;
(iii) new reliance on public transportation systems in order to reduce vehicle emissions, congestion in cities and the health problems caused by polluted air and smog; and
(iv) the growing scarcity of water.

The Earth Summit did provide a potential vision for moving toward sustainable development—that is, toward both greater environmental protection and greater economic justice. The Earth Summit yielded two legally binding treaties: (a) the Framework Convention on Climate Change, and (b) the Convention on Biological Diversity. Also a product of the Summit were a set of non-binding general principles known as the Rio Declaration, a set of non-binding principles on forest management, and the

18. Preamble, Para 1.1, Report of the UN Conference on Environment and Development, 1992.

blueprint for sustainable development entitled Agenda 21. In order to achieve sustainable development, environmental protection was constituted an integral part of the development process. The assembled governments also established the Commission on Sustainable Development (CSD) to integrate environment and development into the UN system while providing a forum to monitor the implementation of summit commitments. The Rio Declaration postulates:

> Human beings are at the centre of concerns for sustainable development. They are entitled to a healthy and productive life in harmony with nature.[19] States have, in accordance with the Charter of the United Nations and the principles of international law, the sovereign right to exploit their own resources pursuant to their own environmental and developmental policies, and the responsibility to ensure that activities within their jurisdiction or control do not cause damage to the environment of other States or of areas beyond the limits of national jurisdiction.[20] The right to development must be fulfilled so as to equitably meet developmental and environmental needs of present and future generations.[21]

All States and all people were made responsible to cooperate in the essential task of eradicating poverty of the people of the world[22] and the special situation and needs of developing countries were given special priority.[23] To create a global partnership to achieve environmental goals, it was declared that:

> States shall cooperate in a spirit of global partnership to conserve, protect and restore the health and integrity of the Earth's ecosystem. In view of the different contributions to global environmental degradation, States have common but differentiated responsibilities. The developed countries acknowledge the responsibility that they bear in the international pursuit of sustainable development in view of the pressures their societies place on the global environment

19. Principle 1, the Rio Declaration on Environment and Development, 1992.
20. Principle 2, *ibid.*
21. Principle 3, *ibid.*
22. Principle 5, *ibid.*
23. Principle 6, *ibid.*

and of the technologies and financial resources they command.[24] States should cooperate to strengthen endogenous capacity-building for sustainable development by improving scientific understanding through exchanges of scientific and technological knowledge, and by enhancing the development, adaptation, diffusion and transfer of technologies, including new and innovative technologies.[25]

The Earth Summit held at Rio De Janeiro, Brazil in June 1992 was primarily held to discuss the problems of global warming, depletion of the ozone layer, deforestation, air and marine pollution and other environmentally interrelated threats facing the earth. The United Nations Framework Convention on Climatic Change (UN FCCC) was opened for signature at this Summit. It was formed in March 1994, and aims stabilising the greenhouse gas concentrations at levels that would prevent dangerous human interference with the climate system. In December 1997, in Kyoto, Japan, nations of the world took a first major step in order to protect our globe from the phenomena of global warming caused by the emission of excessive amounts of Green House Gases into the atmosphere. These nations adopted the Kyoto Protocol on Climatic Change and opted to use modern, innovative and cost-effective techniques and mechanisms to protect the environment.

The Convention on Biological Diversity, 1992 is a legally binding instrument on the parties. The Convention on Biological Diversity was opened for signature at the Earth Summit, and made a start towards redefinition of money supply measures that did not inherently encourage destruction of natural eco-regions and so-called uneconomic growth. It was adopted due to increased threat to genetic resources caused by the new development of biotechnology. Mainly there were three objectives of the convention: (i) conservation of biological diversity,[26] (ii) sustainable use of components of biological diversity, and (iii) fair and equitable sharing of benefits arising out of the utilization of

24. Principle 7, *ibid.*
25. Principle 9, *ibid.*
26. "Biological diversity" means the variability among living organisms from all sources including, *inter alia*, terrestrial, marine and other aquatic ecosystems and the ecological complexes of which they are part; this includes diversity within species, between species and of ecosystems.

generic resources and appropriate transfer of relevant technology.

The objectives of this Convention are, the conservation of biological diversity, the sustainable use of its components and the fair and equitable sharing of the benefits arising out of the utilization of genetic resources, including by appropriate access to genetic resources and by appropriate transfer of relevant technologies, taking into account all rights over those resources and to technologies, and by appropriate funding.[27]

Each Contracting Party were made responsible to (a) Develop national strategies, plans or programmes for the conservation and sustainable use of biological diversity; (b) Integrate, as far as possible and as appropriate, the conservation and sustainable use of biological diversity into relevant sectoral or cross-sectoral plans, programmes and policies.[28]

Being conscious of the intrinsic value of biological diversity and of the ecological, genetic, social, economic, scientific, educational, cultural, recreational and aesthetic values of biological diversity and its components and also of the importance of biological diversity for evolution and for maintaining life sustaining systems of the biosphere, the convention affirmed that the conservation of biological diversity is a common concern of humankind. It recognized the sovereign rights of States over their biological resources and imposed responsibility on them for conserving their biological diversity and for using their biological resources in a sustainable manner because being threatened and significantly reduced by human activities. This makes generic resources subject to ownership of the State but "Generic Resources are no more the common heritage of mankind".[29] The authority to determine access to genetic resources rests with the national governments and is subject to national legislation. Each Contracting Party shall endeavour to create conditions to facilitate access to genetic resources for environmentally sound uses by other Contracting Parties and the genetic resources provided by a Contracting Party are only those that are provided by Contracting Parties that are countries of origin of such

27. Article 1, the Convention on Biological Diversity, 1992.
28. Article 6, *ibid.*
29. Article 1, the International Understanding on Plant Genetic Resources, 1983, *op. cit.*, S.K. Verma, "Biodiversity and Intellectual Property Rights," 39 J.I.L.I. (1997) 203.

resources.[30] Access shall be on mutually agreed terms and shall be subject to prior informed consent. Each contracting Party shall take legislative, administrative or policy measures with the aim of sharing in a fair and equitable way the results of research and development and the benefits arising from the commercial and other utilization of genetic resources with the contracting Party providing such resources.

For the sustainable use of components of Biological Diversity each Contracting Party shall:

(a) integrate consideration of the conservation and sustainable use of biological resources into national decision-making;
(b) adopt measures relating to the use of biological resources to avoid or minimize adverse impacts on biological diversity;
(c) protect and encourage customary use of biological resources in accordance with traditional cultural practices that are compatible with conservation or sustainable use requirements;
(d) support local populations to develop and implement remedial action in degraded areas where biological diversity has been reduced; and
(e) encourage cooperation between its governmental authorities and its private sector in developing methods for sustainable use of biological resources.[31]

Public education and awareness is an important aspect of global partnership of this convention and the Contracting Parties are liable to:

(a) promote and encourage understanding of the importance of the conservation of biological diversity, as well as its propagation through media, and the inclusion of these topics in educational programmes; and
(b) cooperate with other States and international organizations in developing educational and public awareness programmes with respect to conservation and sustainable use of biological diversity.

30. Article 15, *supra* n. 27.
31. Article 10, *ibid*.

**Johannesburg Summit, 2002**

At the 1992 Earth Summit in Rio, the international community adopted Agenda 21, an unprecedented global plan of action for sustainable development. But the best strategies are only as good as their implementation. Ten years later, the Johannesburg Summit presents an exciting opportunity for today's leaders to adopt concrete steps and identify quantifiable targets for better implementing Agenda 21. Johannesburg Summit, 2002—the World Summit on Sustainable Development —brought together tens of thousands of participants, including heads of State and Government, national delegates and leaders from non-governmental organizations (NGOs), businesses and other major groups to focus the world's attention and direct action toward meeting difficult challenges, including improving people's lives and conserving our natural resources in a world that is growing in population, with ever-increasing demands for food, water, shelter, sanitation, energy, health services and economic security. The purpose of the summit was to evaluate the obstacles to progress and results achieved since the 1992 United Nations Conference on Environment and Development. The summit was expected to build a knowledge gained over the past decades, and provide a new impetus for commitments of resources and specific action towards global sustainability. There was commitment to build a humane, equitable and caring global society, cognizant of the need for human dignity for all. Members assumed a collective responsibility to advance and strengthen the interdependent and mutually reinforcing pillars of sustainable development—economic development, social development and environmental protection—at the local, national, regional and global levels.

The summit started with much fanfare as the opening sentence of the Secretary General, Mr. Kofi Annan indicates:

> Not far from conference room, in Lesotho, Malavi, Mozambic, Swazilamd, Zambia and Zimbabwe, 13 million people are threatened with famine. If any reminder were needed of what happens when we fail to plan for and

> protect the long-term future of our planet, it can be heard in the cries for help of those 13 million souls.[32]

The Secretary-General identified five major areas requiring special attention, namely water, energy, health, agriculture and biodiversity whereas lack of resources in developing countries to bear the cost of shifting to the sustainable path of development and lack of coherence and consistency across a range of policy areas dealing with sustainable development were identified as major reasons for a slow pace of progress.

The Declaration contains some broad statements. It re-affirmed the commitment to sustainable development. The declaration assumed collective responsibility to advance and strengthen the interdependent and mutually reinforcing pillars of sustainable development—economic development, social development, and environmental protection—at local, national, regional, and global levels.

The declaration identified certain challenges. It recognized poverty eradication, changing consumption and production patterns, and protecting and managing the natural resource base for economic and social development as overarching objectives of and essential requirements for sustainable development. The ever-increasing gap between the developed and developing worlds pose a major threat to global prosperity, security, and stability. Loss of biodiversity, increasing desertification, adverse impact of climate change, frequent and devastating natural disasters and air water and marine pollution are serious challenges. Globalization has added a new dimension to these challenges. The rapid integration of markets, mobility of capital and significant increase in investment flows around the world have opened new challenge and opportunity for the pursuit of sustainable development. But benefits and costs of globalization are unevenly distributed, with developing countries facing special difficulties in meeting this challenge.

The declaration clearly sounds a warning while stating:

> "We risk the entrenchment of these global disparities and unless we act in a manner that fundamentally change their

32. http//www.un.org/events/wssd/statement/sgE.html *op. cit.* Md. Hussain, K.S., "World Summit on Sustainable Development, Johannesburg: An Appraisal," *Indian Journal of International Law*, 348-69, (2002), (Vol. 42).

lives. The poor of the world may lose confidence in their representatives and the democratic systems to which we remain committed, seeing their representatives as nothing more than sounding brass or tinkling cymbals."

The declaration contains a section entitled, 'Our Commitment to Sustainable Development'. The plan of implementation consists of eleven chapters. Apart from the introductory chapter, the plan contains specific chapter on poverty eradication; changing unsustainable patterns of consumption and production; protecting and managing the natural resource-base of economic and social development; sustainable development in a globalizing world; health and sustainable development; sustainable development of small island developing States; sustainable development for Africa, other regional initiatives, means of implementation; and institutional framework for sustainable development. The following are merely a reaffirmation of the Millennium Development Goals:

1. To halve, by 2015, the proportion of the world's people whose income is less than 1 dollar a day and the proportion of people who suffer from hunger and, by the same date, to halve the proportion of people without access to safe drinking water.[33]
2. By 2020, to achieve a significant improvement in the lives of at least 100 million slum dwellers, as proposed in the "Cities without slums" initiative.[34]
3. To develop programmes and initiatives to reduce, by 2015, mortality rates for infants and children under 5 by two-thirds, and maternal mortality rates by three quarters, of the prevailing rate in 2000.[35]
4. To ensure that, by 2015, children everywhere, boys and girls alike, will be able to complete a full course of primary schooling.[36]

---

33. Para 7(a), "Poverty Eradication" the Plan of Implementation, the World Summit on Sustainable Development, Official Documents, Johannesburg Declaration on Sustainable Development, *Indian Journal of International Law*, Oct.-Dec. 2002, (Vol. 42) (No. 4).
34. Para 11, *ibid*.
35. Para 54 (f), *ibid*.
36. Para 116 (a), *ibid*.

In addition to these, a commitment was made to halve the proportion of people who do not have access to basic sanitation, by the year 2015. A world solidarity fund to eradicate poverty and to promote social and human development in the developing countries was mooted. It stresses the voluntary nature of the contributions and the need to avoid duplication of existing United Nation's Funds, and encouraging the role of the private sector and individual citizen relative to Governments in funding the endeavors. Between Stockholm and Johannesburg, the nations of the world have met on several occasions to deliberate and formulate policies for the protection of environment, but what is actually needed implementation of these policies with moral support.

## CONCLUSION

Environmental right which is third generation of human rights is prime important not only on national but on international level also. Environment should not sacrifice for the sake of development. However, from the above discussion it appears that attempt is being done to make balance between development and environment. Indian Judiciary has also tried to make balance between development and environment but it has also its limitations. So the time has come and we should be sincere for the protection of environment.

# PART III

# Consumers and the Corporate Sectors

CHAPTER 6

# Protection of Consumers: A Human Rights Perspective

*Dr. C.P. Upadhyay*

## INTRODUCTION

The consumer protection laws have originated and developed as a natural response to the recognition of the rights of consumers to be protected against exploitation by business class. The term consumer protection has undergone several changes with growing consumerism, emergence of the welfare state concepts and industrial revolution in almost all the countries of the world. Therefore, protection of consumers has been a continuous process with different dimensions more often than not slow and compromising. But the modern legislations have initiated an era of clear distinction of consumer rights and their protection with system of enforcement. This paper focuses on examining the consumer's rights in the backdrop of Universal Declaration of Human Rights and other covenants and conventions on consumer issues and on presenting a brief overview of the changing perspectives on key issues of consumer protection. In the beginning, the doctrine of 'laissez faire' dominated the economic scene all over the world, individualistic approach was adopted and least interference in the freedom of contract to maintain the sanctity of contract was maintained. It was thought that consumers are competent and skilled enough to safeguard their interests. The maxim 'Caveat Emptor' let the buyer beware was a rule. The globalization bought in an era of consumerism where in order to maintain social harmony legal intervention was called for; consequently exceptions to the doctrine of caveat emptor came to be recognized and became more prominent than the doctrine itself. Thus, doctrine of 'caveat emptor' was converted in 'caveat vendittor' let the seller beware.

Thus, need for protecting the interest of consumers, new dimensions to consumer justice was added. Due to increase in international trade and commerce consumer protection has attained enormous international dimensions. U.N. Secretary General emphasized that "with regard to consumer protection international cooperation is needed because the development of consumer protection policies no longer require that measures be taken only at national level."[1] The Crusade for the consumers right started in USA in 1927 and subsequently in 1936 Union of Consumers of United States of America was formed. In due time world-wide consumer associations, unions and organizations were established in several countries as, Japan, France, Germany, Australia, New Zealand, Malaysia and U.K., etc. The then President of USA, Mr. John F. Kennedy introduced a bill[2] on consumer right and outlined four rights of consumers, namely:

1. Right to safety
2. Right to be informed
3. Right to choose
4. Right to be heard

Later on three consumer rights were added by IOCU,[3] namely:

1. Right to redress
2. Right to healthy environment
3. Right to consumer education

All the above seven rights have been incorporated in the United Nations Charter of human rights. Article 27 of the Universal Declaration of Human Rights read as under:

1. Everyone has the right freely to participate in the cultural life of the community to enjoy the arts and share in scientific advancement and its benefits.

---

1. Report of the Secretary General, "International Activities for Consumer Protection." In IOCU, Proceedings of the International Seminar on Law and the Consumer, Hongkong, Jan. 06-10-1980.
2. This bill of consumer right is now regarded as *'magna carta'* of the rights of consumers.
3. International organization of consumers union.

2. Every one has right to protection of the moral and material interests resulting from any scientific, literary or artistic production of which he is the author."[4]

The term consumer does not cover 'public at large' under it. Though all the consumers do come under the head public but the *vice versa* is not true. Consumer is rather relative term and there are two categories of consumers—voluntary and involuntary consumers. Consumerism aims at giving protection to the voluntary consumers only. The problems of protecting involuntary consumers[5] has to be taken up by government directly.[6] In this way we see that rights of consumers come at par with rights of human being, i.e. human rights.[7] Thus, we find that in a globalizing human future consumer protection law is dedicated to human rights and amelioration of human suffering as ways of servicing the future of human rights.

## HISTORICAL BACKGROUND

For effective solution of consumer-related problems it is necessary to take insight into historical growth. Consumerism has already marched much forward in USA and England in comparison to India. Initially the provisions regarding protection of consumers came to be incorporated in certain laws only in the ordinary process of legislation. All laws passed worldwide relating to contract, sale goods, public distribution systems and prohibition on sale and purchase of certain commodities fall in this category.

The historical development of Indian legal system reveals that consumer interest was protected in the past also. During ancient period under the law of crimes there were provision to ensure standard weights and measures, to prevent adulteration

4. Article 27 of Universal Declaration of Human Rights.
5. Voluntary consumers are the persons who come under the definition of consumer under the Act. Involuntary consumers are the public at large who are not covered by the def. but in wide sense they are consumers.
6. Involuntary consumers are protected by Environment Protection Act, Motor Vehicles Act, etc.
7. Human rights are the rights that are inherent in people by virtue of being human being and are essential for complete development of human personality.

and to control the quality of goods.[8] During medieval period position of consumers was not satisfactory but freedom of contract, sanctity of contract and exception to 'caveat emptor' rule were recognized. In pre-independent India, gradually the common law principles came to be applied and India witnessed a plethora of laws[9] for protection of consumers. These laws transformed the socio-economic scene from duty based to a right-based society. After independence under new constitution we adopted welfare state concept, mixed economy was also adopted in which public and private sectors were to work together. During the second half of nineteenth century for protection of consumers, legislative era started. Since then a considerable number of enactment and special laws[10] have been framed. Now like other countries of the world this process is in advanced stage after the UN guidelines for Consumer Protection Act, 1985.

## INTERNATIONAL LEVEL EFFORTS FOR CONSUMER PROTECTION

Due to increase in international trade and commerce the consumer protection has attained international dimensions. Involvement of multinationals in production and distribution of goods and services have raised various issues which call for inter-governmental cooperation. Several international organizations have been actively contributing to develop a global consumer cooperation for effective programmes at international level.

Inter-governmental organizations are participating in the process of protection of consumers. In 1974, the World Health Organization adopted a resolution to frame a code for marketing prices of substitutes of breast milk.[11] The expert committee of the WHO is also active for the protection of consumers and has prepared a list of drugs considered "most essential" to ensure basic health care of the majority of the people.[12] Food and

8. V.K. Gupta: Kautilya Jurisprudence, p. 67.
9. Indian Contract Act, Transfer of Property Act, Specific Relief Act.
10. Food Adulteration Act, 1954, Drug & Cosmetics Act, 1940, MRTP Act, 1969, Ply. Act, Carriers Act, Motor Vehicle Act, Competition Act, 2002, etc.
11. *Northern India Patrika*, March 16, 1988.
12. Report of WHO Expert Committee, Technical Report Series No. 615, 1977.

Agricultural Organization (FAO) is also pursuing the consumer objectives and preparing special programmes for food. ILO[13] promotes the interest of workers as consumers by providing them education and welfare facility at work place which strengthens the cooperative consumerism. The food science control and consumer protection group of the FAO has played an important role in protection of consumer's interest by promoting food processing to meet established standards, conservation of food resources, increasing food production, raising food quality and improving marketing and distribution systems.

The UNIDO[14] has made contributions with regard to safety of consumers by providing machinery of quality control to improve the quality of goods and products. United Nations International Children Emergency Fund (UNICEF) has done appreciable work for infants and children by encouraging breast feeding over powder milk for infants. For the protection of consumers and to restrict the business practices having adverse effect on consumers certain equitable principles and rules have been evolved. The third Adhoc Group of Experts on restrictive business practice of UNCTAD[15] identified certain restrictive business practices, affecting consumers. Certain consumer-related issues focussed the attention as fixation of prices, resale price, refusal to sell, acquisitions, mergers and take over agreements between enterprises, supply of spare parts replacement and after sale service.[16] The UNCTAD prepared a study giving a comprehensive analysis of the role of trade marks in consumer decisions and its conesquences for developing countries.

For protection of consumer's interest efforts have been made on regional level also. Council of European Union has developed interest in consumer information and co-ordination of consumer policies in member states. Organization for Economic Cooperation and Development (OECD) constituted committee on consumer policy to study governmental consumer protection policy in member countries. Its report highlighted the principles for providing more consumer information and protection.[17] In

---

13. International Labour Organization.
14. United Nations Industrial Development Organization.
15. United Nations Conference on Trade and Development.
16. Dr. Gurbax Singh, Law of Consumer Protection (1991), p. 7.
17. OECD, Consumer Protection in the Field of Consumer Credit (Paris, 1977).

Scandinavian countries Inter-Scandinavian Committee on consumer matters coordinates information on consumer protection.

The consumer groups of the world have formed an organization known as International Organization of Consumers' Union which acts as central coordinating and regulation agency. It is having membership from over 50 countries as well as government financed consumer councils labour unions and similar groups possesses a consultative status with various international agencies. The International Chambers of Commerce[18] also deliberated the issues of consumer protection and established an International Council on Advertising Practice and drafted a code of advertising practice.[19]

Every year the 15 March is observed as the "World Consumer Rights Day" because on this day in 1962, the President of USA John F. Kennedy declared four consumer rights. Internationally the problem of consumers was realized by Economic and Social Council in 1977. On April 9, 1985 the UN General Assembly, with due negotiations in the UN Economic and Social Council adopted by consensus a set of guidelines on consumer protection.[20] They provided a framework to strengthen policy and legislation to protected consumers and also to promote international cooperation in this field. The guidelines have identified the main concerns in consumer protection with reference to consumer's basic needs, safety, choice, information, consumer education, redressal representation and healthy environment. A perusal of the objectives of these guidelines makes clear that there should be concrete consumer protection policy in each country. Promotion of 'Sustainable Consumption Patterns' is a very vital issue. Such policy should take note of need to eradicate poverty, fulfilment of basic human needs of all members of society. These objectives cannot be attained without an effective legal system. Thus, legal system of a country should take note of general consumer safety and advancement of economic interest of consumers. Presently, the most important areas of concern are food, clothing, shelter, healthcare, drinking water, sanitation, energy and transportation. If, these goods and

18. ICC was established in 1920 in Paris.
19. International Code of Advertising Practice, Commission on Marketing, Advertising and Distribution (1997).
20. Resolution No. 39/248, dated April 9, 1985, see Appendix-I.

services not given primary attention may result in denial of basic human treatment to people as consumers. The important measures to empower consumers are rights to information, education, representation and redressal.

## POSITION IN INDIA

After independence we adopted welfare state concept under our new constitution. Rights of Indians public were to be protected through legislative consciousness. In India, consumer movement started in 1960 which travelled a long distance to reach the middle class consumers in 1980. In 1969, MRTP Act was enacted to prevent the concentration of economic power to the common detriment and to prohibit monopolistic and restrictive trade practices which were prejudicial to public interest. In 1956, Insurance Companies were nationalized for utilization of money collected by them in the interest of society. Nationalization of 14 banks in 1970 denotes government's sensitivity towards consumer problems. In 1977, a high powered Expert Committee under Chairmanship of Justice Rajinder Nath Sachar laid emphasis on social responsibility of business concern and public corporation. On the recommendation of committee the concept of unfair trade practice was brought in MRTP Act in 1984 for the protection of consumers. In view of the guidelines by U.N. resolution and due to immense pressure of consumer protection organization, a revolutionary law for better protection of consumers was passed in 1986.[21] The object and purpose of the Act is to render simple, inexpensive and speedy remedy to the consumers. The importance of the Act lies in promoting welfare of the society inasmuch as it attempts to remove the helplessness of a consumer which he faces against powerful business described as a network of rackets.[22]

Prior to the Consumer Protection Act, 1986, consumer interests were protected by certain Acts, e.g. Indian Penal Code, 1860, Indian Contract Act, 1872, Sale of Goods Act, 1930, Law of Torts, Transfer of Property Act, 1882, Specific Relief Act, 1963, Prevention of Food Adulteration Act, 1954, Standards of Weights and Measures Act, 1976, The Bureau of Indian Standard Act,

21. Know as Consumer Protection Act, 1986.
22. *LDA v. M.K. Gupta*, AIR 1994 SC 787, observation of J.R.M. Sahai.

1986, Drugs & Cosmetics Act, 1940, Indian Telegraph Act, 1858, etc.

In addition to above stated enactments protection of interest of consumers has constitutional mandate also. Though Constitution of India does not contain any explicit provision on the subject of consumers, there are several provisions having direct bearing on consumer interests. As a part of fundamental freedom the Constitution of India guarantees under Article 19(1)(g) freedom of profession, trade or business, thereby ensuring that state can not prevent a citizen from carrying on a business except by a law imposing a reasonable restriction under Article 19(2). Article 21 guarantees every person life with dignity free from all kinds of exploitation. Article 38 mandates the state to bring about a social order in which social, economic and political justice shall inform all the institutions of life. Article 39(b) and (c) support the whole public distribution system and administrative mechanism to control hoarding and profiteering in India. According to this provision state is required to direct its policy so that ownership and control of material resources of the community are so distributed as best to sub-serve the common good and operation of the economic system should not result in concentration of wealth and means of production to the common detriment. Article 43 obligates the state to secure by suitable legislation for all workers a living condition ensuring a decent standard of life. Article 47 requires the state to take steps to raise the level of nutrition and standard of living to improve public health and to prohibit consumption of intoxicating drinks or drugs which are injurious to health. Most of the subjects concerning consumer protection have been placed in the concurrent list so that centre and states both may make provisions for better quality and efficiency of consumers.

In the beginning consumers were fully competent and sufficient in guarding their interests. Consumer was the king of market, he was treated as sovereign. By the end of $19^{th}$ century, the globalization brought an era of consumerism where consumers started facing exploitation at the hands of strong business class. The increase in emphasis on consumerism in recent years has given the appearance that philosophy of government protection of consumers from certain business practices is a modern development. But there are many examples of such governmental activities which have been part of law for many years.[23] Function of the most of the administrative agencies are related to consumer protection.[24] 'Consumerism' the term used to describe the activities of government, designed to protect consumer is not a recent development. Thus, consumerism is a movement directed to protect the consumers to ensure in terms of satisfaction that the consumer gets best return in exchange for the money he spends.

Business, consumers and government live on each other, live-off each other and because of each other. Consumer satisfaction is the end for which the means are producers and government.[25] The lawyers use the term protection in two different senses: in liberal sense it means to prevent a consumer from suffering harm, in other sense protection means to recompense the loss suffered by consumer in monetary terms. Thus, consumers protection may means either the precaution of things being wrong for the consumer or it may mean the prevention of financial redress for the consumer when the things have gone wrong.[26]

Every right is based on the interest but all interests are not protected by law.[27] Due to start of consumerism, the process of converting the interests of consumers into legal rights started. Passing the four stages, i.e. identification, recognition of interests, ensuring of consumer rights and ensuring adequate relief to consumers, we can find the rights of consumers protected under the law.[28] In the light of U.N. guidelines that government should establish or maintain legal machinery to enable the consumer or organization to obtain redress through formal or informal procedures that are expeditious, inexpensive[29] and accessible. Consumer Protection Act, 1986 in India provides for establishment of consumer protection councils at national, state and

23. Corley, Black and Reed, the Legal Environment of Business, 513.
24. Gurjeet Singh, Green Consumerism in India: The Challenges Ahead (1998) 1, CPJ 10 (Journal Section).
25. Joyeeta Gupta, Consumerism: Emerging Challenge and Opportunities, Consumer Confrontation, Vol. 3, 1987, pp. 2-11.
26. J.A. Jolowing, "The Protection of the Consumer and Purchaser of Goods under English Law," 1969, *Modern Law Review*, Vol. 32, pp. 1-2.
27. Salmond on Jurisprudence by P.J. Fitzerald, 12th ed., London Sweet & Maxwell, 1966, p. 220.
28. Consumer Protection Act, 1986.
29. UN Guidelines under sub-head, "E-measures Enabling Consumers to Obtain Redress."

district level.[30] The objects of these councils shall be to promote and protect the rights of the consumer.[31]

## RIGHTS OF CONSUMERS AS HUMAN RIGHTS

Human rights which belong to human being are posed a mankind's increasing demand for a decent civilized life in which the inherent dignity of each human being will receive respect and protection. Human rights are fundamental in nature and affect our daily life in various ways. No doubt, bread, clothes and house are indispensable in a man's life but other things are also necessary. In other sense human rights are minimal material conditions that shape our life in various ways. It implies political and economic self-determination. According to political self-determination people may pursue freely their civil and political rights. According to economic self-determination people may pursue freely their economic, social and cultural development which also includes permanent sovereignty over national resources[32]. Thus, human rights may be classified in various ways. At international level most common division is that of Civil and Political Rights and Economic, Social and Cultural Rights.

Civil and Political Rights are inspired by the political philosophy of liberal individualism and economic and social doctrine of *laissez faire*. These rights are also called as traditional rights because they came first in the concept of rights. Since these rights developed first in the order of rights, these rights are also called first generation of human rights. These rights are also said to be negative rights. Negative in the sense that, in order to ensure these rights to the people, states need not take affirmative action. It favours abstention rather than intervention of government in the quest of human dignity and includes freedom from racial discrimination, right to life and liberty, freedom from slavery and servitude, etc.[33]

30. Sections 4, 7, 8-A of C.P. Act, 1986.
31. Sections 6, 8, and 8-B of the C.P. Act, 1986.
32. See G.A. Res. No. 1803 (xviii) of the December 1962 on permanent sovereignty over Natural Resources.
33. See Universal Declaration of Human Rights and International Covenant on Civil and Political Rights.

Economic, social and cultural rights are also said to be programmatic rights. These rights are counter part to civil and political rights because one is complementary to other. Civil and political right is meaningless unless a person has economic and social rights as well. Since, these rights come at second number also called as second generation of human rights. These rights are conceived more positive than negative because in order to ensure these rights to people the state has to take "affirmative action."

Third generation of human rights is also called as collective rights. International law recognises certain collective rights exercised jointly by individuals who are grouped into larger communities including people and nations. These collective rights reconceptualise value demands associated with the two earlier generations of rights. As it is proclaimed that, "everyone is entitled to a social international order in which the rights and freedoms set-forth in this declaration can be fully realised."[34] This generation of right embraces several rights. Some of these rights reflect the emergence of third world nationalism and its demand for a global redistribution of power and wealth.

These rights include right to political economic, social and cultural self-determination,[35] the right to economic and social development[36] and the right to participate in and benefit from 'the common heritage of mankind.'[37] Other third generation rights include: the right to peace, right to healthy and balanced environment, etc. All these rights require concerted efforts of all actors, the individual, the state, public and private bodies and the international community.[38]

## CONCLUSION

The contemporary world under the aegis of liberalization, free market and open trade has led to limitless industrial development turning the whole world into a global village market. The goals of development for all, wealth for all, health

34. Article 28 of Universal Declaration of Human Rights.
35. Article 1 of International Covenant on Civil and Political Rights.
36. See Article of the Declaration on the Right to Development.
37. Such as resources scientific, technical and other information and progress, cultural traditions, sites and monuments.
38. See Lectures by Vasak, tenth study session of the International Institute of Human Rights.

for all, clean environment for all and consumer justice for all seem to become a near possibility in twenty-first century. With the rising revolution in human expectations and desires towards consumerism has led to state regulation and protection of consumer interests in harmony with opposing interests of businessmen and manufacturers. Consumer jurisprudence is study of legal principles, precepts and judicial decisions which control, regulate and protect the interests of consumers in effective realization and administration of consumer justice. Consumer jurisprudence has also become a variant of human rights jurisprudence encompassing some basic rights of man like right to live and life, right to health, right to information and other due process rights conducive to freedom of trade and business within framework of business concerning consumer justice.[39] Consumer protection like the environmental protection has become a duty and right to save the community from consumer hazards. Consumer's Protection (his life, health, safety and welfare) has become an essential component of individual liberty, an element of due process of law and variant of human right claimed by consumers.

The Constitution of India too indirectly includes consumer justice in its preamble and directive principles of state policy. As a result of liberalization, decontrol of Indian economy, it has become duty of government to assure and guarantee basic consumer rights to public because all human beings are consumers whether they are young or old, rich or poor, literate or illiterate. Consumer Protection Act, 1986 has given a new Copernican turn to Indian consumer jurisprudence giving enough scope to judiciary to spin consumer jurisprudence around constitutional values of equality, liberty and right to life. Judiciary has responded to the need of consumer justice and generated consumer awareness. Judiciary has been expounding new principles on consumer rights to prevent the menace of consumer exploitation. Social engineering theory was expounded for establishing a correlationship between duties of businessmen and rights consumers. Courts further gave a new turn to consumer jurisprudence and said that consumerism consists of

39. Fundamental of Jurisprudence, Dr. S.N. Dhyani second edition, Central Law Agency (July 1979), p. 394.

several consumer rights such as right to safety, right to be heard, right to know, right choose, etc.[40] Supreme Court gradually invented new legal devices, doctrines and principles for the protection of rights of consumers and adopted the doctrine of strict liability, diluted the *mens-rea* in matters relating consumer wrongs.

40. *Palghat Municipality v. S.R. & Mills* (1975) Cr. L.J. 479 (Ker).

# PART IV
# Corporate Social Responsibility

CHAPTER 7

# Corporate Social Responsibility and Corporate Governance in India

*Dr. Pradip Kumar Das, and Rajib Hassan*

## DEFINITION AND MEANING OF CORPORATE SOCIAL RESPONSIBILITY

Corporate Social Responsibility has become very popular today nationally and internationally. Trade and business is closely related with the people specifically and society at large. Corporate sector earns huge profit from this society through various business activities. But generating wealth in a manner that is socially and environmentally sustainable must be the basic objective of business houses. We are leaving in the era of globalization. In this globalized age it is very important to do business ethically, morally and with concern for the society. Corporate sector should realize that they have a great role to play for the development of the society. The business class should render their support to the oppressed, downtrodden, have-nots, helpless, weaker sections and the timing million of the society. However, the term 'corporate social responsibility' is also known as corporate responsibility, corporate citizenship, and sustainable responsible business or corporate social performance.

Corporate Social Responsibility is the responsibility of an organization for the impacts of its decisions and activities on society and the environment, through transparent and ethical behaviors that is consistent with sustainable development and the welfare of society and takes into account the expectations of stake holders. It can be described as the continuous commitment by corporations towards the economic and social development of communities in which they operate[1]. According to the world Business Council For Sustained Development: "Corporate Social Responsibility is the continuing commitment by business to behave ethically and contribute to economic development while improving the quality of life of the work force and their families as well as of the local community and society at large"[2]. It is an effort by organizations to take responsibility for the impact of their activities on—customers, suppliers, employees, shareholders, communities and stakeholders, as well as the environment. Corporate community involvement and corporate social responsibility is a genuine attempt by a company to build meaningful relationships between the corporate sector and the rest of society. The notion of companies looking beyond profits to their role in society is generally termed Corporate Social Responsibility (CSR). It refers to a company linking itself with ethical values, transparency, employee relations, compliance with legal requirements and overall respect for the communities in which they operate. It goes beyond the occasional community service action, however, as CSR is a corporate philosophy that drives strategic decision-making, partner selection, hiring practices and ultimately, brand development[3]. CSR is a means of analyzing the interdependent relationship that exist between business and economic system, and the communities within which they are based. It is a means of discussing the extent of any obligations a business has to its immediate society; a way of proposing policy ideas on how those obligations can be met; as well as a tool by which the benefits to a business for meeting those obligations can be identified[4]. The aim of CSR is to build a sustainable business which requires healthy economics, markets and communities.

1. http://www.csr_weltweit.de/uploads/tx_jpdownloads/sudip_Emerging_Trends_In_Corporate_Social_Responsibility (Accessed on 18-09-2010).
2. Shubham BPL, Corporate Social Responsibility—An Overview, http://hubpages.com/hub/corporate-social-responsibility-an-overview (Accessed on 18-09-2010).
3. http://www6.miami.edu/ethics/pdf_files/csr_guide.pdf (Accessed on 18-09-2010).
4. *Ibid.*, 3.

## IMPORTANCE OF CSR

The main aims for CSR are[5]:

"(a) *Enlightened self-interest*: creating a synergy of ethics, a cohesive society and a sustainable global economy where markets, labour and communities are able to function well together.

(b) *Social Investment*: contributing to physical infrastructure and social capital is increasingly seen as a necessary part of doing business.

(c) *Transparency and trust*: business has low ratings of trust in public perception. There is increasing expectation that companies will be more open, more accountable and be prepared to report publicly on their performance in social and environmental arenas.

(d) *Increased public expectations of business:* Globally companies are expected to do more than merely providing jobs and contributing to the economy through taxes and employment".

The world Economic Forum has recognized the importance of corporate social responsibility by establishing the Global Corporate Citizenship Initiative. The initiative expects to increase businesses engagement in and support for Corporate Social Responsibility as a business strategy with long-term benefits both for the companies themselves as well as society in general. However, CSR creates a positive image amongst the people for the company and people use to give special respect to the company. It creates short-term employment opportunities by taking various projects like construction of parks, schools, hospitals, etc. CSR may help to get pollution free environment. CSR cultivates a sense of loyalty and trust amongst the employees in the organizational ethics. It enhances the operational efficiency of the company and is often accompanied by increases in productivity. Employees are more motivated and as a result production is increased. The CSR is particularly important within a globalized world because of the way brands are built-on perceptions, ideas, and concepts that usually appeal to higher values. CSR is a means to match corporate operations with

---

5. http://www.asocio.org/policy/corporate%20social%20Responsibility.pdf. (Accessed on 16-09-20100)

stakeholder values and demands, at a time when these values and demands are constantly evolving. "The twenty-first century will be the century of the social sector organization"[6]. So, CSR has become a crucial to get success in business.

## CSR IN INDIA

The concept of corporate Social Responsibility is not very new in India. Indian business has traditionally been responsible. The business sector in India practices various methods of discharging its social responsibility. Indian business enterprises have a long tradition of working within the values that have defined our nation's character. India's ancient wisdom inspires people to work for the larger objectives of the well-being of all stakeholders. M.K. Gandhi described large business as 'trusts' of the 'wealth of the people' and thus emphasized on the greater social purpose that industrial wealth should serve in independent India. Again, in the early days of the post-independence period, the Indian state under the heavy influence of Nehruvian socialism encouraged private industries to play a crucial effective role in the socio-economic development of the backward and weaker sections of the society[7]. In the 1990's, the government of India initiated reforms to liberalize and deregulate the Indian economy by tackling the shortcomings of the "mixed economy". The Government tried to integrate India into the global market. India has become an important economic and political power in the process of globalization. This new changing situation has also influenced the Indian CSR agenda. Open economy system was introduced in the Indian economy during the Rajiv Gandhi and Narashima Rao Government. This was the beginning of the economic liberalization and the free market economy in India. In this liberalized market economy the importance of CSR of various private enterprises was felt necessary. However, in India though the concept CSR was not

6. Peter F. Drucker, Founder of the Drucker Foundation, http://www.miami.edu/ethics/pdf_files/csr_guide.pdf (Accessed on 18-09-20100.
7. Sudip Mahapatra and Kumar, Visalaksh, Emerging Trends in Corporate Social Responsibility: Perspectives and experiences from post-liberalised India, http://www.csr-weltweit.de/uploads/tx_jpdownloads/sudip-Emerging_Trends_In_Corporate_social_Responsibility (Accessed on 18-09-2010).

new, by and large, it was materialized after 1990. Before 1990, various welfare programmes or initiatives were introduced not as a duty or responsibility but as a form of charity[8]. Many Industrial groups like the Tatas or Birlas set-up charitable trusts that provide only financial grants for different purposes. But there were some exceptional circumstances where some corporations took up more active role like the establishment of the Birla Institute of Technology by Birlas and some other educational institutions by various corporate Groups. But, in the post-liberalization phase there was a shift from this philanthropy-based model of Corporate Social Responsibility to a stakeholder participation-based model[9]. In this stakeholder model, the corporation has certain obligation and duties towards the community in which the corporation is present. This changing attitude has also recognized the role of the companies in the area of human rights, business ethics, environmental policies, corporate contributions, community development, corporate governance and environment protection, etc. Today, CSR in India has gone beyond merely charity and donations and is approached in a more organized fashion. It has become an integral part of the corporate strategy. CSR programms are ranged from overall development of the society to supporting specific causes like education, environment, healthcare, etc. Mr. Narayan Murthy, Chairman and Chief Mentor of Infosys underlines the significance of CSR. "For benefit of globalization and technology to reach the poor, the private sector, Philanthropic Institutes and Individuals should cooperate and establish partnership with Government Institutions. This would lift millions of our people out of the poverty, provide them with opportunities and make them participate in the process and progress of globalization."[10] At present, various corporate houses in India have involved themselves in various corporate social responsibilities. For example, organizations, like, Bharat Petroleum Corporations Ltd., Maruti-Suzuki India Ltd., and Hindustan Unilever Ltd. adopt villages where they carry on various developmental activities. They provide better medical

8. *Ibid.*
9. *Ibid*
10. Shubham BPL, Corporate Social Responsibility: An overview; http://www.hubpages.com/hub/corporate-social-responsibility-an-overview (Accessed on 18-09-2010).

facilities, build schools and houses and help the villagers become self-reliant by teaching them vocational and practical training skills. Various other corporate houses have also taken various projects and initiatives to fulfil CSR. Recently the Government of India is also thinking seriously over the issue of CSR. Very recently (on Monday, 3rd May, 2010) Corporate Social Responsibility Awards, 2009-10 was announced by the Government of India. Mr. Anand Sharma, Union Minister of Commerce and Industry, felicitated fourteen organizations, for their exemplary performance in the field of corporate social responsibility (CSR)[11]. FICCI-SEDF congratulates the five award winners as well as nine certificates of appreciation winners of the Business World FICCI-SEDF Corporate Social Awards 2009-10[12]. These five large enterprises were: Tata Steel Limited, Bharti Airtel Ltd., Smaat Aqua Technologies Pvt. Ltd., Elin Appliances Pvt. Ltd., Multi-Commodity Exchange of India Ltd.[13] The Ministry of Corporate Affairs, Govt. of India, has also issued a voluntary guideline for corporate social responsibility in 2009. The main reason behind this is to encourage India corporations in the Corporate Social Responsibility (CSR).

CSR policy should normally cover the following core elements in India[14]:

(a) Care for all stakeholders;
(b) Ethical functioning;
(c) Respect for workers' Rights and Welfare;
(d) Respect for Human Rights;
(e) Respect for environment; and
(f) Activities for social and Inclusive Development.

Besides the above, the following steps should also be taken in order to make CSR policy effective in India:[15]

11. http://www.ficci-sedf.org/CSR-Awards-Report2010.pdf (Accessed on 18-09-2010).
12. *Ibid.*
13. *Ibid.*
14. Corporate Social Responsibility Voluntary Guidelines, 2009, Ministry of Corporate Affairs, Government of India, http://www.mca.gov.in/Ministry/latestnews/CSR_voluntary_Guidelines_24dec.2009.pdf (Accessed on 25-09-2010).
15. Dr. Shankar Adawal, Corporate Social Responsibility, http://www.insidereports.com/storypage.asp?storyID=20014487

(a) Incorporation of a section on social actions in annual reports of companies;
(b) Appointment of an independent social accounting committee to measure monitors, evaluate and report impact of CSR in annual reports;
(c) Separate department to look after the CSR;
(d) Periodic training programmes and awareness camps to train personnel on CSR;
(e) Linkage between CSR and financial success should be established; and
(f) A certain percentage of profit should be earmarked for social development that should reflect in the annual balance sheet of companies.

## CORPORATE GOVERNANCE

Over the last two decades, corporate governance has been a highly fashionable topic in company law and has generated an enormous literature[16]. The subject came to prominence in the United States with the work leading to the publication of the American Law Institute's *Principle of Corporate Governance* in 1994 and in the UK the topic is associated above all with the Cadbury Committee Report of 1992 and its associated Code of British Practice[17]which has provided a focal point for the subsequent spread of corporate governance enhance codes throughout Europe. In the era of liberalization and lesser bureaucratic controls combined with globalization of corporations and corporate markets a number of new issues relating to control mechanism in corporate governance are being raised. With the effect of globalization the dimension of the business corporations has extended to a large extent. It is undoubtedly admitted that the success and existence of such business corporations largely depend upon good corporate governance. Corporate governance has recently come into prominence in the business world, the term 'corporate governance' and its daily usage is a new phenomenon of the last fifteen years or so. The development of corporate governance is a global occurrence and as such is a complex area including legal, cultural, ownership and other

16. Gower and Davies' Principles of Modern Company Law, Seventh edn. Thomson- Sweet and Maxwell, 2003, p. 291.
17. *Ibid.*

structural differences. In the words of Shri N.R. Narayana Murthy, Chief Mentor, Infosys Limited, "Corporate governance is maximizing the shareholder value in a corporation while ensuring fairness to all stakeholders, customers, employees, investors, vendors, the government and the society-at-large. Corporate governance is about transparency and raising the trust and confidence of stakeholders in the way the company is run. It is about owners and the managers operating as the trustees on behalf of every shareholder—large or small."[18]

## Meaning

Corporate governance is a system by which companies are directed and controlled keeping in view all relevant aspects of business activities. It is needed to create a corporate culture of social consciousness and openness. According to our Ex-Prime Minister Mr. Atal Bihari Vajpayee—corporate governance is a multidisciplinary phenomenon. It involves Board of Directors, Shareholders, Stakeholders, Customers, Employees and Society at large. Corporate governance is a conscious, deliberate and sustained effort on the part of entity to strike a judicious balance between its own interest and the interests of various constituents on the environment in which it is operating. Adrian Cadbury in UK emphasizes, "Corporate governance basically, has to do with power and accountability: who exercise power, on behalf of whom and how the exercise of power is controlled."[19]

## Corporate Governance—No Longer a Luxury but a Necessity[20]

Today, in the present commercial context, corporate governance is no longer a luxury but has become a necessity. The Board of Directors of organizations is required to play a vital role in the strategic affairs of an organization. The responsibility and accountability of the top members of the organizations have come into the forefront in recent years.

---

18. http://www.nfcgindia.org (Accessed on 12-10-2010).
19. Adrian Cadbury, Corporate Governance and Chairmanship, Oxford University Press.
20. *Ibid.*

### Corporate Governance as a Way of Life[21]

Corporate governance today is a way of life and not merely a set of rules. A way of life that necessitates taking into account the shareholder's interest in every business decision. Good governance implies that institution is run for optimal benefits of the stakeholders in it. Even in a competitive environment, the expectations all around are of fair play and effort to excel by ethical means. Indeed, ethical conduct promotes corporate success. It motivates the employees. Good corporate governance and ethical conduct is good policy for achieving success.

### Basic Essentials for Good Corporate Governance

However, following are the basic essentials of good corporate governance:

- Accountability of the Board of Directors and their constituent responsibilities to the ultimate owners, i.e. shareholders.
- A key element of good governance is transparency. Transparency requires the right to information, timeliness and integrity of the information produced.
- System of checks and balances and greater simplicity in process of governance.
- Clarity of responsibility to enhance accountability.
- Adherence to the rules. Corporate action needs to conform to letter and spirit to the codes.

### Reasons for Interest in Corporate Governance

However, following are some of the reasons which are responsible for increasing interest in corporate governance:

- Directors must realize that their job is to represent the shareholders and other stakeholders.
- There is rise of institutional investors and to safeguard their interest good corporate governance is necessary.
- In the wake of globalization, there are numerous take over moves in the corporate world.
- Advent of investigating reporting in business journalism.
- Activism of regulatory bodies such as SEBI, etc.

---

21. *Ibid.*

**Mechanisms of Corporate Governance in India**[22]

In India, there are six mechanisms to ensure corporate governance:

(a) *Companies Act:* Companies in our country are regulated by the Companies Act, 1956, as amended up-to-date. The companies Act is one of the biggest legislations with 658 sections and 14 schedules. The arms of the Act are quite long and touch every aspect of a company's insistence. But to ensure corporate governance, the Act confers legal rights to shareholders to:

- Vote on every resolution placed before an annual general meeting;
- To elect directors who are responsible for specifying objectives and laying down policies;
- Determine remuneration of directors and the CEO;
- Removal of directors; and
- Take active part in the annual general meetings.

(b) *Securities Law:* The primary securities law in our country is the SEBI Act. Since its setting up in 1992, the board has taken a number of initiatives towards investor protection. One such initiative is to mandate information disclosure both in prospectus and in annual accounts. While the Companies Act itself mandates certain standards of information disclosure, SEBI Act has added substantially to these requirements in an attempt to make these documents more meaningful.[23]

(c) *Discipline of the Capital Market:* Capital market itself has considerable impact on corporate governance. Here in lies the role the minority shareholders can play effectively. They can refuse to subscribe to the capital of a company in the primary market and in the secondary market; they can sell their shares, thus depressing the share prices. A depressed share price makes the company an attractive takeover target.[24]

22. www.indianmba.com/Faculty_Column/FC974/fc974.html (Accessed on 12-10-2010; 1:25pm)
23. *Ibid.*
24. *Ibid.*

(d) *Nominees on Company Boards:* Development banks hold large blocks of shares in companies. These are equally big debt holders too. Being equity holders, these investors have their nominees in the boards of companies. These nominees can effectively block resolutions, which may be detrimental to their interests. Unfortunately, the role of nominee directors has been passive, as has been pointed out by several committees including the Bhagwati Committee on takeovers and the Omkar Goswami Committee on corporate governance.[25]

(e) *Statutory Audit:* Statutory audit is yet another mechanism directed to ensure good corporate governance. Auditors are the conscious-keepers of shareholders, lenders and others who have financial stakes in companies. Auditing enhances the credibility of financial reports prepared by any enterprise. The auditing process ensures that financial statements are accurate and complete, thereby enhancing their reliability and usefulness for making investment decisions.[26]

(f) *Codes of Conduct:* The mechanisms discussed till now are regulatory in approach. They are mandated by law and violation of any provision invites penal action. But legal rules alone cannot ensure good corporate governance. What is needed is self-regulation on the part of directors, besides of course, the mandatory provisions.[27]

## Theories of Corporate Governance[28]

The theories underlying the development of corporate governance date from much earlier and are drawn from a variety of disciplines including finance, economics, accounting, law, management and organizational behavior. The main theories which effected the development of corporate governance may be discussed as under:

---

25. *Ibid.*
26. *Ibid.*
27. *Ibid.*
28. Haslinda Abdullah; Faculty of Economics & Management, University Putra Malaysia and Benedict Valentine; Graduate School of Management, University Putra Malaysia; www.ejournals.com (Accessed on 12-10-2010; 1:05pm).

- *Agency Theory:* A significant body of work has built up in this area within the context of the principal-agent framework. Agency theory identifies the agency relationship where one party, the principal delegates work to another party, the agent. Much of agency theory as related to corporations is set in the context of the separation of ownership and control. In the context of a corporation, the shareholders [owners] are the principal and the directors are the agents.
- *Transaction Cost Economics:* Transaction Cost Economics [TCE] is often viewed as closely related to agency theory. TCE views the firm as a governance structure whereas agency theory views the firm as the nexus of contracts. Hart indicates that, in a world of incomplete contracts [where agency problems are also present], governance structure does have a role. Governance structure can be seen as a mechanism for making decisions that have not been specified in the initial contract.
- *Stakeholder Theory:* Stakeholder theory takes account of a wider group of constituents rather than focusing on shareholders only. A consequence of focusing on the shareholders only is that the maintenance of enhancement of shareholder value is paramount, whereas when a wider stakeholder group such as employees, providers of credit, customers, suppliers, government and local community is taken into account, the overriding focus shareholder value becomes less self-evident.
- *Stewardship Theory:* Stewardship theory draws on the assumptions underlying agency theory and TCE. The work of Donaldson and Davis [1991] cautioned against accepting agency theory as a given and introduced an alternative approach to corporate governance-Stewardship theory. As per Stewardship Theory, directors are regarded as the stewards of the company's assets and will be predisposed to act in the best interest of the shareholders.

**Periodical Development of Corporate Governance in India**

Following a devastating economic downturn and social unrest in 1990-91, the Government of India introduced a programme of reforms to open up the economy and encourage greater reliance on market mechanisms and less reliance on government. Further reforms were aimed at making the public sector more efficient. There were also reforms to the Banking sector to bring it into in line with the international norms and to the Securities market, with the SEBI becoming the regulator of the securities market. However, all the reforms above led to a much improved environment in which corporate governance was able to develop. India has a range of business forms, including public limited companies which are listed on the Stock Exchange, domestic private companies and foreign companies.

- *1998 Standards:* The Confederation of Indian Industries (CII) published a *"Desirable Code of Corporate Governance"*[29] in 1998 and number of forward looking companies took its recommendations on Board. However, many companies have still poor practices.

*Kumar Mangalam Birla Committee Report, 2000*[30]

SEBI formally established the Committee on Corporate Governance in May 1999, chaired by Shri Kumar Mangalam Birla. The Report of the KM Birla Committee on corporate governance [hereinafter referred as the Report] was published in 2000. The Report emphasizes the importance of corporate governance to future growth of the capital market and the economy. Three key aspects underlying corporate governance are defined as accountability, transparency and equality of treatment for all stakeholders.

- Corporate governance has several claimants—shareholders and other stakeholders—which include suppliers, customers, creditors, and the bankers, the employees of the company, the government and the society at large. This Report on Corporate Governance has been prepared by the Committee for SEBI, keeping in view primarily the interests of a particular class of stakeholders, namely, the shareholders, who together

29. www.nfcgindia.org/desirable_corporate_governace_cii; (Accessed on-12-10-2010;12:40pm)
30. www.sebi.gov.in/commreport/corpgov.html (Accessed on 12-10-2010; 12:25pm.)

with the investors form the principal constituency of SEBI while not ignoring the needs of other stakeholders.

- *The Committee therefore agreed that the fundamental objective of corporate governance is the "enhancement of shareholder value, keeping in view the interests of other stakeholder"*. This definition harmonizes the need for a company to strike a balance at all times between the need to enhance shareholders' wealth whilst not in any way being detrimental to the interests of the other stakeholders in the company.
- In the opinion of the Committee, the imperative for corporate governance lies not merely in drafting a code of corporate governance, but in practicing it. Even now, some companies are following exemplary practices, without the existence of formal guidelines on this subject. Structures and rules are important because they provide a framework, which will encourage and enforce good governance; but alone, these cannot raise the standards of corporate governance. What counts is the way in which these are put to use. *The Committee is thus of the firm view, that the best results would be achieved when the companies begin to treat the code not as a mere structure, but as a way of life.*
- It follows that the real onus of achieving the desired level of corporate governance, lies in the proactive initiatives taken by the companies themselves and not in the external measures like breadth and depth of a code or stringency of enforcement of norms. The extent of discipline, transparency and fairness, and the willingness shown by the companies themselves in implementing the Code, will be the crucial factor in achieving the desired confidence of shareholders and other stakeholders and fulfilling the goals of the company.

*Some Essential Features of the Report*

I. *Board of Directors*: This section of the Code covers the composition of the Board and independent directors. The Board provides leadership and strategic guidance for the company is at all times accountable to the shareholders.

The Code recommends that not less than 50% of the Board is comprised of non-executive directors; where there is a non-executive chairman, then at least 1/3rd of the Board should be independent.

II. *Nominee Directors*: The Indian system allows for nominee directors to be put forward by financial or investment institutions to safeguard their investment in the company. The Code allows this practice to continue but stated that such nominees should have the same responsibility as other directors and be accountable to the shareholders generally.

III. *Chairman of the Board*: Whilst recognizing that the roles of the Chairman and Chief Executive are different, the Code recognizes that the roles may be combined and performed by one individual in some instances.

IV. *Audit Committee*: There are a number of recommendations in the Code in relation to audit committees including the recommendation that a qualified and independent audit committee is established to help to enhance confidence in the company's disclosures.
The committee should comprise a minimum of 3 members all of whom are non-executive, with a majority being independent; it should be chaired by an independent director.

V. *Remuneration Committee*: A remuneration committee should be established to make recommendations on executive director's remuneration. The committee should be comprised of at least 3 non-executive directors and chaired by an independent director.

VI. *Board Procedures*: Mandatory requirements in relation to board meetings are:
First, that they should be held at least four times a year with a maximum gap of four months between any two meetings;
Secondly, that a director should not be involved in more than 10 committees or act as chairman of more than 5 committees across all companies with which he is a director.

VII *Management*: A mandatory recommendation is that there should be disclosure in the Annual Report, either as part of the 'Director's Report' or as a 'Management Discussion and Analysis Report', about the company's position, its outlook, performance and relevant areas of interest to shareholders.

There should also be disclosure of any material financial/commercial transaction in which management has a personal interest that may have a potential conflict with the interest of the company.

VIII *Shareholders*: Shareholders are entitled to be able to participate effectually in the Annual General Meeting. Therefore, in support of this aim, it is mandatory recommendation that, on the appointment of a new and on the re-appointment of existing directors, the shareholders are provided with relevant information about the directors.

IX *Manner of Implementation*: There are mandatory recommendations that a company should have a separate section on corporate governance in its Annual Report.

After the Kumar Mangalam Birla Committee Recommendations, the Murthy Committee Recommendations, 2003 also play an important role in the expansion of the concept Corporate Governance in India[31]. With the goal of promoting better corporate governance practices in India, the Ministry of Corporate Affairs, Government of India, has set-up National Foundation For Corporate Governance (NFCG) in partnership with Confederation of Indian Industries (CII), Institute of Company Secretaries of India (ICSI) and Institute of Chartered Accountants of India (ICAI). However, the mission of National Foundation For Corporate Governance (NFCG) are as below[32]:

(a) To foster a culture for promoting a good governance, voluntary compliance and facilitate effective participation of different stakeholders;
(b) To create a framework of best practices, structure, processes and ethics; and
(c) To make significant difference to Indian corporate sector by raising the standard of Corporate Governance in India towards achieving stability and growth.

Good corporate governance is vital because of its role in attracting foreign investment. It is a medium whereby society can

---

31. www.highbeam.com/doc/1G1-167305801.html (Accessed on 12-10-2010.
32. http://www.nfcgindia.org (Accessed on 12-10-2010).

be sure that large corporations are well-run institutions to which investors and lenders can confidently deposit their funds. It creates safeguards against corruption and mismanagement, while promotes fundamental values of a market economy in democratic society. Good corporate governance practices are also a *sine qua non* for sustainable business that aims at generating long term value to all its shareholders and other stakeholders. The position and goals of the Indian Corporate sector has changed a lot after the liberalization of 1990's. Since then, we have witnessed wide-ranging changes in both laws and regulations, and a major positive transformation of the corporate sector and the corporate Governance[33]. Some aspects of corporate Governance have also been enshrined in the law that is administered by the Ministry of Corporate affairs, SEBI and other sectoral regulators. However, a transparent, ethical and responsible corporate Governance framework essentially emerges from the intrinsic will and passion for Good Governance ingrained in the business entity[34]. The Ministry of Corporate Affairs has, in recent times, initiated a number of initiatives for growth and development of the corporate sector. The endeavor of the ministry is to administer the Companies Act and the activities of the corporate sector with enlightened regulation. With this vision the Ministry is now focusing its concern on a generic issue of tremendous importance not only to Corporate India but to the nation as a whole, that of good corporate governance practices, essential to ensure inclusive growth, wherein every section of society enjoys the fruits of the corporate growth. Sound and efficient corporate governance practices are the basis for stimulating the performance of companies maximizing their operational efficiency, achieving sustained productivity as well as ensuring protection of shareholder's interests[35]. However, the CII Code Recommendations, 1997, the Kumar Mangalam Birla Committee Recommendations, 2000 and the Murthy Committee Recommendations, 2003 have widened a more sophisticated understanding of Corporate Governance in India.

---

33. R. Chakrabarti, W. Megginson, P. Yadav, Corporate Governance in India, December 8, 2007, CFR: Working Paper No. 08-02; www.cfr-cologne.de/download/.../cfr-08-02.pdf (Accessed on 12-10-2010).
34. http://www.mca.gov.in/Ministry/latestnews/CG_voluntary_Guidelines_2009_24december2009.pdf (Accessed on 12-10-2010).
35. *Supra* note 33.

## CONCLUDING REMARKS

In the post-liberalization period, the importance of Corporate Social Responsibility (CSR) in India and corporate governance are increasing day-by-day. CSR is good business sense and an effective approach in doing business in a globalised world where companies are increasingly relying on brand strength. Again, good Corporate Governance practices increase company's value and stakeholders' trust resulting into rapid development of capital market, the economy and also help in the evolution of a vibrant and constructive shareholders' activism. Both of these concepts are very important and widely discussed today in the corporate world. The Ministry of Corporate Affairs, Government of India, has examined various committee reports and other suggestions from various corners with regard to Corporate Governance in this context. Keeping in mind that, the subject of Corporate Governance may go well beyond the law and that there are inherent limitations in enforcing many aspects of Corporate Governance through legislative or regulatory means, it has been considered necessary that a set of voluntary guidelines called "Corporate Governance—Voluntary Guidelines, 2009" which are relevant in the present context, are prepared and distributed for consideration and adoption by corporate[36]. However, these guidelines provide for a set of good practices which may be voluntarily adopted by the public companies[37]. Business cannot succeed in a society which fails. As business is established in the society so it must have some duty towards the society. In the age of information revolution and growing emphasis on transparency, customers of any product or service are unlikely to feel satisfied in buying from a company that is seen to violate the expectations of ethical and socially responsible behavior. Companies that pay genuine attention to the principles of socially responsible behavior are favoured by the public and preferred for their goods and services. CSR is aimed at the welfare of communities; employees and their families. Its aim is to active social development, higher economic growth and social engineering to reduce social inequalities. It creates a sense of pride in employees and shareholders. Companies with CSR Schemes are highly regarded in the society by the government,

---

36. *Ibid.*
37. *Ibid.*

the media and the common people. However, as per Government of India's CSR implementation guidance[38] companies should allocate specific amount in their budgets for CSR activities. In the words of S.V. Sudhakar, Vice-Chancellor of Dr. B.R. Ambedkar University[39], Corporate Social Responsibility (CSR) should be made mandatory for a company. However, it is really controversial whether it should be made compulsory or not. The importance of CSR in this globalized world cannot be denied. It is no longer a luxury but a necessity today. There should be a balance between the responsibility of the corporate to solve socio-economic problems of the society and profit-making intention of the corporate. In line with Corporate Social Responsibility Voluntary Guidelines, 2009 of Corporate Affairs, Government of India, and considering the socio-economic condition of India, it can be suggested that CSR in India should not be made compulsory but voluntary.

38. http://www.mca.gov.in/Ministry/latestnews/CSR_voluntary_Guidelines_24dec2009.pdf. (Accessed on 25-09-2010).
39. The statement was made in a national seminar on CSR, *The Hindu*, Feb. 20, 2010; www.thehindu.com/2010/02/20/stories/2010022062660600.htm (Accessed on 24-09-2010).

# CHAPTER 8

# Corporate Social Responsibility and Legal Regulations in India: An Overview

*Dr Sukanta Sarkar*

## INTRODUCTION

Corporate law is especially doctrinally challenging because it incorporates and builds upon several areas of law. Contract, property, tort, trust, civil procedure, professional responsibility, and federal securities law, courts are example.[1] As corporate social disclosure and reporting became part of the accounting problematic, several theories, approaches or perspectives have been provided in the literature in order to approach this sort of disclosure.[2] The overarching ideological system of beliefs of government officials and ruling parties or coalitions, may also be another determinant of Corporate Social Responsibility (CSR). In countries with leftist political ideologies firms might have better CSR because all major stakeholders expect companies to be socially and environmentally responsible. In other words, collective social consciousness might encourage firms to attach greater importance to CSR.[3] In recent decades, a growing number

1. Faith Stevelman (2009), "Globalization and Corporate Social Responsibility: Challenges for the Academy," *Future Lawyers and Corporate Law*, Vol. 53, pp. 819-20.
2. Nafez Abu-Baker (2000), "Corporate Social Reporting and Disclosure Practice in Jordan: An Empirical Investigation," *Dirasat Administrative Sciences*, Vol. 27, No. 1, p. 251.
3. Ioannis Ioannou and George Serafeim (2010), What Drives Corporate Social Performance? International evidence from social, environmental and governance scores, Retrieved from http://www.hbs.edu/faculty/Pages/item.aspx?num=38373

of academics as well as top executives have been allocating a considerable amount of time and resources to Corporate Social Responsibility (CSR) strategies.[4] The idea of CSR is necessary for the goal of society's sustainable development.[5] The U.N. High Commissioner for Human Rights (UNHCHR) observed that *"there are gaps in understanding the nature and scope of the human rights responsibilities of business."*[6]

Business and society are interdependent. The well-being of one depends on the well-being of the other.[7] It is impossible to consider organizations apart from the society in which they exist.[8] In the olden days, management is seeking for survival and profits. Nowadays, management concerns managing financial and non-financial results with awareness of risk and maintenance of transparency.[9] Business is facing challenging times world-wide. Management of business has progressed rapidly in last 50 years.[10] As a result, corporate social performance (CSP) has possessed equal importance of corporate financial performance (CFP). In the last twenty years, there has been a sea change in the nature of the triangular relationship

---

4. Beiting Cheng, Ioannis Ioannou and George Serafeim (2011), Corporate social responsibility and access to finance, p. 2, Retrieved from http://papers.ssrn.com/sol3/papers.cfm?abstract_id=1847085
5. Yakup Selvi, Eva Wagner and Ahmet Türel (2010), "Corporate social responsibility in the time of financial crisis: Evidence from Turkey," *Annales Universitatis Apulensis Series Oeconomica*, 12(1), p. 281.
6. Radu Mares (2010), Defining the limits of corporate responsibilities against the concept of legal positive obligations, p. 1158, Retrieved from http://docs.law.gwu.edu/stdg/gwilr/PDFs/40-4/40-4-7-Mares.pdf
7. Dr. D'Silva Bernadette, Dr. D'Silva Stephen and Miss Bhuptani Roshni (2012), Corporate social responsibility—An innovation to a strategic business success: An empirical study, Maratha Mandir's Babasaheb Gawde Institute of Management Studies, p. 1, Retrieved from http://www.mmbgims.com/docs/full_paper/42_PS_Rao_pp.pdf
8. Nazan Yelkikalan and Can Kose (2012), "The effects of the financial crisis on corporate social responsibility," *International Journal of Business and Social Science*, Vol. 3, No. 3, p. 293.
9. Shirley Yeung (2011), "The Role of Banks in Corporate Social Responsibility," *Journal of Applied Economics and Business Research*, 1(2), p. 103.
10. Shoubhagya Ranjan Mahakud (2012), Corporate Social Responsibility: Indian Perspectives, Retrieved from http://www.indianmba.com/Occasional_Papers/OP194/op194.html

between companies, the state and the society.[11] Most Multinational Corporations (MNCs) identify CSR as a business tool to promote a positive image to business stakeholders and as a way to improve the quality of life among citizens of the host countries.[12] Pressure from internal and external stakeholders strongly influences companies to maintain a positive, CSR reputation.[13]

CSR has developed immensely over the last decade and has brought about the growth of many voluntary initiatives and Codes of Conduct, as expressions of the willingness of corporations to abide by human rights and contribute to sustainable development. Despite these initiatives, there are continuous reports of human rights violations by corporations. In the eyes of many, this leaves no choice but to introduce legally binding minimum CSR standards. The first truly international attempt to introduce such standards was initiated by the UN Sub-Commission on Human Rights with the Draft UN Norms on the Responsibilities of Transnational Corporations and Other Business Enterprises with Regard to Human Rights (UN Norms).[14]

---

11. Parul Khana and Gitika Gupta (2011), "Status of Corporate Social Responsibility: In Indian Context," *Sri Krishna International Research & Educational Consortium*, Vol. 2, Issue 1, p. 178, Retrieved from http://www.skirec.com/images/download/apjrbm/APJRBM-VOL2-ISSUE-1-JAN-2011/2.13%20PARUL%20KHANNA%20%20Paper-_Corporate_Social_Responsibility-1%5B1%5D.pdf
12. Nattavud Pimpa (2011), Multinational Corporations: Corporate social responsibility and poverty alleviations in Thailand, The First International Conference on Interdisciplinary Research and Development, 31 May to 1 June 2011, Thailand, Retrieved from http://www.inrit2012.com/inrit2011/Proceedings2011/02_83_24C_Nattavud%20Pimpa_%5B8%5D.pdfhttp://www.inrit2012.com/inrit2011/Proceedings2011/02_83_24C_Nattavud%20Pimpa_%5B8%5D.pdf
13. Nagib Salem Bayoud, Marie Kavanagh and Geoff Slaughter (2012), "Corporate Social Responsibility Disclosure and Corporate Reputation in Developing Countries: The Case of Libya," *Journal of Business and Policy Research*, Vol. 7, No. 1, p. 145.
14. Marianna Linnik and Sune Skadegaard Thorsen (2008), ILO and CSR—minimum human rights standards for corporations, Governance, International Law & Corporate Social Responsibility, p. 105, Retrieved from http://www.ilo.org/inst/lang--en/index.htm

## WHAT IS CORPORATE SOCIAL RESPONSIBILITY?

Corporate social responsibility is not a difficult concept and can be explained as: Corporate—means organized business; social—means everything dealing with the people and Responsibility—means accountability between the two.[15] It is generally used to describe business's efforts to achieve sustainable outcomes by committing to good business practices and standards.[16] Corporate Social Responsibility is one of the important aspects of civilized society in which every individual is continuously receiving different experiences from the society.[17] The concept of CSR captures the dynamics of the relationship between business and society. The core theme of CSR is to deal, interact and relate with stakeholders with an ethical approach that is not harming or hurting any stakeholder.[18] CSR is defined as the economic, legal, ethical, and discretionary expectancies that society has of organizations at a given point in time. Legal responsibilities refer to the framework of legal requirements which businesses need to meet while practicing economic duties. Ethical responsibilities are the defined appropriate behavior by established norms that businesses should follow, and philanthropic responsibilities reflect the common desire to see businesses get actively involved in the betterment of society.[19] As

---

15. Jadhav, Amrita and Koli, Amita C. (2012), Corporate Social Responsibility and Women Empowerment, p. 1, Retrieved from http://www.mmbgims.com/docs/full_paper/20_AMITA%20KOLI_pp.pdf
16. Dr. Naringrekar, Satish (2012), Corporate Social Responsibility and Corporate Governance, Maratha Mandir's Babasaheb Gawde Institute of Management Studies, p. 1, Retrieved from http://www.mmbgims.com/docs/full_paper/17_Sirajuddin_pp.pdf
17. Sandeep Gupta and Dr. Parul Khana (2011), "Corporate Social Responsibility: An Analysis in SME's at Faridabad Region," *ZENITH: International Journal of Multidisciplinary Research*, Vol. 1, Issue 8, p. 261.
18. Dr. Rajesh Kumar Shastri and Anushree Singh (2012), An Empirical Study on Corporate Social Responsibility Practices of Indian Public Sector Companies, National Conference on Emerging Challenges for Sustainable Business, 2012, p. 443, Retrieved from http://domsiitr.info/allpaper/05%20An%20Empirical%20Study%20on%20Corporate%20Social%20Responsibility_Rajesh%20Kumar%20Shastri_GM023.pdf
19. Gresi Sanje Dahan and Isil Senol (2012), "Corporate Social Responsibility in Higher Education Institutions: Istanbul Bilgi University Case,"

anticipated, the meaning of CSR was largely framed to reflect the local realities.[20]

A widely quoted definition by the World Business Council for Sustainable Development states that: "*Corporate social responsibility is the continuing commitment by business to behave ethically and contribute to economic development while improving the quality of life of the workforce and their families as well as of the local community and society at large.*"[21] The UK Government's (2004) CSR report indicates that: "*Corporate Social Responsibility has moved from the margins to the mainstream, from the arena of charity to the arena of corporate strategy: the emphasis is no longer just on external giving but now on internal business processes, the focus is less on how companies give money away, to focussing on how companies make money.*"[22] Milton Friedman said that "*the basic mission of any business is to produce, with profit, goods and services, making the business to achieve its maximum contribution to society and, infact, to be socially responsible.*"[23] The European Multistakeholder Forum defines CSR as "*a concept whereby companies integrate social and environmental concerns in their business operations and in their interactions with their stakeholders on a voluntary basis*".[24]

---

*American International Journal of Contemporary Research*, Vol. 2, No. 3, p. 97.

20. Kenneth M. Amaeshi, Bongo C. AdiChris Ogbechie and Olufemi O. Amao (2006), Corporate Social Responsibility (CSR) in Nigeria: Western Mimicry or Indigenous Practices?, No. 39-2006, ICCSR Research Paper Series, ISSN 1479-5124, p. 22, Retrieved from http://195.130.87.21:8080/dspace/bitstream/123456789/1091/1/39-Corporate%20Social%20Responsibility%20%28CSR%29%20in%20Nigeria%20western%20mimicry%20or%20indigenous%20practice.pdf
21. Geetika Singh (2012), Corporate Social Responsibility: The Vedic Perspective, National Conference on Emerging Challenges for Sustainable Business, 2012, p. 527, Retrieved from http://domsiitr.info/allpaper/09%20Corporate%20Social%20Responsibility-The%20Vedic_Geetika_GM014.pdf
22. Kwesi Amponsah-Tawiah and Kwasi Dartey-Baah (2012), "Corporate Social Responsibility in Ghana," *International Journal of Business and Social Science*, Vol. 2, No. 17, p. 108.
23. Jucan Cornel Nicolae and Jucan Mihaela Sabina (2011), "Dimensions and Challenges of Social Responsibility," *Annales Universitatis Apulensis Series Oeconomica*, 12(1), p. 238.
24. Jolde Cosmin, Belu Mihaela and Iamandi Irina Eugenia (2012), Corporate Social Responsibility in the Romanian Banking Sector, p. 668,

CSR also called corporate conscience, corporate citizenship and sustainable responsible business is generally understood as a way through which a company achieves a balance of economic, environmental and social imperatives.[25] The concept of CSR originated in the 1950s in the USA and the concept came into prominence in public debate during the 1960s and 1970s. At that time US had lots of pressing social problems like poverty, unemployment, race, urban blight and pollution. Corporate Social Responsibility became a matter of utmost importance for diverse groups demanding change in the business. During the 1980s to 2000, corporations generally recognized a responsibility towards society and weighed against the demands of being competitive in a rapidly changing global economy.[26] In the 1960s and 1970s the civil rights movement, consumerism, and environmentalism affected society's expectations of business.[27] In the 1970s, the attention in CSR shifted away from theorizing about what is good for society, to analyzing which demands to business are put forward by society. In 1979, Carroll concluded that CSR relates to society's *expectations*.[28] In the late 1990s, CSR began to gain momentum as pressure from consumers, the media, activists and various public organizations demanded that companies contribute to society.[29] Since the mid-1990s the notion

---

Retrieved from http://steconomice.uoradea.ro/anale/volume/2008/v2-economy-and-business-administration/121.pdf

25. Kwasi Dartey-Baah and Kwesi Amponsah-Tawiah (2011), "Exploring the Limits of Western Corporate Social Responsibility Theories in Africa," *International Journal of Business and Social Science*, Vol. 2, No. 18, p. 126.
26. Dhond, Arvind A. (2010), Corporate Social Responsibility of Indian Business Houses, p. 1, Retrieved from http://www.mmbgims.com/docs/full_paper/3_Arvind_pp.pdf
27. Asiamah Yeboah (2012), "Building and Sustaining Competitive Advantage Through Corporate Social Responsibility (CSR) and Ethics in the Telecommunication Industry in Ghana: A Case Study of MTN, Ghana," *International Journal of Business and Management Tomorrow*, Vol. 2, No. 1, p. 4.
28. Dr. Frans Paul van der Putten (2005), A Research Agenda for International Corporate Social Responsibility, p. 5, Retrieved from http://papers.ssrn.com/sol3/papers.cfm?abstract_id=896672
29. Nancy R. Lockwood (2004), Corporate Social Responsibility: HR's Leadership Role, p. 2.

of CSR has been associated with the terms of *'corporate citizenship'*, *'corporate sustainability'* and *'triple bottom line'*.[30]

**Significance**

Corporate social responsibility is sometimes described as being a tacit contract between business organizations and a hosting community, whereby the community permits the business to operate within its jurisdiction to create job opportunity for its residents and revenue through taxation.[31] Any organization, be it social or commercial, always depend upon the society.[32] Business leaders can be expected to say that CSR is important, especially in today's social and political climate.[33] Many enterprises have adopted CSR practices largely because they believe it will benefit their business in the long-term and improve their competitiveness.[34] CSR is all about adding values which will derives to the outer and inner success of the corporation as it enhances the brand development, partnership selection and decision-making.[35] Now, CSR is being linked with business strategies. Competitive advantage can be gained by

30. Constantina Bichta and Jan Merchant (2003), Corporate Social Responsibility: A Role in Government Policy and Regulation?, p. 7. Retrieved from http://www.bath.ac.uk/management/cri/pubpdf/Research_Reports/16_Bichta.pdf
31. Chima Mordi, Iroye Samuel Opeyemi and Stella Ojo (2012), "Corporate Social Responsibility and Legal Regulations in Nigeria," *Economic Insights—Trends and Challenges*, Vol. 1, p. 2, Retrieved from http://www.upg-bulletin-se.ro/archive/2012-1/1.%20Mordi_Opeyemi_Tonbara_Ojo.pdf
32. Vhankate Bharat S. and Mrs. Vhankate Pradnya B. (2012), Corporate Social Responsibility: A Case of NDTV, Maratha Mandir's Babasaheb Gawde Institute of Management Studies, p. 1, Retrieved from http://www.mmbgims.com/docs/full_paper/40_Bharat_pp.pdf
33. N. Craig Smith (2002), Corporate social responsibility: Not whether, But now?, Retrieved from http://www.london.edu/facultyandresearch/research/docs/03-701.pdf
34. Angeles Moreno and Paul Capriotti (2009), Communicating CSR, Citizenship and Sustainability of the Web, *Journal of Communication Management*, Vol. 13, No. 2, p. 158.
35. Ms. P. Gayathri (2012), The Importance of Corporate Social Responsibility (CSR) by the University Students Towards the Environment, Retrieved from http://www.amfiteatrueconomic.ro/temp/Article_1026.pdf

CSR.[36] Essentially, CSR is the deliberate inclusion of public interest into corporate decision-making.[37] CSR actions have potential to create additional value for corporate. CSR combines the social and environmental aspects in doing business.[38]

There are a many reasons for adopting minimum CSR standards for corporations. First of all, companies themselves would benefit from such initiative. Standards would assist corporations by clarifying their responsibilities, so that companies are no longer subject to arbitrary allegations and demands from various stakeholders. Furthermore, it is no longer enough for only governments to have human rights obligations under international law, as many companies are now more economically powerful and influential than states. Companies represent one-third of the world's one hundred most powerful entities and often the government that host them, especially in the economic developing world, lack of ability to ensure that corporations abide by minimum standards. The introduction of minimum CSR standards internationally would not only ensure that corporations respect the rights of the people and the environment that they affect, but it would also positively impact on the rule of law globally, providing the needed leverage to encourage governments to abide by their international obligations.[39]

---

36. Sweta Singh (2011), "Philanthropy to Corporate Social Responsibility: An Indian Perspective," *Review of International Comparative Management*, Vol. 11, Issue 5, p.993.
37. Poddar Sandeep and Jain Natika (2012), Corporate Social Responsibility: A need of the hour, Maratha Mandir's Babasaheb Gawde Institute of Management Studies, p. 1, Retrieved from http://www.mmbgims.com/docs/full_paper/17_Sirajuddin_pp.pdf
38. Imran Ali, Kashif Ur Rehman, Ayse Kucuk Yilmaz, Sajid Nazir and Jawaria Fatima Ali (2010), "Effects of corporate social responsibility on consumer retention in cellular industry of Pakistan," *African Journal of Business Management*, Vol. 4 (4), p.476.
39. Marianna Linnik and Sune Skadegaard Thorsen (2008), ILO and CSR—Minimum Human Rights Standards for Corporations, Governance, International Law and Corporate Social Responsibility, First edition, p.109, Retrieved from http://www.ilo.org/inst/lang--en/index.htm

## CORPORATE SOCIAL RESPONSIBILITY: GLOBAL PERSPECTIVES

Over the last three decades CSR has evolved from an irrelevant and self-contradictory phenomenon to one of the most widely talked about and universally recognized concepts at the global level.[40]

Bangladesh has made remarkable progress since its independence less than 40 years ago. The other main drivers of the economy are the readymade garment (RMG) industry. Katalyst, a program funded by three European donors and co-implemented by Swiss contact and GTZ. Katalyst is working to stimulate pro-poor growth in many sectors of the economy by increasing the competitiveness of the private sector and supporting micro and small enterprises in a number of urban industrial sectors. Over the last three years, the program has experimented with ways to reduce child labour and improve working conditions by way of sustainable mechanisms.[41]

Children's rights are human rights. Children have the right to be free from child labour and have the right to education. But rights also imply that others have duties. While states have the primary responsibility to respect, protect and fulfil these human rights, it is increasingly recognized that companies have the responsibility to respect the human rights that are enshrined in international treaties and conventions. This was recently reinforced by UN Special Representative on business and human rights John Ruggie in his report to the Human Rights Council.[42]

As one of the largest and most global companies in the world, Coca-Cola took seriously its ability and responsibility to

40. Deborah Blackman, Monica Kennedy and Ali Quazi (2012), Corporate Social Responsibility and Individual Resistance: Learning as the missing link in implementation, p. 3, Retrieved from http://mlq.sagepub.com/content/early/2012/05/24/1350507612444392.abstract?rss=1
41. Peter Roggekamp (2000), Corporate Social Responsibility in Practice: Improving Working Conditions in Bangladesh, pp. 300-2, Retrieved from http://www.accaglobal.com/content/dam/acca/global/PDF-technical/sustainability-reporting/tech-tp-srd.pdf
42. Gerard Oonk (2008), Child Labour, Trade Relations and Corporate Social Responsibility: What the European Union should Do, p. 6, Retrieved from http://www.europarl.europa.eu/meetdocs/2009_2014/ documents/deve/dv/3childlabourtradeandcsr_/3childlabourtradeandcsr_en.pdf

positively affect the communities in which it operated. The company's mission statement, called the Coca-Cola Promise, stated: "*The Coca-Cola Company exists to benefit and refresh everyone who is touched by our business.*" The Company has made efforts towards good citizenship in the areas of community, by improving the quality of life in the communities in which they operate, and the environment, by addressing water, climate change and waste management initiatives. Their activities also included The Coca-Cola Africa Foundation created to combat the spread of HIV/AIDS through partnership with governments, UNAIDS, and other NGOs, and The Coca-Cola Foundation, focused on higher education as a vehicle to build strong communities and enhance individual opportunity. Coca-Cola's footprint in India was significant as well. The Company employed 7000 citizens and believed that for every direct job, 30-40 more were created in the supply chain. Like its parent, Coke India's CSR initiatives were both community and environment-focused. Priorities included education, where primary education projects had been set-up to benefit children in slums and villages, water conservation, where the Company supported community-based rainwater harvesting projects to restore water levels and promote conservation education and health.

Pepsi Cola is also helping in rural areas in their economic development. It further offered to transfer food-processing, packaging, and water-treatment technology to India. Pepsi's bundle of benefits won four Ps for entering a market, Pepsi added two additional Ps, namely, politics and public opinion. Similarly, almost all MNCs like Microsoft, McDonald, Nokia, Unilever, ITC are also adopting social responsibility of business in order to have sustainable market development and growth not only in their countries but also in the host countries.[43]

## CORPORATE SOCIAL RESPONSIBILITY IN INDIA

CSR is not new to India; companies like TATA and BIRLA have been imbibing the case for social good in their operations

43. M. Mohamed Labbai (2007), Social Responsibility and Ethics in Marketing, International Marketing Conference on Marketing & Society, 8-10 April, 2007, IIMK, p. 26.

for decades long before CSR become a popular cause.[44] CSR has become increasingly prominent in the Indian corporate scenario because the organizations have realized that besides growing their businesses it is also vital to build trustworthy and sustainable relationships with the community at large. Another reason fuelling this rapid adoption of CSR is the state of the Indian society and economy. Though India is one of the fastest growing economies, socio-economic problems like poverty, illiteracy, lack of health care, malnutrition, etc. are still ubiquitous and the governments has limited resources to tackle such challenges. This scenario has opened up several areas for business to contribute towards social development. Today, CSR in India has gone beyond merely charity and donations, and is approached in a more organized fashion. It has become an integral part of the corporate strategy. Companies have CSR teams that devise specific policies, strategies and goals for their CSR programs and set aside budgets to support them.[45] In developing economies like India, CSR is seen as part of corporate philanthropy in which corporations augment the social development to support the initiatives of the government.[46] Many CSR initiatives are executed by corporate in partnership with Non-Governmental Organizations (NGOs) who are well versed in working with the local communities and are experts in tackling specific social problems.[47] Corporations are motivated to

44. Rao, P.S. and Surve Shyamkant (2012), Corporate Social Responsibility: Issues and Challenges—An empirical research on Indian context, Maratha Mandir's Babasaheb Gawde Institute of Management Studies, p. 6, Retrieved from http://www.mmbgims.com/docs/full_paper/42_PS_Rao_pp.pdf
45. Dr. R.S. Ramesh and Prof. Puneeta Goel (2012), "Study and Measurement of Corporate Social Responsibility—An Indian Perspectives," *ZENITH: International Journal of Multidisciplinary Research,* Vol. 2, Issue 6, p. 213.
46. Dr. Moon, Urmila (2012), Corporate Social Responsibility in India, Maratha Mandir's Babasaheb Gawde Institute of Management Studies, p. 2, Retrieved from http://www.mmbgims.com/ docs/full_paper/17_Sirajuddin_pp.pdf
47. Ghanshyamdas Saraf (2012), Corporate Social Responsibility and Education in India, Maratha Mandir's Babasaheb Gawde Institute of Management Studies, p. 6, Retrieved from http://www.mmbgims.com/docs/full_paper/17_Sirajuddin_pp.pdf

investing in CSR by a set of hypothesis; the *Business Integrity Thesis*, and the *Slack Resources Theory*.[48]

The leading national and regional/local chambers of commerce and industry of India such as the Confederation of Indian Industries (CII); FICCI; ASSOCHAM, Progress, Harmony and Development Chambers of Commerce and Industry (PHDCCI); and Bombay Chambers of Commerce and Industry (BCCI), have all traditionally been active in mobilizing industry participation in social and environmental issues. They have focused on the involvement of their members on a broad range of issues, including occupational health, quality management, human resources development, technical and vocational training, providing support for entrepreneurs and SMEs, rural development, family planning, HIV/AIDS prevention, alcoholism, education, community development and environmental care. The FICCI was established in 1927 on the advice of Mahatma Gandhi. The CII, on the other hand, was initially called the Engineering and Iron Trades Association (EITA). Established in 1895, it was made up of five engineering firms. FICCI and CII both work closely with the government on policy issues, enhancing efficiency, competitiveness and expanding business opportunities for industry through a range of specialized services and global linkages. During the 1970s and 1980s, both FICCI and CII focused largely on rural development and population issues, and both associations decided to set-up separate bodies to deal with CSR: in 1995, FICCI set-up the Socio Economic Development Foundation (SEDF) and CII the Social Development Council (SDC). This was in the context of the growing demand on industry to help adopt CSR as a tool to ensure corporate participation in social development, and to provide an institutional base for the social activities of the corporate sector. Both SEDF and SDC work closely and in partnership with the government, multi- and bilateral-agencies, and civil society organizations.

The SDC has been focusing on the areas of community development (for livelihood programmes), disaster management, education and literacy, population and health (including

48. Olawari D.J. Egbe and Mr. Fidelis A.E. Paki (2011), "The Rhetoric of Corporate Social Responsibility (CSR) in the Niger Delta," *American International Journal of Contemporary Research*, Vol. 1, No. 3, p. 126.

HIV/AIDS), vocational training and women's empowerment. CII, in partnership with UNDP, has set-up the India Partnership Forum to promote a multi-stakeholder approach to CSR. To help extend the impact of national programmes for the prevention and control of HIV/AIDS, CII has set-up the Indian Business Trust for HIV/AIDS. CII also established the Environmental Management Department (EMD) with a team of well-trained professionals to undertake a range of activities: environmental research; giving policy advice; and organizing practical initiatives, such as training and conducting audits. EMD's thrust is on building in-house capabilities in Indian industry to address environmental issues effectively and proactively.

Other industry associations in India, like PHDCCI, ASSOCHAM and BCCI, have long been working on the issues of social and environmental responsibility with their members. On the occasion of its Platinum Jubilee Celebration, ASSOCHAM started a major initiative on drinking water, asking its members to facilitate the provision of drinking water in 100 villages; by 1996 110 villages were served. The BCCI has been working consistently with its members on issues of population and civic conditions of Mumbai. PHDCCI has major interventions in family welfare and rural development through its two foundations—PHD Rural Development Foundation and PHD Family Welfare Foundation. Additionally, almost all the industry chambers have instituted CSR awards to recognize and encourage the efforts of deserving companies in India.[49]

CSR is not a new concept in India. Corporate like the Tata Group, the Aditya Birla Group, Reliance and Indian Oil Corporation, to name a few, have been involved in serving the community ever since their conception. Many other organizations have been doing their part for the society through donations and charity events, etc. Ever since in the 1970s and the decade of eighties Indian industries and MNC's started setting up units in the Special Economic Zones of Madhya Pradesh, their business houses have been engaged in some sort of community development work. But it was the second half of the current

49. Atul Sood and Bimal Arora (2006), The Political Economy of Corporate Responsibility in India, pp. 22-24, Retrieved from http://books.google.co.in/books/about/The_Political_Economy_of_Corporate_Respo.html?id=cXr1NAAACAAJ&redir_esc=y

decade that the CSR has become a major activity of these units. Some of the major players who are actively involved in CSR in Madhya Pradesh are:

1. Suzlon Foundation
2. Ranbaxy Limited
3. Bridgestone India
4. Grasim Nagda
5. Cummins Turbo Technologies
6. Lupin Pharma
7. Tata International Dewas
8. Crompton Greaves
9. Mafoi Foundation[50]

Tata initiated various labour welfare laws, like the establishment of Welfare Department was introduced in 1917 and enforced by law in 1948 or Maternity Benefit was introduced in 1928 and enforced by law in 1946. The group has always been recognized as a value-driven organization. The group's mission statement states, *"At the Tata group, our purpose is to improve the quality of life of the communities we serve. We do this through leadership in sectors of national economic significance, to which the group brings a unique set of capabilities..."* Different Tata companies have been actively involved in various social works. Like Tata Consultancy Services runs an adult literacy programme, Titan has employed 169 disabled people in blue collar workforce at Hosur, Telco is fighting against Leprosy at Jamshedpur, Tata Chemicals runs a rural development programme at Okhamandal and Babrala, Tata Tea's education programme and Tata Relief Committee (TRC) which works to provide relief at disaster affected areas.

The Tata group has long accepted the idea that CSR makes business sense. This was realized by J.N. Tata way back in 1895, when he stated, *"We do not claim to be more unselfish, more generous or more philanthropic than others, but we think we started on sound and straightforward business principles considering the interests of the shareholders, our own and the health and welfare of our employees... the sure foundation of prosperity."* After decades of corporate

50. Ms Simple Verma and Simranjeet Kaur Sandhar (2012), "Corporate Social Responsibility in Central India," *International Journal of Social Sciences & Interdisciplinary Research*, Vol. 1, No. 4, pp. 81-82.

philanthropy, the efforts of the group in recent years have been directed towards synchronization of the Triple Bottom Line (TBL). Through its TBL initiative, the Tata group aimed at harmonizing environmental factors by reducing the negative impact of its commercial activities and initiating drives encouraging environment-friendly practices.[51]

Similarly, TVS Electronics was involved in CSR during the Tsunami to provide relief measures to the victims. They have also participated with the government to improve sanitation in a village called Tiruvidenthai. Such initiatives will help in improving the conditions of rural people. Satyam Foundation of Satyam Computer Services Ltd., Infosys Foundation of Infosys Technologies Ltd., GE Foundation of the General Electric Company are exemplary instances of the philanthropic commitment of the corporate sector in India.[52] Companies like Wipro, Infosys, Dabur, and ICICI have even framed whistle blowing policy, providing protection to the employees who come to know about any unethical practice going on within the organization, covering a whole gamut of subjects and showing their positive approach towards unethical practices. Public sector aluminum company NALCO has contributed US$ 3.23 million for development work in Orissa's Koraput district as part of its Corporate Social Responsibility (CSR).[53]

Welspun Energy Ltd., (WEL) India's largest solar photovoltaic developer, has been honored by Amity Business School with the *'Amity Corporate Excellence Award for Corporate Social Responsibility'*. The Award recognizes WEL's persistent efforts in empowering India through environmental sustainability and social inclusion. As a vibrant and active corporate

51. Pednekar, Mahesh C. and Dr. Jha, Nishikant (2012), Corporate Social Responsibility and Business Strategy: A Case Study on the Tata Group under Ratan Tata, pp. 1-5, Retrieved from http://www.mmbgims.com/docs/full_paper/5_Mahesh_pp.pdf
52. Dr. Mohammad Khalil Ahmed (2010), Corporate Social Responsibility in Indian Organizations, pp. 2-3. Retrieved from http://www.mmbgims.com/docs/full_paper/14_MOHAMMAD%20KHALIL%20AHMED_2_pp.pdf
53. Dr. Mohammad Khalil Ahmed (2012), The Role of Human Resource Management in Corporate Social Responsibility, p. 4, Retrieved from http://corostrandberg.com/wp-content/uploads/files/CSR_and_HR_Management1.pdf

citizen, Welspun believes Corporate Social Responsibility (CSR) is core to its business.[54] ONGC has allocated around 2 per cent of its net profit towards CSR initiatives during financial year 2010. Some of the key initiatives include: (1) Setting up and running five centres of Gandhi Institute of Computer Education and Information Technology, (2) Ashadeep *"Shiksha Ki Jyot"* project aimed at continued schooling of the girl students belonging to economically weaker sections of society, and (3) *"Varishthajan Swasthya Sewa Abhiyan"* with an objective of providing community-based health services for destitute aged people.

NMDC has been actively participating in various CSR initiatives and has allocated around 2.4% of its net profit in the financial year 2010 towards CSR initiatives. Some of the key CSR initiatives taken by NMDC include: (1) Establishment of a residential school at Nagarnar in Chhattisgarh, (2) Mid-day meal programme for children in the surrounding villages of Donimalai Project, Karnataka covering around 10000 children. Neyveli Lignite Corporation has been actively involved in CSR activity with some of the key initiatives including (1) providing medical services including setting up a hospital with around 360 beds with peripheral dispensaries to provide allopathic and ayurvedic treatments to its employees, their family members and others, (2) Established Neyveli Health Promotion and Social Welfare Society which offer services for the benefit of physically challenged, widows & destitute.[55]

Canara Bank, Indal, Gujarat Ambuja and Wipro are involved in community development work of building roads, running schools and hospitals. ACC has been rendering social service for over five decades. They are setting up schools, health centers, agro-based industries and improving the quality of rural life. BHEL is actively involved in the Welfare of the surrounding communities in helping the organization to earn good will of the local people. BHEL is also providing drinking water facilities, construction of roads and culverts, provision of health facilities, educational facilities, and so on, companies like ONGCs are

---

54. Welspun Energy Awarded for its Corporate Social Responsibility, Retrieved from http://www.indiaprwire.com/pressrelease/oil-energy/20120302113592.htm
55. Public Sector Enterprises in India: Catalyst for Growth, p.16, Retrieved from http://www.indianchamber.org/policy_forms/3.pdf

encouraging sports by placing good players on their pay rolls. TISCO, TELCO and HINDALCO won the award for excelling in CSR, jointly given by FICCI and Business world for the 2003.

Considering the fact that the construction industry is the second largest employer in India after agriculture, employing about 32 million-strong workforce, L&T set out to regulate and promote Construction Vocational Training (CVT) in India by establishing a Construction Skills Training Institute (CSTI) on a 5.5 acre lánd close to its Construction Division Headquarters at Manapakkam, Chennai. CSTI imparts, totally free of cost, basic training in farm work, carpentry, masonry, bar-bending, plumbing and sanitary, scaffold and electrical wireman trades to a wide spectrum of the rural poor.

ITC partnered the Indian farmer for close to a century. It is now engaged in elevating this partnership to a new paradigm by leveraging information technology through its trailblazing *'e-Choupal'* initiative. ITC is significantly widening its farmer partnerships to embrace a host of value-adding activities, viz. creating livelihoods by helping poor tribes make their wastelands productive, investing in rainwater harvesting to bring irrigation to parched dry lands, empowering rural women by helping them evolve into entrepreneurs, and providing infrastructural support to make schools an exciting platform for village children.

India Inc has joined hands to fine-tune all its activities falling under CSR. For this, it has set-up a global platform to showcase all the work done by Indian firms. Confederation of Indian Industry (CII) and the TVS Group collaborated to form the CII-TVS Centre of Excellence for Responsive Corporate Citizenship in 2007. It provides consultancy services and technical assistance on social development and CSR.[56]

Reliance is the only private sector fortune 500 Indian companies. Reliance believes that good governance practices stem from the culture and mindset of the organization. Reliance official policy says that the firm is unequivocally committed to all its stakeholders—employees, costumers, shareholders, investors,

---

56. Dharamshi Pratik and Dr. Bora Chandan (2012), The Role of Corporate Social Responsibility in Developing Economies with Special Reference to India, Maratha Mandir's Babasaheb Gawde Institute of Management Studies, p. 6, Retrieved from http://www.mmbgims.com/docs/full_paper/46_Pratik_%20Dharamshi_pp.pdf

vendors and policy planners. At reliance, every team member is encouraged to ensure that stakeholder's interests are uppermost. Reliance has a well defined policy framework in this regard consisting of values and commitments, code of ethics, business policies, prohibition of insider trading, program of ethics and management.[57]

## HUMAN RIGHTS AND CSR

Human rights form an underlying legal foundation for CSR. Businesses and corporations are part of the entire society and human rights focus on the dignity and worth of the human beings who compose the society. Additionally, human rights form part of international law and corporations are bound by those laws that are applicable to non-state parties. Of course, national laws are also applicable. A current development lies in the area of environmental crimes and humanitarian law. Here, individuals can be held responsible if specific crimes are committed. There are also other human rights standards, all of which serve to enhance human worth and dignity and have become part of the rule of law. In the international arena, human rights are often in a state of flux and satisfactory human rights condition in a country may deteriorate because of an outbreak of civil conflict or some other apocalyptic event. The corporation then has to choose whether to disinvest or risk accusations of collusion with the human rights violators. Very often the corporation may be a supporter of international human rights standards and yet be in a nation where human rights policies are difficult or impossible to implement. However, operating in countries which abuse human rights is a risky business in any case where the company may be at the mercy of the authoritarian government, where the people employed are dissatisfied, and where corruption is generally rampant.[58]

---

57. Debabrata Chatterjee (2010), "Corporate Governance and Corporate Social Responsibility: The Case of three Indian Companies," *International Journal of Innovation, Management and Technology*, Vol. 1, No. 5, p. 507.
58. Karjee, Kshitiz and Kumar, Amit (2012), Corporate Social Responsibility: Path to Social Responsibility and Green Practices, pp. 6-11, Retrieved from http://www.mmbgims.com/docs/full_paper/25_Kshitiz_Karjee_pp.pdf

It is undisputed that these rights should be included as minimum CSR standards. All the rights in the International Bill of Human Rights should be addressed by minimum CSR standards, as they are all vulnerable to being affected by corporations, whether by being affected directly, or by companies being complicit in their violations, for example:

1. The Right to Health
2. The Rights of Indigenous Peoples
3. The Freedom of Expression
4. The Right to Housing.[59]

## LEGAL PERSPECTIVES

International law, and particularly labour law, incorporates various forms of social regulation with or without the status of law and originating from both public and private sources.[60] For decades, the ILO has been working towards the realization of primarily four core labour rights globally: the freedom of association, elimination of compulsory labour, elimination of child labour and the elimination of discrimination.

As far as Companies Act, 1956 is concerned it does not contain any provision regarding corporate social responsibility till recently as in Companies Bill, 2009 twenty-first report by Ministry of Corporate Affairs contained special provision for corporate social responsibility as it clearly specifies that *"There was no mention in the earlier Companies Act about corporate social responsibility. We are just mentioning that there will be a Corporate Social Responsibility Policy in each and every company beyond a certain limit, which are profitable companies and which are of certain size."*[61]

---

59. Marianna Linnik and Sune Skadegaard Thorsen (2008), ILO and CSR—Minimum Human Rights Standards for Corporations, Governance, International Law & Corporate Social Responsibility, First edition, pp. 110-14, Retrieved from http://www.ilo.org/inst/lang--en/index.htm
60. Isabelle Duplessis (2008), Soft International Labour Law: The Preferred Method of Regulation in a Decentralized Society, Governance, International Law & Corporate Social Responsibility, p. 7, Retrieved from http://www.ilo.org/inst/lang--en/index.htm
61. Aniket Pandey (2011), Corporate Social Responsibility and its Enforceability, Retrieved from http://www.mightylaws.in/605/corporate-social-responsibility-enforceability

The Companies Bill of 2009 and the latest Companies Bill of 2011 mandate that companies falling in a certain category allocate at least 2 per cent of their average profits over the previous three years to corporate social responsibility initiatives. These initiatives include eradicating extreme hunger and poverty; promotion of education; promoting gender equality and empowering women; reducing child mortality and improving maternal health; combating the human immuno-deficiency virus, acquired immune deficiency syndrome, malaria and other diseases; ensuring environmental sustainability; employment enhancing vocational skills; social business projects; contribution to the Prime Minister's National Relief Fund or any other fund set-up by the Union Government or the State governments for socio-economic development and relief and funds for the welfare of the Scheduled Castes, the Scheduled Tribes, other backward classes, minorities and women. The CSR initiatives have to be mentioned in the financial statements. The Companies Bill, 2011 has proposed Clause 136(6)(o) that the disclosure of the financial statements contain *inter alia* "the details about the policy developed and implemented by the company on corporate social responsibility initiatives taken during the year".

Every company having a net worth of Rs. 500 crore or turnover of Rs. 1,000 crore has to constitute a *"CSR Committee of the Board"* consisting of at least three directors and out of these three, one has to be an independent director. This is a fool-proof provision ensuring that the committee is not just a quasi-committee addressing the whims of the board, but is in fact, taking up an initiative. The main role of the committee is to formulate and recommend to the board a Corporate Social Responsibility Policy which should indicate the activities to be undertaken by the company. Additionally, the committee has to also recommend the quantum of expenditure to be incurred on these activities. Finally, the committee has to monitor the Corporate Social Responsibility Policy of the company from time to time.[62]

The CSR clause covers all companies that have either net worth in excess of Rs. 500 crore, or turnover of Rs. 1,000 crore or

---

62. *Business Line* (December 18, 2011). New Provisions Mandating Corporate Social Responsibility, Retrieved from http://www.thehindubusinessline.com/industry-and-economy/article2726654.ece

more, or net profit of Rs. 5 crore or more. They have to set aside 2% of the average net profit of the preceding three years for CSR activities. The Companies Bill 2011 makes no exception, though an 'errant' company can explain the reason for not spending the amount in its annual report. Industry fears hefty fines for non-compliance, though there is no mention of penalty in the Bill. They also fear political extortion. Politicians can force companies contribute to their *"trusts"*. They can even demand that a company develops their constituencies.[63]

The Bill is aimed at having a modern legislation for growth and regulation of the Indian corporate sector. It has been amended to ensure that the rate of interest on inter-corporate loans will be the prevailing rate of interest on dated government securities. The bill, long under consideration for a comprehensive revision, is expected to help in curbing a major source of corporate delinquency as Clause 36(c) has been amended to also include punishment for falsely inducing a person to enter into any agreement with a bank or financial institution with a view to obtain credit facilities. In view of various reformatory and contemporary provisions proposed in the Companies Bill, 2011 together with omission of existing unwanted and obsolete compliance requirements, companies in the country would be able to comply with the requirements of the proposed Companies Act in a better and more effective manner.

However, the legal fraternity says that the various provisions and sub-provisions of the Companies' Bill are yet to be framed, putting the entire system in a flux and creating operational hindrances. It is not yet known when and how these legislations will be framed. The Bill takes care of the operational procedures, but the underlying provisions are yet to be framed. To help in curbing a major source of corporate delinquency, Clause 36 (c) of the Companies' Bill has been amended to also include punishment for falsely inducing a person to enter into any agreement with bank or financial institution with a view to obtaining credit facilities. Another prominent drawback of the Bill is with regards to the pledging of assets of an acquired

63. *The Economic Times* (July 22, 2012), New Companies Bill: What India Inc should watch out for, Retrieved from http://articles.economictimes.indiatimes.com/2012-07-22/news/32777534_1_csr-activities-new-companies-bill-corporate-social-responsibility

company to fund the acquisition. Also, under the proposed amendments for pledging of assets of an acquired company to fund the acquisition, directors can be imprisoned up to three years. So, large companies will have various ways to do away with it, but directors of small firms will be caught. Provisions relating to audit of government companies by the Comptroller and Auditor General of India (CAG) have been modified to enable a more effective audit.[64]

## CHALLENGES

There are a number of challenges to the implementation of CSR. They are enumerated below:

1. Maintaining continuous improvements in safety performance throughout the organization.
2. Building a more robust safety culture.
3. Achieving significant reductions in resource use.
4. Reducing waste arising and improving recycling rates.
5. Integration of environmental considerations into supply chain management and purchasing decisions.
6. To strengthen the people management framework to develop a positive and productive working environment.
7. To achieve greater consistency in the management of people processes across the business.
8. To communicate effectively the organization's goals and direction.
9. To improve the employee attitude survey ratings.
10. To achieve greater diversity in the workforce.
11. Build the relationship with business in the community and with Local Authorities.
12. To integrate consideration of environmental and social issues into the purchasing process.[65]

---

64. *The Times of India* (Oct. 5, 2012), Cabinet okays Companies' Bill, Legal experts see loopholes, Retrieved from http://articles.timesofindia.India times.com/2012-10-05/mumbai/34279011_1_companies-bill-corporate-social-responsibility-environment-protection
65. Research Capsule: The Status of Corporate Social Responsibility in India: A Note (2005), Retrieved from http://www.coprocem.org/documents/12corporate_social_responsibility.pdf

In a World Bank Study, it was found that the three key challenges to the implementation of CSR were:

1. Generation of inefficiency and confusion in the buyer CSR codes.
2. Traditional implementation of CSR Strategies not achieving the desired results.
3. Insufficient information about the business benefits of CSR implementation.

The World Bank then proposed some solutions to go forward. Effective implementation of CSR involves active engagement of the public sector, capacity building, empowerment of the workers, development of the standards, and harmonizing them with the firm's objectives and goal, ongoing research, removal of economic barriers to CSR, etc. Public Sector engagement involves host government actions as well as home country government. They must build a sustainable relationship so as to promote CSR. In order to harmonize standards, care must be taken to address implementation guidelines, training and education, sharing information, and monitoring of procedures.[66]

## CONCLUSION

There is a need of such valuable Corporate Social Responsibility campaigns from prominent companies which can surely change fate and face of women in Indian society in the significant areas of education, health, sports, cultural, political, employment and neglected as well as untouched areas of women empowerment which will boost them to live independent and dignified life which they deserve as they are vital and inseparable part of society. The governmental plans and policies are highly skewed and time consuming. If the corporate houses choose to intervene, perhaps India can boast of a real economic boom. The role of a successful company is to contribute to national wealth, generate employment opportunities, promote e-

66. Bhattacharyya, Dipak and Ms. Kumari Priyanka (2012), Corporate Social Responsibility: Its Practices in India, Initiatives, Mechanisms and Issues and Challenges—A Multilateral Approach to the Subject, p. 5, Retrieved from http://www.mmbgims.com/docs/full_paper/16_DIPAK%20 BHATTACHARYYA_pp.pdf

business and e-commerce, bring transparency in management policies, and provide open communication and a safe working environment. In Indian context, such a partnership has enormous potential for strengthening society.

CSR can play a valuable role in ensuring that the invisible hand acts, as intended, to produce the social good. In addition, it seems clear that a CSR programme can be a profitable element of corporate strategy, contributing to risk management and to the maintenance of relationships that are important to long-term profitability.

CHAPTER 9

# Contextualising Corporate Social Responsibility in the Era of Human Rights

*Dr. Uday Shankar and Mr. Divya Tyagi*

## INTRODUCTION

Business has for long been regarded as an activity which brings prosperity to the society.[1] Entrepreneurial freedom therefore has been safeguarded in societies the world over.[2] Advancement in science and technology has made large scale production a reality.[3] At the same time, corporate form of ownership has immensely facilitated pooling of resources (both financial and technical).[4] A combination of both has made it possible for the companies to undertake mega projects. However, all business activity is aimed towards only one goal—maximising the profits for owners of the business. This particular feature when coupled with the financial and technical might of the company, create a situation wherein society's resources (though pooled together as pointed above) end up being exploited blindly for the singular pursuit of profit-making. Here, a further technicality is

1. It is interesting to note that most of the leading civilisations in the history across the world had encouraged prolific business activity. *Laissez faire* society was essentially about maximum entrepreneurial freedom with minimal intervention by the state. And even now brisk business activity is known to result in higher economic growth.
2. For example, the Indian Constitution guarantees right to freedom to carry on trade, business, intercourse as a fundamental right.
3. Industrial revolution evidenced it sufficiently.
4. The characteristic of limited liability conferred by law on the companies is largely responsible for making it a reality.

introduced by a very fundamental canon of corporate law—a company has its own personality which is for all purposes different from its shareholders. And on the top of it all this personality is artificial. The sanctity of this rule is well expressed in the principle that recognition of corporate veil is the rule and lifting of corporate veil is an exception.[5] The implication is that once the resources of the society are exploited by the companies they are in fact being 'entrusted' to an artificial entity whose artificiality is guardedly maintained by the law. So this result into a situation wherein artificial owner, i.e. company acquires tremendous and unprecedented *might*.[6] Most importantly, even though the nations are in the process of learning what becoming global means, companies have learnt it way back.[7] In this sense, companies have outsmarted nations. But a parallel movement is also gaining ground which is expressed through terms like corporate social responsibility (hereinafter CSR)[8] through which companies are asked to use their corporate might not only for private profit but also for the betterment of the society.

However, another major development that the last century has witnessed is the evolution of human rights and the centrality these rights are in the process of acquiring in all human ventures. Companies are also apart from their pursuit of profit are making efforts to justify their might through developing different models of corporate social responsibility. This paper tracks evolution and understand the justification of CSR and the kind of relationship it has with human rights particularly in the context of developing parties.

---

5. Courts across the world has devised exceptions (which are again not exhaustive) to ensure that this principle of corporate veil is not abused to the detriment of the society or anyone who *bona fide* deal with the company. However, it has given on case to case basis (which has its own obvious limitations). Moreover, grounds are not exhaustive and will depend on the facts and circumstances presented before the courts.
6. It is a known fact that annual turnover of leading MNCs exceeds the GDP of many countries in the world.
7. It is well recorded fact that during the colonial era, search for new markets have made companies to undertake oversees ventures, e.g. East India Company; Hudson's Bay Company, Dutch East India Company, etc.
8. Other terms in use for the similar purpose are: corporate ethics; corporate citizenship, etc.

## UNDERSTANDING CSR

In present times CSR is the most talked concept in the academic and commercial spheres. The concept is value laden in the sense of it may be prone to getting ideologically coloured. It means different things to different people. In this sense it is a highly contested concept also. Nevertheless, CSR as a concept is evolving and therefore still continue to be in search of a universally accepted definition.

Philip Kotler and Nancy Lee has defines CSR as "a commitment to improve community well-being through discretionary business practices and contributions of corporate resources."[9]

**Mallen Baker** refers to CSR as "a way companies manage the business processes to produce an overall positive impact on society."[10]

**According to the World Business Council for Sustainable Development,** "Corporate Social Responsibility is the continuing commitment by business to behave ethically and contribute to economic development while improving the quality of life of the workforce and their families as well as of the local community and society at large".[11]

Broadly CSR may be understood as contribution made by a company in the society through its core business activities, its social investment and philanthropy programmes, and its engagement in public policy. This contribution is determined by the manner in which a company manages its economic, social, and environmental impacts and manages its relationships with different stakeholders, in particular shareholders, employees, customers, business partners, governments, communities, and future generations. It is generally understood as voluntary non-binding rules which corporations adhere to their attempt to be socially responsible. It includes voluntary codes, principles and

---

9. Corporate social responsibility—towards a sustainable future available at http://www.in.kpmg.com/pdf/CSR_Whitepaper.pdf accessed on June 11, 2010.
10. Corporate social responsibility—towards a sustainable future available at http://www.in.kpmg.com/pdf/CSR_Whitepaper.pdf accessed on June 11, 2010.
11. Corporate social responsibility—towards a sustainable future available at http://www.in.kpmg.com/pdf/CSR_Whitepaper.pdf accessed on June 11, 2010.

initiatives companies adopt in their general desire to confine corporate responsibility to self-regulation.

## CSR: VARIOUS APPROACHES

Narrow view of CSR found its most vocal expression when Milton Friedman vehemently argued against acknowledging any kind of social responsibility of companies in the following words:

> "the view has been gaining widespread acceptance that corporate officials and labour leaders have a social responsibility that goes beyond serving the interest of their stockholder or their members. This view shows a fundamental misconception of the character and nature of a free economy. In such an economy, there is one and only one social responsibility of business—to use its resources and engage in activities designed to increase its profits so long as it stays within the rules of the game, which is to say, engages in open and free competition, without deception or fraud.... Few trends could so thoroughly undermine the very foundations of our free society as the acceptance by corporate officials of a social responsibility other than to make as much money."[12]

According to him, owners of companies employ executives for the purpose of maximising profits and making money. The moment one acknowledges the social responsibility of companies it implies that the executives of the company at least some times, must subordinate interest of the owners to social objective which effectually means taxing the owners and spending these taxes on social causes. Taxation being the function of government, this doctrine of social responsibility transforms these executives into civil servants and companies into government agencies, thereby diverting business from its proper function in the society.

Theodore Levitt also has opined that "in the end business has only two responsibilities—to obey the elementary canons of face-to-face civility (honesty, good faith, and so on) and to seek material gain."[13]

---

12. Milton Friedman, *Capitalism and Freedom*, 1962, University of Chicago Press, 133.
13. Theodore Levitt, "The Dangers of Social Responsibility," *Harvard Business Review*, 36 (September-October 1958).

## Arguments against Broadening CSR

Apart from the above-mentioned extreme view many arguments advanced against broadening CSR. Few major are summarized as follows[14]:

(i) Companies are permitted to be established by the governments the world over with profit motive.[15] Their activities will by themselves result in betterment of the society as a whole. This is referred to as *invisible hand*. If companies are burdened with obligation of undertaking activities other than making profit, it will politicize basic economic function of the companies and will hamper their ability to satisfy material needs of the society. However, critiques point out that it is difficult to notice the working of this invisible hand making any tangible impact because in dealing of companies with individuals the scales are starkly unevenly tilted in favour of the companies due to their immense *might*.

(ii) Proponents of this view reject "invisible hand" and point out that since companies are structured in a way so as to maximise profits, they will enrich themselves while impoverishing the society, if left to themselves. Therefore, they can only be controlled through stern governmental regulation. This is referred to as *Hand-of-Government* argument. Critiques however point out governmental regulation is by itself riddled with problems. First, putting appropriate regulation in place is difficult as consensus is difficult to forge. Secondly, enforcement is far more challenging particularly against the big companies. It may be expensive and may be get prolonged. At time the costs involved in resorting to judicial intervention may far outweigh the benefits involved. So the objective may not be achieved by law alone. It may give the companies an impression that their only obligation now is to obey the law and they are implicitly permitted to do whatever is not (yet) made illegal.

---

14. For precise reference to these arguments see, William H. Shaw, *Business Ethics*, Fourth edition Thomson Wadsworth, 2005, pp. 166-75.
15. Non-profit companies are also permitted but they are viewed as an exception and not as a rule.

(iii) Corporate executives are best trained for doing business, i.e. maximising profits. Entrusting them with non-economic responsibilities will result in entrusting social welfare in the hands of inept custodian. This is referred to as *Inept-Custodian* Argument.

(iv) If entrusted with social responsibilities, company executives will impose their materialist values on the whole of the society. Thus, broadening CSR will materialise society. This is referred to as *Materialization-of-Society* argument. However, critiques point out that big companies already enjoy huge influence over us. If one goes by the advertisements campaigns for promoting their products they impose their own concepts and ideas over the society. So consumerism and materialism is already imposed (consciously or unconsciously).[16]

However, proponents of the broader view of CSR look at the whole matter differently. They believe that in addition to pursuing profits companies have other obligations too. They do not find fault with profit motive as such but they simultaneously build a case for responsibilities of companies towards their stake-holders as well as to the society at large. This is more so in the light of corporate might and the resulting influence they have over society.

## CSR AND HUMAN RIGHTS: FORCING RELATIONSHIP

Human rights have been quest of every civilisation. Human rights are inalienable rights of every individual which society is under obligation to respect, to protect and to fulfil. Traditionally, State is responsible for promoting and protecting human rights of individual as its existence is based upon such premises. Based upon such premise, international charter of human rights entrusted prime responsibilities on member state to respect ideals of human rights.[17]

The human rights of the citizens have been regarded as the responsibilities of the state. On this ground, companies particularly MNCs have always shirked from owning up any

16. Idea of happiness, beauty, success, fulfilment and hygiene, etc.
17. Universal Declaration of Human Rights, International Covenant on Civil and Political Rights and International Covenant on Social, Economic and Cultural Rights.

responsibility regarding the violations of human rights towards the people of the respective state(s). This situation was heavily skewed in favour of the MNCs and gravely weakened any effort to strengthen human rights. This was so because MNCs wield as much or more power over the people than the governments in the sense that a shift in their policies have huge bearing in controlling their well-being.[18] In the pursuit of bringing more and more FDI these state governments neither the interest nor the resources to monitor corporate behaviour. Further, as more and more companies have undertaken cross-border ventures and have become international in their operations, they have also become ever more independent of government control. The stakeholders of leading MNCs[19] are so widely scattered the world over that their regulation becomes far more challenging even for the most competent of the governments. To top it all companies always have the option of shifting their operations to those states which offer fewer regulatory hassles including human rights compliances.

With rising consciousness about human rights the world over including developing countries one notable accomplishment has been that companies found to their dismay that if they violate human rights and it comes under the public domain that society at large will condemn them and they will find it extremely difficult to do business. But mere condemnation is not enough.

However, despite contrary views, argument in favour of CSR has grown over a period of time. Credit for this has invariably to be given to the efforts made at the international level.

In 1974, the United Nations established a Centre for Transnational Corporations to prepare the Code; it completed a draft in 1983 and another in 1990. While recognizing some rights for investors, these Codes emphasized the need for foreign investors to obey host country law, follow host country economic policies, and avoid interference in the host country's domestic political affairs. In a response to this development, the Organization for Economic Cooperation and Development (OECD), the principal international institution composed of wealthy states, drafted its own set of guidelines for multinational

18. The development of anti-competitive law bears testimony to this fact.
19. E.g. consumer, creditors, shareholders, suppliers, employees, etc.

enterprises. These contained far fewer and weaker obligations on TNEs and were not intended to be binding.[20] OECD guidelines *inter alia* provide that the multinational enterprises should respect human rights of those affected by their activities consistent with the host government's international obligations and commitments.[21] However, end of cold war and rising movement in favour of free trade these attempts took the back seat and is now revived in this new format.[22]

United Nations came out with global compact in 2004. It is a voluntary initiative designed to encourage companies to address human rights, labour rights and environmental and corruption concerns, and to share their experiences in implementing the Global Compact principles. It contained a set of ten principles relating to human rights, labour standards, environment, and anti-corruption. First principle relating to human rights categorically mandates that Businesses should support and respect the protection of internationally proclaimed human rights whereas second requires the business to make sure that it is not complicit in human rights abuses.[23] The fundamental and vitally crucial contribution of this global compact was that it established the relationship between CSR and human rights. It made possible for the first time at the global level to view CSR through the prism of human rights and appreciate it on the parameters of human rights.

United Nations is in the process of developing norms relating to the Responsibilities of Transnational Corporations and Other Business Enterprises with Regard to Human Rights.[24] These norms are based on key international human rights instruments. They attempt to take up the human rights

20. Steven, R., Ratner Corporations and Human Rights: A Theory of Legal Responsibility, 111 Yale L.J. 458, December, 2001.
21. Available at http://www.oecd.org/dataoecd/56/36/1922428.pdf accessed on June 10, 2010
22. See, David Kinley and Rachel Chambers, The UN human rights norms for corporations: the private implications of public international law, *H.R.L. Rev.*, 2006, 6(3), 447-97, 455.
23. Available at http://www.unglobalcompact.org/aboutthegc/thetenprinciples/index.html accessed on June 10, 2010.
24. Norms on the responsibilities of transnational corporations and other business enterprises with regard to human rights available at http://www.unhchr.ch/huridocda/huridoca.nsf/(Symbol)/E.CN.4.Sub.2.2003.12.Rev.2.En accessed on June 10, 2010.

obligations most relevant to companies and apply them directly to TNCs and other business enterprises, within their respective spheres of activity and influence. That said, the Norms make clear that states retain primary, overarching responsibility for human rights protection. The rights covered by the Norms are, broadly, equality of opportunity and non-discriminatory treatment; the right to security of persons; labour rights; respect for national sovereignty and human rights, including prevention of bribery and corruption; consumer protection; economic, social and cultural rights; and environmental protection.[25]

Drafting of these norms is regarded as a unique endeavour in the sense that it attempts to detail each duty and obligation under the umbrella of human rights and thus to provide a broader-based indicative check-list for companies to follow. Whereas the Global Compact is a voluntary initiative designed to encourage companies to address human rights, labour rights and environmental and corruption concerns, and to share their experiences in implementing the Global Compact principles these norms certainly go beyond.[26]

All these developments are clear pointer to the fact that so far as the activities of multinational enterprises are concerned distinct attempts are underway to make them accountable for their actions through the emerging human rights jurisprudence.

## CSR IN DEVELOPING COUNTRIES

CSR should be conceived differently in developing countries from their counterpart in developed countries. This is due to the fact that many of these countries are growing economies and so offer themselves as very lucrative growth markets particularly for MNCs. The situation is so grave that these countries competed amongst themselves to invite more and more foreign investment (both direct and indirect) and in this goal are prepared to make all sorts of compromises to appease foreign investors – which may result in violation of one or more human

25. David Kinley and Rachel Chambers, The UN human rights norms for corporations: the private implications of public international law, *H.R.L. Rev.*, 2006, 6(3), 447-97, 449.
26. David Kinley and Rachel Chambers, The UN human rights norms for corporations: the private implications of public international law, *H.R.L. Rev.*, 2006, 6(3), 447-97, 465.

rights of their people. Another aspect relates to environment. These are the countries which are home to vast bio-diversity which they are under pressure to preserve as developed countries have already lost theirs. But since developing countries are also following more or less the same model of development that has been followed by the developed countries, therefore, they are facing the conflict between preservation of environment and highest economic growth within shortest span of time.

Certain factors are recognised as drivers for CSR in developing countries. There drivers are classified as internal and external. Internal drivers *inter alia* include:

(i) The nature, focus and extent of CSR heavily depends the socio-economic development. It varies significantly according to their development needs. Therefore, the conception of CSR will invariably vary in developing countries from the developed ones. In developed countries of the west CSR priorities on areas like consumer protection, fair trade, green marketing, climate change, etc. Contrary to this, the challenges of poverty alleviation, infrastructure bottlenecks, educational backwardness will determine how CSR is shaped up in developing countries. This will make importing western models of CSR not much suitable for developing countries and will imply the need for developing *sui generis* models suitable to the priorities of developing countries.

(ii) CSR is also viewed as a way to plug the 'governance gaps'. As governments in developing countries are found wanting in their track records of fulfilling the mandate of living conditions of their ever increasing populations (a large portion of it living in poverty line) bottom of the pyramid approach[27] towards CSR maintains that companies can assume this role.

(iii) CSR in developing countries cannot be divorced from the socio-political reform process, which often drives business behaviour towards integrating social and ethical issues. For instance, the adoption of policy of LPG

27. See, C.K. Prahalad, *The Fortune at the Bottom of the Pyramid: Eradicating Poverty Through Profits*, Wharton School Publishing, 2009.

in India after 1991 has brought the social responsibility of companies in greater focus than ever before.

(iv) Disasters that cripple countries or a part thereof also have encouraged CSR activities. For instance, Tsunami is a classic case in point.

(v) Gaining access to the markets of developing countries is also encourages the companies to undertake and engage in CSR activities.

(vi) Cultural traditions too have a huge bearing and drives the companies to undertake CSR activities.

External drivers include:

(i) Various codes and standards regarding CSR which has been developed at the international level so far have proved to be crucial drivers for CSR in developing countries.

(ii) As governmental control over the companies are proving insufficient in developing countries, stakeholders (trade unions, consumers, business associations, development agencies, NGOs media, etc.) activism has become another very crucial driver for CSR.

(iii) Certain standards (regarding labour standards and human rights at least in certain sectors) being imposed by multinationals on their supply chains in developing countries has also led to adherence of CSR standards.

(iv) A tendency is emerging to screen the foreign investments. There is now a tendency coming up to screen these investments on the altar of CSR performance. In this sense, socially responsible investment (SRI) is becoming another driver for CSR in developing countries.

The goal set out in the Millennium Development Goals of creating a world with less poverty, hunger and disease, greater survival prospects for mothers and their infants, better educated children, equal opportunities for women, and a healthier environment[28] constitute as much a challenge for the governments of developing countries as it is a challenge for the companies which are doing business in such countries. This is so

28. Available at http://www.un.org/millenniumgoals accessed on June 10, 2010.

because such companies are doing business for profits amidst oceanic and killing poverty.

## CSR: AN INDIAN EXPERIENCE

Though the term CSR the concept as such is not new to India. People in India have known Companies like the Tata Group, the Aditya Birla Group, etc. for their commitment towards the social cause while they do business. A number of industrialists have played their part in India's freedom movement. Over a period of time many other companies have also taken up one or the other social cause alongwith their business through donations and charity events. In fact, the approach of the companies towards CSR has been largely philanthropic. Thus, the philanthropic approach is still widespread.

One thing about CSR in India is unmistakable. Companies now approach it in a more organized fashion. It is slowly becoming an integral part of the corporate strategy. Companies have CSR teams that devise specific policies, strategies and goals for their CSR programs and set aside budgets to support them. In most of the cases these strategies are more tuned to the company's business expertise, e.g. organizations like BPCL, Maruti Suzuki and HLL and scores of others adopt villages where they focus on holistic development. They provide better medical and sanitation facilities, build schools and houses, and help the villagers become self-reliant by teaching them vocational and business skills. This was done on encouraging scale in the aftermath of Tsunami devastated certain parts of Indian coast. Whereas there are others like GlaxoSmithKline Pharmaceuticals' CSR programs primarily focus on health and healthy living. They work in tribal villages where they provide medical check-up and treatment, health camps and health awareness programs. They also provide money, medicines and equipment to non-profit organizations that work towards improving health and education in under-served communities.[29]

Interestingly, many CSR initiatives are executed by companies in partnership with Non-governmental organizations (NGOs) who are well versed in working with the local

29. Bhagwant Corporate Social Responsibility in India – Putting Socio-Economic Development on a Fast Track available at http://www.csrindia.info/story.php?aid=168 accessed on June 11, 2010

communities and are experts in tackling specific social problems, e.g. SAP India in partnership with Hope Foundation, an NGO that works for the betterment of the poor and the needy throughout India, has been working on short and long-term rebuilding initiatives for the tsunami victims. Together, they also started *The SAP Labs Center of HOPE* in Bangalore, a home for street children, where they provide food, clothing, shelter, medical care and education.[30]

While the Indian understanding of CSR shows a slight shift from traditional philanthropy to sustainable business, philanthropic CSR patterns are still apparent in many Indian companies. In addition, the imbalance between the internal and external CSR dimensions is still huge.[31]

The Indian CSR agenda continues to be dominated by community development activities, particularly in the areas of health and education. While most Indian companies view their community development projects as important contributions to the existing development challenges in their region of operation, many stakeholders are more critical of this approach.[32] Where community development is concerned, Indian stakeholders' criticism focuses on the following aspects:

(i) a company's community development approach based on the argument that it needs to "give something back to society" lacks transparency and specific standards;
(ii) community development approaches often amount to little more than window-dressing and must be compared to violations of social and environmental standards within companies;

30. Bhagwant Corporate Social Responsibility in India – Putting Socio-Economic Development on a Fast Track available at http://www.csrindia.info/story.php?aid=168 accessed on June 11, 2010
31. Tatjana Chahod *et al.*, Corporate Social and Environmental Responsibility in India—Assessing the UN Global Compac's Role available at http://www.die-gdi.de/CMS- Homepage/openwebcms3.nsf/(ynDK_contentByKey)/ENTR-7BMDUB/$FILE/Studies%2026.pdf accessed on June 11, 2010
32. Tatjana Chahod *et al.*, Corporate Social and Environmental Responsibility in India—Assessing the UN Global Compac's Role available at http://www.die-gdi.de/CMS- Homepage/openwebcms3.nsf/(ynDK_contentByKey)/ENTR-7BMDUB/$FILE/Studies%2026.pdf accessed on june 11, 2010

(iii) public authorities in local communities very often lack the required know-how and experience to negotiate business-driven commitment to community development; and

(iv) very few companies disclose their motivation and business interests when engaging in community development.[33]

Debate over CSR in India got heated up few years back on the issue of providing reservation to members of scheduled castes and scheduled tribes in jobs in private sector. Vociferous demands were made that the government should enact law to make it mandatory for the companies to reserve certain percentage of posts in the recruitment as has been the case for government jobs. It was argued vehemently that as the state has withdrawn itself from many sectors of the economy in pursuance of the policy of privatisation after 1991, so the jobs which were erstwhile provided by the government are now being provided by the companies in the private sector. Consequently, reservation mandated under Article 16 of the Indian constitution as the companies are not covered by the definition of the State under Article 12. Therefore, an implied fraud is being committed on the Indian constitution.

Indian corporate sector represented by CII opposed mandatory job reservation for weaker sections of the society in the private sector as this would affect competitiveness of corporate India.[34] It assured the government that they will develop and structure their recruitment policies in such a way that scheduled castes and tribes candidates are also enabled to take up jobs in those companies. Since then CII is emphasising creation of capabilities through scholarships, coaching programmes and funding entrepreneurs. In fact, Tata group of companies is following the policy of hiring from disadvantaged sections particularly the scheduled castes and scheduled tribes

33. Tatjana Chahod *et al.* Corporate Social and Environmental Responsibility in India—Assessing the UN Global Compac's Role available at http://www.die-gdi.de/CMS- Homepage/openwebcms3.nsf/(ynDK_contentByKey)/ENTR-7BMDUB/$FILE/Studies%2026.pdf accessed on June 11, 2010.

34. No job reservation in private sector: CII available at http://timesofindia.indiatimes.com/articleshow/749046.cms accessed on June 11, 2010

communities without sacrificing merit in the spirit of positive discrimination.[35]

However, recently Indian Prime Minister has stated that Reserving jobs in private sector is part of the national Common Minimum Programme of UPA-I and a national dialogue has been initiated with political parties and industry to see how it be better implemented. He emphasised that in order to take forward the affirmative action an atmosphere is needed to be created so that trade and industry participants help the government on this issue. He assured that the government is working hard towards that while at the same time acknowledging that it needs to be taken forward fast.[36]

Furthermore, Ministry of Corporate Affairs has recently come out with a set of voluntary guidelines regarding CSR in India.[37] Preamble to these guidelines acknowledge that CSR is purely voluntary (i.e. beyond any statutory obligation) and the underlying idea behind the guidelines is to provide guidance to the companies. Preamble also expresses the hope that more and more companies will make sincere efforts in complying with these guidelines. Importantly those companies which fail to comply for certain genuine reasons will report to the stakeholders that part of the guidelines which it is unable to comply fully or partly. Preamble expresses the hope that India Inc. will respond positively in complying with these guidelines. Preamble also states that although the guidelines have been prepared in Indian context however companies with overseas operations may also comply with the guidelines. Preamble also is categorical about its voluntary nature as it is a prescriptive road map not being intended for regulatory or contractual use.

---

35. Kala Vijayraghavan & M.V. Ramsurya Tatas lead India Inc in "positive discrimination" hiring available at http://cii.in/Affirmative_ActionDetail.aspx?enc=lM9ggWqHZMzbDxYzuDsBxNFNtjAFpKwccvpdPVewxHamZmAW/plOKh6pXySUnpsrBSgjeHUwXxL2vMNCSNLyGMLfFCoY07818yzlWLIMv7tFP9qKVRDURaiIYUhOdniXDtHKAWb4ZTqazYw91fHKcg== accessed on June 11, 2010.
36. Government to Push for Job Reservation in Private Sector available at http://www.businessworld.in/bw/2010_05_24_Govt_To_Push_For_Job_Reservation_In_Pvt_Sector.html, Accessed on June 11, 2010.
37. Corporate Social Responsibility Voluntary Guidelines, 2009 available at HTTP://WWW.TAXMANN.COM/TAXMANNFLASHES/FLASHBN22-12-09_2.HTM accessed on June 14, 2010.

Guidelines recognises the fundamental principle that each business entity should formulate CSR policy to guide its strategic planning. CSR initiatives should be an integral part of overall business policy and should be aligned with its business goal. This principle is vital because unless CSR initiatives are so harmonised they continue to be perceived as a burden. The principle further mandates that such policy should be formulated in consultation with executives at different levels. This is also very important because any meaningful implementation at the ground level will depend on how far corporate executives share the orientation required for such initiatives. How much they identify themselves with the objective underlying this policy and how far they see it as a business sense.

Such CSR policy should cover the core elements namely—all stakeholders, ethical functioning, worker's rights and welfare, human rights, environment, activities for social and inclusive development. In the context of human rights the guidelines provide "Companies should respect human rights for all and avoid complicity with human rights abuses by them or by third party".[38] With regard to implementation, guidelines provide that CSR policy should contain implementation strategy consisting of project identification, time bound targets, monitoring mechanisms. For this purpose companies may partner with local authorities, business associations and civil society/non-Government organizations. Independent evaluation may also be incorporated in such strategy. Companies should provide for specific budgetary allocation. Companies should disseminate the CSR—policy, activities and progress to all the stakeholders as well as the public at large.

The preamble of guidelines provides that depending on the adoption of these guidelines by the companies in India and other feedbacks, government will review them after one year.

Through these guidelines a process is started in India. This is a welcome move but one which has taken long time (almost twenty years after India started liberalising). Indian companies have got time now to mature after LPG and it high time for them to go beyond piecemeal efforts towards CSR. However, one feels that with these voluntary set of guidelines India has entered into

38. Corporate Social Responsibility Voluntary Guidelines, 2009 available at HTTP://WWW.TAXMANN.COM/TAXMANNFLASHES/FLASHBN2 2-12-09_2.HTM accessed on June 14, 2010.

a transitional phase of moving from voluntary approach to mandatory approach towards CSR. Corporate Affairs Minister too has stated that government is exploring all options including legislations in order to make more companies adopt CSR and with this end in view new clauses covering CSR may be inserted in the companies bill provided consensus may be arrived at.[39] So the message is loud and clear—CSR in India is moving albeit slowly towards mandatory instruction through legislative intervention. But the concern is that corporate freedom should not be suffocated through this effort. Also the law, as and when it comes up, must address the human rights concerns of the people.

## CONCLUSION

Human rights law provide a sound basis on which models of CSR may be built. This is so because human rights law represent the consensus of the global community. Also CSR performance may be as assessed on the parameter of human rights. It will also facilitate comparisons of CSR performance across different jurisdictions.

India is globally regarded as a vibrant democracy. For the last twenty years, Indian companies have also gained sufficient experience of doing business in a liberalised economic environment. Perhaps realising this fact, Government of India has indicated that it is soon likely to come out with the law mandating CSR for Indian companies. Challenge for such a law will be to meet the mandate of human rights standards while at the same time keeping the entrepreneurial freedom intact.

39. India may make CSR a law available at http://igovernment.in/site/india-may-make-csr-law-37213 accessed on June 11, 2010.

CHAPTER 10

# Corporate Responsibility Towards Human Rights: An Analysis

*Dr. R.D. Dubey and Ms. Priya Roy*

*"Law must constantly be on the move adapting itself to the fast-changing society and not lag behind."*

—***Justice P.N. Bhagwati***[1]

## INTRODUCTION

Mahatma Gandhi had always insisted that World would become truly independent and a better place to live, only when the poorest of its people would be free from human suffering. An overwhelming concern for the poor, a multidimensional view of poverty and human deprivations, the focus on freedoms, the need to expand opportunities and ensure its equal distribution are fundamental to a strong human development perspective

Human dignity cannot be achieved through the constitutional protection unless the guarantee under the Law extends to the development and promotion of its components like 'decent livelihood, great and valuable traditions and culture' of the countrymen. There can never be advancement in a society as such, unless its citizens have been in a position to enjoy the basic fundamental freedom of 'Life and Personal Liberty'.

Such dynamism of Law arises out of the inarticulate major premises seeking the most from their rulers so as to provide social and economic justice which has now been raised to the status of basic Human Rights and the violation of such human

1. *National Textile Workers' Union v. P.R. Ramakrishnan*, (1983) 1 SCC 228.

rights causes the downfall of the Government. Welfare society inculcates both economic and social justice. The concept thus takes within its sweep the objective of removing all inequalities and affording equal opportunities to all citizens in social affairs as well as economic activities. Social and economic justice not only promotes the growth and development of a citizen's personality but also mitigates the sufferings of the poor and weaker sections in a society. It is the *'grundnorm'* for any State, a legal system to exist, develop and prosper in every aspect.

In today's modern globalized era, social and economic justice can have only one meaning and that is the creation of a 'social order' in which every human gets a decent life. Such a socio-welfare order is created by certain political and historical forces and most importantly, the judiciary plays a supportive and auxiliary role by upholding our modern Constitution in its true spirit, by giving it teeth and content, by throwing-up modern ideas and creating awareness among the people.

Economic players, especially companies that operate across national boundaries have gained unprecedented power and influence across the world economy. Companies cause harm by directly abusing human rights, or by colluding with others who violate human rights. Despite this potential to cause significant harm, there are few effective mechanisms at national or international level to prevent corporate human rights abuses or to hold companies to account. This means those affected by their operations—often already marginalized and vulnerable—are left powerless, without the protection to which they are entitled or meaningful access to justice.

During the last decade, human rights have become central to the conceptualization and evaluation of business ethics and corporate responsibility in the globalized economy. A growing commitment by increasing number of private corporations to respect for human rights in their business practices has been supported by political initiatives such as the United Nations Global Compact programme and by the work of non-governmental organisations including Human Rights Watch and Amnesty International. This emerging will to take human rights seriously in business practice has raised urgent new questions concerning the extent, definition and specification of the legal and ethical responsibilities of companies and investors for the safeguarding of human rights within their sphere of influence.

## PARADIGM DEVELOPMENT OF HUMAN RIGHTS

The fundamental rights that humans have by the fact of being human, and that are neither created nor can be abrogated by any government. Although they were defined first by the Scottish philosopher John Locke (1632-1704) as absolute moral claims or entitlements to life, liberty, and property, the best-known expression of human rights is in the Virginia Declaration of Rights in 1776 which proclaims that "All men are by nature equally free and independent and have certain inherent rights, of which, when they enter a state of society, they cannot, by any compact, deprive or divest their posterity."[2]

Human rights are the most basic and essential natural rights, which are universally accepted and are inalienable. Human rights are those minimal rights which every individual must have against the State or other public authority by virtue of being a member of the human family irrespective of any other consideration. As stated at the outset, the concept of human rights is as old as the ancient doctrine of 'natural rights' founded on natural law, though the expression 'human right' is of the recent origin, emerging from (post-Second World War) International Charters and Conventions.[3]

Amartya Sen points out that human rights are the ethical claims which are constitutively linked with importance of human freedom, and the robustness of an argument that a particular claim can be seen as a human right has to be assessed through the scrutiny of public reasoning, involving opening impartiality.[4]

In short, the expression human right denotes all such rights are inherent in human nature and without which the very existence of human life is unacceptable. Human rights are the eternal part of the human behaviour and are immensely essential for the individuals to live and develop a respectable life. These are the inalienable rights which belong equally to all members of the human family and as such, which should be protected by rule of law.

---

2. http://www.businessdictionary.com/definition/human-rights.html visited on 07/03/2013.
3. D.D. Basu, Human Rights in the Constitutional Law, Wadhwa & Company, 2005, p. 8.
4. Amartya Sen, Idea of Justice, Oxford University Press, 2009, p. 365.

Human rights are commonly understood as "inalienable fundamental rights to which a person is inherently entitled simply because she or he is a human being." Human rights are thus conceived as universal and egalitarian. *The idea of human rights* states, "if the public discourse of peacetime global society can be said to have a common moral language, it is that of human rights." Despite this, the strong claims made by the doctrine of human rights continue to provoke considerable scepticism and debates about the content, nature and justifications of human rights to this day. Indeed, the question of what is meant by a "right" is itself controversial and the subject of continued philosophical debate.[5]

Multinational companies play an increasingly large role in the world, and have been responsible for numerous human rights abuses. Such companies may be larger than the economies of some of the states within which they operate, and can wield significant economic and political power. No international treaties exist to specifically cover the behaviour of companies with regard to human rights, and national legislation is very variable.

## CORPORATIONS AND ITS GROWING RESPONSIBILITY

Corporations are the most common form of business organization, and one which is chartered by a state and given many legal rights as an entity separate from its owners. This form of business is characterized by the limited liability of its owners, the issuance of shares of easily transferable stock, and existence as a going concern. The process of becoming a corporation, called incorporation, gives the company separate legal standing from its owners and protects those owners from being personally liable in the event of the company being sued. Incorporation also provides companies with a more flexible way to manage their ownership structure. In these respects, corporations differ from sole proprietorships and limited partnership. Multinational companies play an increasingly large role in the world, and have been responsible for numerous human rights abuses. Although the legal and moral environment surrounding the actions of governments is reasonably well developed, that surrounding multinational companies is both controversial and ill-defined.

5. http://en.wikipedia.org/wiki/Human_right visited on 10/03/2013.

*Jean Ziegler,* Special Rapporteur of the UN Commission on Human Rights on the right to food once stated in a report in 2003, "The growing power of transnational corporations and their extension of power through privatization, deregulation and the rolling back of the State also mean that it is now time to develop binding legal norms that hold corporations to human rights standards and circumscribe potential abuses of their position of power."[6]

Society is increasingly concerned about how business activities have impacts on human rights. Company stakeholders, ranging from employees and customers to investors and governments, expect and demand that companies integrate human rights in their business practices. In an effort to respond to these calls, companies have committed themselves to voluntary initiatives such as the United Nations Global Compact and by referring to human rights in their codes of business principles. Yet for many companies it remains a challenge to embed human rights in their day-to-day operations. In some of the places they do business, the rule of law is non-existent, not enforced or in conflict with international human rights. As a result, merely respecting local law may not always be a sustainable approach.

A recent report by WWF states that if we continue at current levels of consumption we will use up all of the Earth's resources within 50 years, and we will need two more planets to meet our resource needs. We either take urgent action to save the planet, or we get-off. The UN Environmental Programme agrees that "the state of the planet is getting worse." They say, "there is a growing gap between the efforts of business and industry to reduce their impact on the environment and the worsening state of the planet."

Corporations carry out some of the most horrific human rights abuses of modern times, but it is increasingly difficult to hold them accountable. Economic globalization and the rise of transnational corporate power have created a favourable climate for corporate human rights abusers, which are governed principally by the codes of supply and demand and show genuine loyalty only to their stockholders. Global Exchange developed in 2012 a list of some of the world's worst corporate

---

6. *Ibid.*

abusers which were indulged in the acts of human rights violations including that of the harassment, environmental degradation, violently repressing political rights, releasing toxins into pristine environments, destroying homes, discrimination, and causing widespread health problems. It has enlisted top ten corporations as human rights abusers, these are:

(i) **Bank of America** for funding of environmentally harmful coal industry, excessive campaign contributions;
(ii) **Chevron** for damaging ecosystem and people of Ecuador, repression of protest to oil extraction, Brazil spill;
(iii) **Century International Arms** for producing Romanian AKs, which are frequently smuggled into Mexico;
(iv) **Halliburton** for hydraulic fracturing, involvement in the Gulf spill, bribery in Nigeria;
(v). **The Hershey Company** for refusing to use fair trade labour and continuing to support labour that violates human rights standards;
(vi) **Monsanto** for promotion of mono-cropping, involvement in government, refusing to label product, bankrupting small farms;
(vii) **Pacific Rim** for mining in El Salvador;
(viii) **TransCanada** for plans to construct Keystone XL Pipeline;
(ix) **Veolia** for operations in Israel, high prices and bad service, privatization of water; and
(x) **Wal-Mart** for unfair treatment of employees, use of sweatshop labour, bribery in Mexico.[7]

In August 2003 the Human Rights Commission's Sub-Commission on the Promotion and Protection of Human Rights produced the draft titled, *Norms on the responsibilities of transnational corporations and other business enterprises with regard to human rights*. These were considered by the Human Rights Commission in 2004, but have no binding status on corporations and were not monitored.

7. http://www.globalexchange.org/corporateHRviolators visited on 09/03/2013.

Until recently, no common understanding or standard existed by which companies could understand their response-bilities in such contexts. However, in June 2008, the United Nations made an important contribution to the business and human rights debate. It unanimously endorsed the framework Protect, Respect and Remedy, proposed by the Special Representative of the UN Secretary-General on Business and Human Rights, *Professor John Ruggie*. It consists of three pillars:

1. The state duty to protect against human rights abuses, including those by business;
2. The corporate responsibility to respect human rights; and
3. The need for better access to remedy when corporate-related abuses have occurred.

The Guiding Principles highlight what steps States should take to foster business respect for human rights; provide a blueprint for companies to know and show that they respect human rights, and reduce the risk of causing or contributing to human rights harm; and also to constitute a set of benchmarks for stakeholders to assess business respect for human rights. The Framework provided an authoritative focal point around which the expectations and actions of the various players could converge in this debate—business, government, civil society, investors and beyond. The Guiding Principles provide practical and concrete recommendations to governments and companies on the policies and processes they may put in place to manage these risks. And in particular for companies, the systems to help integrate respect for human rights throughout the enterprise to help meaningfully prevent and address their involvement in human rights abuse.[8]

The framework has received wide uptake by governments, business, civil society and others. It represents the first formal affirmation of the responsibilities of business with respect to human rights by the United Nations. International human rights standards have traditionally been the responsibility of governments, aimed at regulating relations between the State and individuals and groups. But with the increased role of corporate actors, nationally and internationally, the issue of

8. http://blogs.law.harvard.edu/corpgov/2011/04/09/un-guiding-prin ciples-for-business-human-rights visited on 09/03/2013.

business impact on the enjoyment of human rights has been placed on the agenda of the United Nations. Over the past decade, the United Nations human rights machinery has been considering the scope of business human rights responsibilities and exploring ways for corporate actors to be accountable for the impact of their activities on human rights. As a result of this process, there is now greater clarity about the respective roles and responsibilities of governments and business with regard to protection and respect for human rights. Most prominently, the emerging understanding and consensus have come as a result of the UN "Protect, Respect and Remedy" Framework on human rights and business, which was elaborated by the Special Representative of the UN Secretary-General on the issue of human rights and transnational corporations and other business enterprises, building on major research and extensive consultations with all relevant stakeholders, including States, civil society and the business community. On 16 June 2011, the UN Human Rights Council endorsed Guiding Principles on Business and Human Rights for implementing the UN "Protect, Respect and Remedy" Framework, providing—for the first time—a global standard for preventing and addressing the risk of adverse impacts on human rights linked to business activity.[9]

## GUIDING PRINCIPLES ON BUSINESS AND HUMAN RIGHTS: IMPLEMENTING THE 'PROTECT, RESPECT AND REMEDY' FRAMEWORK[10]

These Guiding Principles apply to all States and to all business enterprises, both transnational and others, regardless of their size, sector, location, ownership and structure. These Principles are understood as a coherent whole and read, individually and collectively, so as to achieve tangible results for affected individuals and communities, and thereby also contribute to a socially sustainable globalisation.

It has been specifically mentioned in the Guiding Principles that nothing in it should be read as creating new international law obligations, or as limiting or undermining any legal

9. http://www.ohchr.org/EN/Issues/Business/Pages/BusinessIndex.aspx visited on 07/03/2013.
10. Publishing House, United Nations, Geneva, 2012, GE.11-46529, HR/PUB/11/4.

obligations a State may have undertaken or be subject to under international law with regard to human rights. These Guiding Principles should be implemented in a non-discriminatory manner, with particular attention to the rights and needs of, as well as the challenges faced by, individuals from groups or populations that may be at heightened risk of becoming vulnerable or marginalized, and with due regard to the different risks that may be faced by women and men.

The Office of the United Nations High Commissioner for Human Rights (OHCHR) has supported the six-year long process that led to the Principles under the stewardship of the Special Representative. Before their endorsement by the Human Rights Council, the High Commissioner stated that, "These Guiding Principles clarify the human rights responsibilities of business. They seek to provide the first global standard for preventing and addressing the risk of adverse human rights impact linked to business activities. If endorsed, the Guiding Principles will constitute an authoritative normative platform which will also provide guidance regarding legal and policy measures that, in compliance with their existing human rights obligations, States can put in place to ensure corporate respect for human rights."[11]

These Guiding Principles are grounded in recognition of:

(a) States' existing obligations to respect, protect and fulfil human rights and fundamental freedoms;

(b) The role of business enterprises as specialized organs of society performing specialized functions, required to comply with all applicable laws and to respect human rights; and

(c) The need for rights and obligations to be matched to appropriate and effective remedies when breached.

There are in all 31 Guiding Principles, to be obligated and imposed by the State as well as by the enterprises, some of these important principles are discussed hereinafter. Chapter II deals with the States' responsibility to protect and respect human rights against abuse by third parties, including business enterprises. Chapter III mentions the corporate responsibility to respect human rights which is further categorised into

11. Statement to the Employers' Group at the International Labour Conference, 7 June 2011 from The Corporate Responsibility to Respect Human Rights: An Interpretative Guide, 2012.

foundational and operational principles. While Chapter IV lays down the principles for access to remedy in case of any business-related human rights abuse.

**Principle 1:** The States must protect against human rights abuse within their territory and/or jurisdiction by third parties, including business enterprises. This requires taking appropriate steps to prevent, investigate, punish and redress such abuse through effective policies, legislation, regulations and adjudication.

It has been laid in the very first foundational principle that it is the duty of the State to protect against any kind of human rights violation by enterprises, for which proper action must be taken through policing, legislating and adjudicating.

**Principle 3:** In meeting their duty to protect, States should,

(a) Enforce laws that are aimed at, or have the effect of, requiring business enterprises to respect human rights, and periodically to assess the adequacy of such laws and address any gaps;

(b) Ensure that other laws and policies governing the creation and ongoing operation of business enterprises, such as corporate law, do not constrain but enable business respect for human rights;

(c) Provide effective guidance to business enterprises on how to respect human rights throughout their operations; and

(d) Encourage, and where appropriate require, business enterprises to communicate how they address their human rights impacts.

**Principle 4:** States should take additional steps to protect against human rights abuses by business enterprises that are owned or controlled by the State, or that receive substantial support and services from State agencies such as export credit agencies and official investment insurance or guarantee agencies, including, where appropriate, by requiring human rights due diligence.

This principle has been placed so as to evade the possibility of claiming any kind of sovereign immunity by the enterprises and thereby imposing the liability for human rights violation on the enterprises whether it is an instrumentality of the State or not.

**Principle 7:** Because the risk of gross human rights abuses is heightened in conflict affected areas, States should ensure that business enterprises operating in those contexts are not involved with such abuses, including by:

(a) Engaging at the earliest stage possible with business enterprises to help them identify, prevent and mitigate the human rights-related risks of their activities and business relationships;

(b) Providing adequate assistance to business enterprises to assess and address the heightened risks of abuses, paying special attention to both gender-based and sexual violence;

(c) Denying access to public support and services for a business enterprise that is involved with gross human rights abuses and refuses to cooperate in addressing the situation; and

(d) Ensuring that their current policies, legislation, regulations and enforcement measures are effective in addressing the risk of business involvement in gross human rights abuses.

**Principle 10:** States, when acting as members of multilateral institutions that deal with business-related issues, should

(a) Seek to ensure that those institutions neither restrain the ability of their member States to meet their duty to protect nor hinder business enterprises from respecting human rights;

(b) Encourage those institutions, within their respective mandates and capacities, to promote business respect for human rights and, where requested, to help States meet their duty to protect against human rights abuse by business enterprises, including through technical assistance, capacity-building and awareness-raising; and

(c) Draw on these Guiding Principles to promote shared understanding and advance international cooperation in the management of business and human rights challenges.

**Principle 11:** Business enterprises should respect human rights. This means that they should avoid infringing on the human rights of others and should address adverse human rights impacts with which they are involved.

**Principle 12:** The responsibility of business enterprises to respect human rights refers to internationally recognized human rights—understood, at a minimum, as those expressed in the International Bill of Human Rights and the principles concerning fundamental rights set out in the International Labour Organization's Declaration on Fundamental Principles and Rights at Work.

**Principle 13:** The responsibility to respect human rights requires that business enterprises,

(a) Avoid causing or contributing to adverse human rights impacts through their own activities, and address such impacts when they occur; and
(b) Seek to prevent or mitigate adverse human rights impacts that are directly linked to their operations, products or services by their business relationships, even if they have not contributed to those impacts.

**Principle 14:** The responsibility of business enterprises to respect human rights applies to all enterprises regardless of their size, sector, operational context, ownership and structure. Nevertheless, the scale and complexity of the means through which enterprises meet that responsibility may vary according to these factors and with the severity of the enterprise's adverse human rights impacts.

Such principles make it clear that all the enterprises of whatever size and operation are responsible for any kind of human rights violation. They are under an obligation to protect and respect human rights.

**Principle 15:** In order to meet their responsibility to respect human rights, business enterprises should have in place policies and processes appropriate to their size and circumstances, including:

(a) A policy commitment to meet their responsibility to respect human rights;
(b) A human rights due diligence process to identify, prevent, mitigate and account for how they address their impacts on human rights; and

(c) Processes to enable the remediation of any adverse human rights impacts they cause or to which they contribute.

Business enterprises need to know and show respect towards human rights, by following certain policies and processes which are elaborately mentioned from Principles 16 to 24.

**Principle 16:** As the basis for embedding their responsibility to respect human rights, business enterprises should express their commitment to meet this responsibility through a statement of policy that:

(a) is approved at the most senior level of the business enterprise;
(b) is informed by relevant internal and/or external expertise;
(c) stipulates the enterprise's human rights expectations of personnel, business partners and other parties directly linked to its operations, products or services;
(d) is publicly available and communicated internally and externally to all personnel, business partners and other relevant parties; and
(e) is reflected in operational policies and procedures necessary to embed it throughout the business enterprise.

**Principle 17:** In order to identify, prevent, mitigate and account for how they address their adverse human rights impacts, business enterprises should carry out human rights due diligence. The process should include assessing actual and potential human rights impacts, integrating and acting upon the findings, tracking responses, and communicating how impacts are addressed. Human rights due diligence:

(a) Should cover adverse human rights impacts that the business enterprise may cause or contribute to through its own activities, or which may be directly linked to its operations, products or services by its business relationships;
(b) Will vary in complexity with the size of the business enterprise, the risk of severe human rights impacts, and the nature and context of its operations; and

(c) Should be ongoing, recognizing that the human rights risks may change over time as the business enterprise's operations and operating context evolve.

**Principle 18:** In order to gauge human rights risks, business enterprises should identify and assess any actual or potential adverse human rights impacts with which they may be involved either through their own activities or as a result of their business relationships. This process should

(a) Draw on internal and/or independent external human rights expertise; and
(b) Involve meaningful consultation with potentially affected groups and other relevant stakeholders, as appropriate to the size of the business enterprise and the nature and context of the operation.

**Principle 19:** In order to prevent and mitigate adverse human rights impacts, business enterprises should integrate the findings from their impact assessments across relevant internal functions and processes, and take appropriate action.

(a) Effective integration requires that (i) responsibility for addressing such impacts is assigned to the appropriate level and function within the business enterprise; (ii) internal decision-making, budget allocations and oversight processes enable effective responses to such impacts.
(b) Appropriate action will vary according to (i) whether the business enterprise causes or contributes to an adverse impact, or whether it is involved solely because the impact is directly linked to its operations, products or services by a business relationship; (ii) the extent of its leverage in addressing the adverse impact.

**Principle 20:** In order to verify whether adverse human rights impacts are being addressed, business enterprises should track the effectiveness of their response. Tracking should (a) be based on appropriate qualitative and quantitative indicators; (b) draw on feedback from both internal and external sources, including affected stakeholders.

**Principle 21:** In order to account for how they address their human rights impacts, business enterprises should be prepared to communicate this externally, particularly when concerns are raised by or on behalf of affected stakeholders. Business enterprises whose operations or operating contexts pose risks of severe human rights impacts should report formally on how they address them. In all instances, communications should (a) Be of a form and frequency that reflect an enterprise's human rights impacts and that are accessible to its intended audiences; (b) Provide information that is sufficient to evaluate the adequacy of an enterprise's response to the particular human rights impact involved; (c) In turn not pose risks to affected stakeholders, personnel or to legitimate requirements of commercial confidentiality.

**Principle 22:** Where business enterprises identify that they have caused or contributed to adverse impacts, they should provide for or cooperate in their remediation through legitimate processes.

**Principle 23:** In all contexts, business enterprises should (a) Comply with all applicable laws and respect internationally recognized human rights, wherever they operate; (b) Seek ways to honour the principles of internationally recognized human rights when faced with conflicting requirements; (c) Treat the risk of causing or contributing to gross human rights abuses as a legal compliance issue wherever they operate.

**Principle 24:** Where it is necessary to prioritize actions to address actual and potential adverse human rights impacts, business enterprises should first seek to prevent and mitigate those that are most severe or where delayed response would make them irremediable.

These principles clearly describe the obligations undertaken by the business enterprises. It also explains the protective procedures to be applied, importance of the judicial and extra-judicial steps to resolve the human rights violation instances and its various methods.

**Principle 25:** As part of their duty to protect against business-related human rights abuse, States must take appropriate steps to ensure, through judicial, administrative, legislative or other appropriate means, that when such abuses occur within their territory and/or jurisdiction those affected have access to effective remedy.

**Principle 26:** States should take appropriate steps to ensure the effectiveness of domestic judicial mechanisms when addressing business-related human rights abuses, including considering ways to reduce legal, practical and other relevant barriers that could lead to a denial of access to remedy.

**Principle 27:** States should provide effective and appropriate non-judicial grievance mechanisms, alongside judicial mechanisms, as part of a comprehensive State-based system for the remedy of business-related human rights abuse.

In order to ensure the effectiveness of the non-judicial grievance system, the criteria have been set out in Principle 31, which must be meted out. National human rights institutions have an important role to play in this regard. Various other judicial and non-judicial mechanisms are endowed with the responsibility to regularise the human rights violations. States also have an extra obligation to consider ways to address any imbalances between the parties to business-related human rights claims and any additional barriers to access, faced by individuals from groups or populations at heightened risk of vulnerability or marginalization.

**Principle 31:** In order to ensure their effectiveness, non-judicial grievance mechanisms, both State-based and non-State-based, should be:

(a) *Legitimate:* enabling trust from the stakeholder groups for whose use they are intended, and being accountable for the fair conduct of grievance processes;

(b) *Accessible:* being known to all stakeholder groups for whose use they are intended, and providing adequate assistance for those who may face particular barriers to access;

(c) *Predictable:* providing a clear and known procedure with an indicative time frame for each stage, and clarity on the types of process and outcome available and means of monitoring implementation;

(d) *Equitable:* seeking to ensure that aggrieved parties have reasonable access to sources of information, advice and expertise necessary to engage in a grievance process on fair, informed and respectful terms;

(e) *Transparent:* keeping parties to a grievance informed about its progress, and providing sufficient infor-ma-tion about the mechanism's performance to build confidence in its effectiveness and meet any public interest at stake;

(f) *Rights-compatible:* ensuring that outcomes and remedies accord with internationally recognized human rights;

(g) *A source of continuous learning:* drawing on relevant measures to identify lessons for improving the mechanism and preventing future grievances and harms;

Operational-level mechanisms should also be:

(h) *Based on engagement and dialogue:* consulting the stakeholder groups for whose use they are intended on their design and performance, and focusing on dialogue as the means to address and resolve grievances.

Above are some of the important Principles laid down by the UN for the state and the business enterprises to respect, protect and adjudicate the instances of the human rights violations. These principles are been laid in lieu of the growing abuse of human rights due to the advent of the globalisation and growing corporatisation. These are very recently laid, in the year of 2008 and 2011, and suffer from the biggest lacuna of not having the sanctional applicability but still it could not be devalued since it forms the basic norms of various legislations and the judicial pronouncements.

*Martin Lipton* of Wachtell, Lipton, Rosen and Katz has remarked that the "*Guiding Principles* insightfully marries aspirations with practicality. It identifies a host of tangible opportunities for Nations and businesses to contribute to the goal of preventing human rights abuses. In short, Guiding Principles encapsulates the Special Representative's stated commitment to "principled pragmatism," reflecting the world's fundamental human rights expectations in a balanced way that takes account of the varied, complex global business landscape."[12]

12. http://blogs.law.harvard.edu/corpgov/2011/04/09/un-guiding-principles-for-business-human-rights visited on 09/03/2013.

## CORPORATE RESPONSIBILITY AND HUMAN RIGHTS: IMPLICATIONS IN INDIA

In the recent past, India has witnessed some significant judicial rulings that are related to corporate disasters. The most relevant amongst these is the 'Bhopal gas tragedy'. In the case pertaining to the female employee in Bangalore, who was raped and killed by the transport driver of her company, the Supreme Court allowed the prosecution of the Managing Director under the Shops & Establishment Act. Furthermore, in yet another ill-famed case of the 'Uphar Cinema hall fire tragedy', the High Court and the Supreme Court ruled that the compensation was to be paid by the owners of the cinema hall to the victims' family. Scandals related to the appalling practices of multinational corporations like Union Carbide (now DOW), Enron, Coke, Cadbury, and others may have shocked the nation and the world in the recent past.[13]

In Bhopal, more than 8,000 people died in the first three days after 40 tonnes of lethal gas spilled out from Union Carbide's pesticide factory in December 1984. People woke in their homes to fits of coughing, their lungs filling with fluid. 520,000 people were exposed to poisonous gases. 150,000 victims were chronically ill, and even now one person dies every two days. Union Carbide merged with Dow Chemical Corporation two years ago and has ceased to exist as an entity while the present owners Dow refuse to accept any pending liabilities in Bhopal including clean-up of the abandoned site.

In Kodaikanal, Hindustan Lever, a subsidiary of Unilever Plc, an Anglo-Dutch multinational dumped mercury waste from its thermometer factory in the surrounding forests and on an innocent local community. When the scandal was exposed, first the company denied that there was a problem and later fudged facts and figures until the Indian authorities forced them to come clean. Since then Unilever has retrieved and sent back to USA some of the waste for disposal but are shying away from compensating affected workers and further environmental remediation measures. Ship-owning companies (and indeed, their countries) like Bergesen (Norway), and Chandris (Greece) meanwhile, regularly violate international and national laws and

13. http://www.greenpeace.org/india/en/news/corporate-accountability visited on 09/03/2013.

dump their hazardous wastes at ship-breaking yards in India, Pakistan, China, Turkey and Bangladesh. The voluntary guidelines issued by International Marine Organisation are not enough and it is imperative that these guidelines are made mandatory to make the ship-owners liable and responsible.

Monsanto, one of the world's largest pesticide companies, continues to sell its genetically engineered seeds to farmers around the world despite growing evidence of failure of crops like Bt cotton, that has reduced once well-to-do farmers in the developing world to penury and poverty while the threat of contamination of indigenous species by GE seeds increases every day. Bayer AG, a German transnational continues to manufacture and sell phased out pesticides like Methyl Parathion (brand name Folidol/Metacid) in Asia despite an assurance to their European investors and stakeholders that they would stop manufacturing these organo-phosphate poisons.

It is quite evident from the above few examples that our world is increasingly ruled and ruined by large multinational corporations. In the era of globalization, multinational companies increasingly move around assets, products and wastes on a global chessboard to maximize their profits and minimize their costs. These companies are using differences and loopholes in national environmental, health laws and other labour sectors to the detriment of local communities.

The gap between the world's rich and poor has widened. Instead of providing developing countries with the tools for sustainable development, corporations have pushed their dirty technologies and polluting industries on to some of the world's poorest countries. In the past ten years, corporations have not only resisted environmental challenges, they have lobbied to water down international treaties and have maintained their unsustainable practices in all sectors.

Current systems of governance in Asia (as elsewhere) are proving to be deficient against the activities of abusive multinational corporations. To roll back the excessive powers of corporations and to pressure governments to check corporate abuse and prosecute corporate crimes, greater public participation is a must. Corporations need to be held accountable for their actions that are destroying the planet, destroying people's lives around the globe. We must stand up to the corporations. Our governments must agree on international, legally binding rules for corporate responsibility, accountability and liability: a set of rules that business must follow, and governments must enforce them.

The world needs corporations to be held accountable to the following laws—no matter where they operate in the world. 'Greenpeace' emphasis upon the Indian Government to endorse the Bhopal Principles on Corporate Responsibility, which call on Multinational Corporations to:

- Accept liability for environmental damage and compensate victims of pollution;
- Accept liability for the damage, no matter when it happens, what the cause or who in the corporation is responsible;
- Accept responsibility for damage and injury beyond national borders including accidents in the oceans and atmosphere;
- Ensure that they do not infringe upon basic human rights;
- Disclose all information regarding releases into the environment to the public;
- Protect human and social rights including the highest standards for rights to health care and a clean environment;
- Avoid influence over governments, combat bribery and practice transparency;
- Allow states to maintain their sovereignty over their own food supply;
- Implement a precautionary principle and take preventative action before environmental damages or health effects are incurred; and
- Promote and practice clean and sustainable development.

In India, howsoever, in the streamline of various International Conventions and the agreements there are plethoras of legislations so as to make corporations liable for the human rights infringements. Being a signatory member of the UN, India is under an obligation to follow and apply various regulations respecting and protecting human rights. Starting from environment to labour and to sexual harassment there are many legislations imposed by the State but due to poor administration and deep-rooted corruption, the corporate violators escape out the liability, under such practical circumstances the biggest rescuer emerges in the form of the judiciary. By interpreting the different Constitutional provisions, international agreements and legislations the courts, especially the Supreme Court has provided with many landmark judgements to held enterprises including corporations liable for infringing the various human rights including that of the clean environment, water, payment of wages, sexual harassment, gender justice, working conditions, etc.

The Indian Government acceded to the ICESCR on 10 July 1979, on the same day it acceded to the ICCPR. The Government of India, upon accession to the Covenant, made three declarations to the ICESCR. No indication has been given of plans to either remove or amend the Declarations.[14]

The Constitution of India recognizes many fundamental freedoms contained in the International Covenant on Civil and Political Rights, including the right to life, equality, and freedom of expression, and the right to seek judicial redress for violation of these rights. Economic, social and cultural rights are not given automatic judicial protection, but are contained in the Constitution's Directive Principles of State Policy (DPSPs) in Part IV. These have been referred to as 'the precursor to the economic, social cultural rights specified in the ICESCR, 1966' by the National Commission to Review the Working of the Constitution.[15] In the Directive Principles, however, one finds an even clearer statement of social revolution. They aim at making the Indian masses free from the passivity engendered by centuries of coercion by society.[16]

However, as the ultimate authority on constitutional law, the Supreme Court has taken an active role in developing the power of judicial review as an integral part of its work. These decisions are binding 'on all Courts within the territory of India',[17] and 'all authority, civil and judicial, in the territory of India shall act in

14. SAHRDC, Human Rights and Humanitarian Law: Developments in India and International Law, New Delhi, Oxford University Press, 2008.
15. *Ibid.*, at 377.
16. Granville Austin, The Indian Constitution—Cornerstone of a Nation, (11th impression), New Delhi, Oxford University Press, 2007.
17. The Constitution of India, Article 141.

aid of the Supreme Court of India'[18]. Failure to do so is punishable with Contempt of Court[19]. It is though the power of judicial review that the Supreme Court has been capable of expanding the scope of economic, social and cultural rights from DPSPs to rights enforceable before the Courts.

The relaxing of the rule of *locus standi* to allow for Public Interest Litigation (PIL) further enable the Court to enforce ESCRs, i.e., Economic, Social and Cultural Rights. The judiciary initiated PIL in 1978-79 in the wake of widespread violations of human rights during the emergency period. This development allowed for any individual approach the Courts for the protection of constitutional rights of other individuals or groups and to resolve issues of common concern, opening the Supreme Court to those 'who are living in desperation, who are helpless victims of an exploitative society and who do not have an easy access to justice'.[20]

Consequently, the combination of PIL and the expansion of the nation of the right to life allowed the Courts to overcome the question of justifiability and to address economic, social and cultural rights as more than just directives of state policy. This supports the principle that all human rights are indivisible, interdependent and interrelated. There is a subtle shift from a neutralist adversarial judicial role to an inquisitorial, affirmative judicial role and the judicial process changed from an adversarial, bilateral process to a polycentric, conflict-resolving process.

It is clearly the duty of the judiciary to promote a social order in which justice, economic and political informs all the institutions of the national life. This was also made clear in *Kesavananda case* by Justice Mathew that the DPSPs nevertheless are fundamental in the governance of the country and all the organs of the State, including the judiciary are bound to enforce those directives. The fundamental Rights themselves have no fixed content; most of them are mere empty vessels into which each generation must pour its content in the light of its experience.

The SC has a duty to interpret statutes with social welfare benefits in such a way as to further the statutory goal and not to

18. *Ibid.*, Article 144.
19. *Ibid.*, Article 129.
20. *S.P. Gupta v. President of India and others,* AIR 1982 SC 149.

frustrate it. In doing so, this court should make an effort to protect the rights of the weaker sections of the society in view of the clear constitutional mandate.[21]

It was also further emphasised in the case that any attempt to dilute the Constitutional imperatives in or order to promote the so called trends of "Globalisation", may result in precarious consequences. It is the judges' duty, being constitutional invigilators and statutory interpreters, to consider Part IV as one of the trinity of the nation's appointed instrumentalities in the transformation of the socio-economic order and also to uphold the constitutional focus on social justice without being in any way misled by the glitz and glare of the globalisation.[22]

In *C.E.S.C. Limited v. Subhash Chandra Bose,*[23] in the 'minority view' Ramaswami, J., referred to Article 25(2) of the UDHR, Article 7(b) of ICESCR and Article 39(e) of Indian Constitution and held that the right to health and medical care as a fundamental right. The health and strength of a worker is an integral facet of right to life. The aim of fundamental rights is to create an egalitarian society to free all citizens from coercion or restrictions by society and to make available for all. To the tillers of the soil, wage earners, labourers, wood-cutters, rickshaw pullers, scavengers and hut dwellers, the civil and political rights are mere 'cosmetic rights'. Socio-economic and cultural rights are their means and relevant to them to realize the basic aspirations of meaningful right to life. Our Constitution also reinforces such rights compendiously as social-economic justice, a bed-rock to an egalitarian social order. The right to social and economic justice is thus fundamental right.

Ramaswami, J., while delivering the judgment advocated the same view in *Consumer Education & Research Centre and Others v. Union of India & Others*[24] and opined 'the jurisprudence of personhood or philosophy of the right to life envisaged under Article 21, enlarges its sweep to encompass human personality in its full blossom with invigorated health which is a wealth to the workman to earn his livelihood, to sustain the dignity of person and to live a life with dignity and equality.' It was further

21. *Harjinder Singh v. Punjab State Warehousing Corporation,* AIR 2010 SC 1116.
22. *Ibid.*
23. (1992) 1 SCC 441.
24. (1995) 3 SCC 42.

observed that the State be it Union or State Government or an industry, public or private, is enjoined to take all such actions which will promote health, strength and vigour of the workmen during the period employment and leisure and health even after retirement as basic essentials to live the life with health and happiness. Facilities for medical care and health to prevent sickness ensure stable manpower for economic development and would generate devotion to duty and dedication to give the worker's best physically as well as mentally in production of goods or services. Health of the worker enables him to enjoy the fruits of his labour, keeping him physically fit and mentally alert for leading a successful life, economically, socially and culturally. Medical facilities to protect the health of the workers are, therefore, the fundamental and human rights to workmen.

The Court thus allowed the petition and directed following directions to all the industries:

(1) To maintain and keep health records of every worker upto a minimum period of 40 years from employment or 15 years after retirement or cessation;
(2) The Membrane Filter test to detect asbestos fibre should be planted in accordance with Vienna Declaration;
(3) All the factories are directed to compulsorily insure health coverage to every worker;
(4) Governments are directed to review the standards of permissible exposure limit value of fibre/CC in consonance with the international standards, which is to be continued after every 10 years and also when so required by ILO directives;
(5) Governments are directed to consider inclusion of such of those small-scale factory or industries to protect health hazards of workers engaged in manufacture of asbestos or its ancillary; and
(6) Appropriate authority must send workers examined by ESI hospital concerned to the National Institute of Occupational Health for re-examination. In case of positive finding, each of the suffering workers be entitled to compensation of rupees one lakh payable by the establishment concerned within three months.[25]

25. *Ibid.*, at 73-74.

Ramawamy, J., in the case of *LIC of India & another v. Consumer Education & Research Centre and others,*[26] emphasized the importance of insurance for workers, and stated that it would be thus well-settled law that the Preamble, Chapters of Fundamental Rights and Directive Principles accord right to livelihood as a meaningful life, social security and disablement benefits are integral schemes of socio-economic justice to the people, in particular to the middle class and lower middle class and all affordable people. Life insurance coverage is against disablement or in the event of death of the insured economic support for the dependants, social security to livelihood to the insured or the defendants. The appropriate life insurance policy within the paying capacity and means of the insured to pay premia is one of the social security measures envisaged under the Constitution to make right to life meaningful, worth-living and right to livelihood as a means for sustenance.

When the public sector undertaking was closed and it lead to poverty, ill-health and other such deteriorating conditions of its workers, the Court took up the matter and issued necessary guidelines to mitigate the extreme hardship of the employees in the case of *Kapila Hingorani v. State of Bihar*[27]. It held the government of Bihar to be responsible by lifting the corporate veil and stated that the financial stringency may not be a ground for not issuing requisite directions when a question of violation of fundamental right arises. The Constitutional mandate of State cannot be permitted to be circumvented on the ground of lack of economic capacity or financial incapacity. However, no rule to make the State vicariously liable is made but has been emphasized by the Court that the State cannot escape its liability when a human rights problem of such magnitude involving the starvation deaths and/or suicide by the employees has taken place by reason of non-payment of salary to the employees of public sector undertakings for such a long time. Interim directions were passed to deposit a sum of Rs. 50 crores for disbursement of salaries to the employees.

This was a landmark case on the vital issue of the 'instrumentality of the State'. In it the State was held liable for the human right abuse done by the corporation, though it was not

26. (1995) 5 SCC 482.
27. (2003) 6 SCC 1.

vicariously liable. The concept of instrumentality or agency of the government is not limited to a corporation created by a statute but is equally applicable to a company or a society.

While explaining the rule of 'equal work equal pay' the Supreme Court stated that "we have interpreted and applied the doctrine even more widely to prevent discriminatory pay scales within an organization which is owned by or is an instrumentality of the State, provided that the different pay-scales exist in one organization, are applied to employees doing work of equal value, and there is no rational explanation for the difference.[28] Thus, the court emphasises the need of equal pay for similar work to be maintained by the State and its instrumentalities including the different enterprises.

On the issue of sexual harassment, the following case is very important, though it does not involve corporation, since it lays guidelines for protection to female workers wheresoever they are been employed. A three-judge Bench of the Supreme Court in *Vishaka v. Union of India*,[29] made a significant contribution in evolving the code against sexual harassment for the women workers at the workplace. While emphasizing the need to have guidelines the Supreme Court observed that in the instances of sexual harassment which results in violating of fundamental right of women workers under Articles 14, 19 and 21, an effective redressal requires that some guidelines should be laid down for the protection of these rights to fill the legislative vacuum. These guidelines must be strictly observed at all work places for the preservation and enforcement of the right to gender equality of the working women. These directions according to the Court would be binding and enforceable in law until suitable legislation is enacted to occupy the field. However, these guidelines will 'not prejudice' any rights available under the Protection of Human Rights Act, 1993.

The Court further added that a writ of *mandamus* in such a situation, if it is to be effective, needs to be accompanied by directions for prevention; as the violation of fundamental rights of this kind is a recurring phenomenon. The fundamental right to carry on any occupation, trade or profession depends on the

28. *Associate Banks Officers' Association v. State Bank of India*, AIR 1998 SC 32.
29. (1997) 6 SCC 241.

availability of a 'safe' working environment. Right to life means life with dignity.[30]

Some of the important guidelines issued by the Court were as following:

(1) it shall be the duty of the employer or other responsible persons in workplaces or other institutions to prevent or deter the commission of such acts and to provide the procedures for the resolution;
(2) the rules/regulations of Government and Public Sector bodies relating to conduct and discipline should include rules/regulations prohibiting sexual harassment and provide for appropriate penalties;
(3) appropriate work conditions should be provided in respect of work, leisure, health and hygiene to further ensure that there is no hostile environments towards women workers;
(4) appropriate disciplinary action should be initiated by the employer in accordance with the rules; and
(5) an appropriate complaint mechanism should be created in the employer's organization for readdress of the complaint[31].

The Court opined on the issue relating to as to what constitutes sexual harassment in the recent case of *D.S. Grewal v. Vimmi Joshi*,[32] by stating that even writing of a sensuous letter to a female employee expressing love to her, admiring her qualities and beauty and extending unsolicited help to her besides sexual advances will all amount to sexual harassment. It was further held that while dealing with such issues of female employee's grievance it must ought to have been looked into according to the directions given in *Vishaka's case*, Articles 14, 15, 16, 21, 42, 51, 51-A(e)(f), 141 and 144 of the Constitution to be harmoniously interpreted and even Protection of Women against Sexual Harassment at Workplace Bill, 2007 be regarded. In violation of such guidelines the Court held the management of the school where the female employee was working to be liable and ordered to pay compensation of Rs. 50,000 to her.

30. *Ibid.*
31. *Ibid.*
32. (2009) 2 SCC 210.

The working conditions and benefits of female workers especially the maternity benefits, was emphasized by the Supreme Court in the case of *Municipal Corporation of Delhi v. Female Workers (Muster Roll) & others.*[33] The Court observed that the female workers who are engaged by the Corporation on muster roll have to work at the site of construction and repairing of roads. Their services have also been utilized for digging of trenches. It is in this background and in the background of the Preamble, Articles 14 and 15(3) in Part III and Articles 38, 39(a)(c), 42 and 43 in Part IV of the Constitution of India that one can determine whether the denial of maternity benefit by the petitioner is justified in law or not. A woman employee, at the time of advanced pregnancy cannot be completed to undertake hard labour as it would be detrimental to her health and also to the health of the foetus. It is for this reason that it is provided in the Maternity Benefit Act, 1961 that she would be entitled to maternity leave for certain period prior to and after delivery. There is nothing contained in the Act which entitles only regular women employees to the benefit of maternity leave and not to those who are engaged on casual basis or on muster roll on daily-wage basis. A just social order can be achieved only when inequalities are obliterated and everyone is provided what is legally due. Women who constitute almost half of the segment of the society have to be honoured and treated with dignity at places where they work to earn their livelihood.

Mostly the corporations are involved in the environment degradation thereby infringing the human right of the maximum persons. The judiciary having no uniform application of legislation has developed various principles to held these corporations liable for the damage done and to restore the same. In *Indian Council for Enviro-Legal Action v. Union of India,*[34] the court held that the 'polluter pays principle' was explained as once the activity carried on is hazardous or inherently dangerous, the person carrying on such activity is liable to make the loss caused to any other person by his activity irrespective of fact whether he took reasonable care while carrying on his activity. The polluting enterprise is absolutely liable to compensate for harm caused to the environment and is also liable to pay

33. (2000) 3 SCC 224.
34. (1996) 3 SCC 212.

the cost of restoring the environmental degradation—reversing the damaged ecology.

The court again declared in the famous case of *Nitrite Ltd. v. State of Gujarat*[35] that the compensation to be awarded must have some broad correlation not only with the magnitude of the risk and the capacity of the enterprise, but with the harm caused by it. Liability arises only where it is proved that some damage has been caused to the man and material or to the environment by the industrial unit through its activity.

The *Union Carbon Carbide Corporation v. Union of India,*[36] is the landmark case in which the Supreme Court while furthering the 'absolute liability' principle observed that where an enterprise is engaged in hazardous or inherently dangerous activity and harm results to anyone on account of an accident in the operation of such hazardous or inherently dangerous activity, for example, in the case escape of toxic gas, the enterprise is strictly and absolutely liable to compensate all those who are affected by the accident and such liability is not subject to any exceptions. This case established the rule of corporate liability for the damage done in any manner due to its activity and most importantly it brought forward the ugly face of the human rights abuse by the corporations.

The greatest problem faced by India before the ILO supervisory bodies in recent years have been the existence of bonded labour in the country which amounts to forced labour. The ILO Committee of Experts has noted the problem in the identification of bonded labour in the country and the debate over their number—varying between the Government assertion that their number was in lakhs and that of independent non-governmental organizations which have placed the number at around 5 million. The ILO Committee of Experts has pointed out that there has been no comprehensive survey on the magnitude of bonded labour in the country.[37]

The bonded labour system is the relic of feudal exploitative system resulting in domination of a few socially and economically powerful persons over large number of illiterate, socially and economic weak people. At times, several generations

35. (2004) 6 SCC 402.
36. AIR 1990 SC 273.
37. Kamal Sankaran, 'Human Rights and the World of Work,' 40 JILI 284 (1998).

worked under bondage for the repayment of a party sum, which had been taken by some remote ancestors. This system implied infringement of basic human rights and destruction of the dignity of human labour.[38]

Attempts have been made, from time to time, by the international community to eradicate forced labour. A number of treaties were entered into for putting an end to the slave traffic through international co-operation. The most important one was the Slavery Convention of 1926 framed under auspices of League of Nations. Article 4 of the Universal Declaration of Human Rights prohibited 'slave trade'; Article 4 of the European Convention of the Human Rights and Article 8 of the International Covenant on Civil and Political Rights, 1966 also prohibited forced or compulsory labour. Two Conventions adopted by the International Labour Organization are the main instrument to carry on its crusade against forced labour:

(1) The Forced Labour Convention, 1930.
(2) The Abolition of Forced Convention, 1957.

The order to prevent exploitation of bonded labour the Constitution contains several provisions. Article 23(1) of the Constitution prohibits traffic in human beings and other similar forms of forced labour. Further, Article 21 guarantees the right to life and personal liberty. Apart from these, several provisions of Part IV direct the State to provide humane conditions of work and protection of socio-economic interests of weaker sections.[39]

The landmark case relating to several inhuman issues of bonded labour has been elaborately for the first time was discussed in *Bandhua Mukti Morcha v. Union of India.*[40] In a letter addressed to one of the judges of the Supreme Court, it was pointed out that a large number of labourers were languishing under abject conditions of bondage for about ten years. The Court treated it as a writ petition and held that their fundamental rights under Article 21 were violated.

Bhagwati, J., observed that 'when a complaint is made on behalf of workmen that they are held in bondage and are working and living in miserable conditions without any proper

38. Suresh C. Srivastava, 'Constitutional Protection to Weaker and Disadvantaged Section of Labour,' 42 JILI 232 (2000).
39. *Ibid.*
40. (1984) 3 SCC 161.

or adequate shelter, without meals and with only dirty water from a nullah to drink, it is difficult how such a complaint can be thrown out on the ground that it is not violative of the fundamental right of the workmen. The right to live with human dignity enshrined in Article 21 derives its life breath from the Directive Principles of State Policy, particularly clauses (e) and (f) of Article 39 and Articles 41 and 42.

The Court further held such right includes protection of the health and strength of workers, men and women and of the tender age of children against abuse, opportunities and facilities for children to develop in a healthy manner and in conditions of freedom and dignity; educational facilities, just and humane conditions of work and maternity relief benefits. The court also interpreted the provisions of the Bonded Labour System (Abolition) Act, 1976 in its true spirit of providing socio-economic benefits of such social welfare legislations. The Court accordingly pointed out that the Government, Social action groups, NGOs and groups with record of honest service for SC/STs, agricultural labourers and unorganised workmen should be involved in the task of release of such labourers. Directives were also issued against the Government of Haryana to constitute vigilance committees to free and rehabilitate such labourers within a period of three months.[41]

In *Neeraja Chaudhury v. State of M.P.*,[42] the Court took the matter more seriously and now merely non-implementation of the provision of the Act was considered as violative of Article 21. Bhagwati, J., observed that it is the plainest requirement of Articles 21 and 23 of the Constitution that bonded labour must be identified and released and on release they must be suitably rehabilitated.

This multi-dimensional judicial strategy for the identification and release of bonded labourer included evolution of the concept of Public Interest Litigation, adoption of the technique of directions and appointment of monitoring agency to oversee the observance of directions. This shows the deep concern of the Supreme Court for the cause of bonded labourers. From the traditional role of enforcing the law by interpreting various provisions, the Court went ahead in applying the result of social

41. *Ibid.*
42. (1984) 3 SCC 243.

research with the object of seeing how the society may be changed through the process of law.[43]

It is a tyranny that though our highest judiciary provided such landmark judgment for the upliftment of bonded labourers, the menace is still very much prevalent but again our judiciary at times has taken up the issue and provides adequate relief. The best example of such is the following case.

In *P.U.C.L. v. State of Tamil Nadu,*[44] the Supreme Court stated that 'it does appear to us that no significant progress has been made by the authority concerned' and thus considered it appropriate to make certain directions for their development: (1) to identify the bonded labourers and update the existing list of such; (2) to identify the employers exploiting the bonded labourers; (3) to extinguish and discharge any existing debt and/ bonded liability and to ensure them an alternative means of livelihood; (4) to provide employment, educate shelter, food, education to the children of bonded labourers and medical facilities to the bonded labourers and their families as part of rehabilitation package

Justice Krishna Iyer once stated that "the hallmark of culture and advance of civilization consists in the fulfilment of our obligation to the young generation by opening up all opportunities for every child to unfold its spiritual. It is the birth right of every child that cries for justice from the world as a whole."

In a civilized society, the importance of child welfare cannot be underestimated because the welfare of the entire community, its growth and development, depends on the health and well-being of its children. Children are a "supremely important national asset" and the future well-being of the nation depends on how its children grow and develops. However, these wishful and optimistic sayings look shallow and no more than a rigmarole when one encounters the reality of child labour and exploitation in the unorganised and organised sectors of the economy.[45]

Children are the most vulnerable section of any society. They

43. B.P. Dwivedi, 'Changing Dimension of Personal Liberty in India', Allahabad, Wadhwa & Co., 1998 at 187.
44. (1994) 5 SCC 116.
45. Mamata Rao, 'Law Relating to Women and Children', Allahabad, Eastern Book Co., 2008 (second ed.) at 413.

are exploited in various ways. To protect them from exploitation and provide them opportunities for harmonious development the United Nations has focused its attention on their problems since 1946, when the Geneva Declaration of 1924 was recommended to be treated as binding on the peoples of the post-Second World War.[46]

The basic rights of family, care, education of every child has been widely provisioned under the UDHR, ICCPR, ICESCR, Convention on the Rights of Child, and various instruments of UNICEF. The UN Convention on Rights of the Child proclaims that every child has the inherent right to life and the State Parties shall ensure to the maximum extent possible for the survival and development of the child.[47] The Convention further mandates the state parties to recognize the right of the child to be protected from economic exploitations and from performing any work that is likely to be harmful to the child's health or physical, mental, spiritual, moral or social development.[48] The ILO has also been instrumental in protecting the rights of children and laying down conditions and standards regarding wages and welfare of working children.

'Child Labour' is a complex and a controversial issue. Unfortunately, it is a global phenomenon. In almost all societies, children work in some way, through the type and form of their involvement in the work varies. Child labour includes children prematurely leading adult lives, working long hours for law wages, under conditions damaging to their health and development, frequently deprived of meaningful education that could open up for them a better future. Child labour is therefore all work that places children at risk. The evil of child employment in agriculture and industrial sector is a product of economic, social and among others, inadequate legislative measure. The founding fathers of the Constitution, being aware of the likely exploitation by different profit-makers for their personal gain specifically prohibited employment of children in certain employment.

The Convention on the Rights of the Child, 1989 (CRC) is

46. U. Chandra, 'Human Rights,' Allahabad, Allahabad Law Agency Publications, 2007 (Seventh ed.) at 267.
47. Article 6.
48. Thomas Paul, 'Child Labour-Prohibition v. Abolition: Untangling the Constitutional Tangle', 50 JILI 143 (2008).

first globally binding treat protecting children's civil, political, economic, social and cultural rights. It represents a 'quantum leap' in the legal dimension of children's right from the previous international instruments concerning children rights. After the advent of CRC, the child is no longer considered as merely a vulnerable human being, needing special care and assistance but as subjects of fundamental rights and freedoms having the same spectrum of right as adults.[49]

India's abiding interest in the welfare of children is an expression of the country's commitment to the welfare of its single most populous group. Articles 23, 24, 37(e) and 39(f) of the Indian Constitution prohibits employment of children into any form of hazardous or forced labour. Article 15(3) enables the State to make special provisions for children. Articles 21A and 45 provides for free and compulsory education to children in the age group of 6-14 years.[50]

Apart from the Constitutional obligation, the States as well as the Centre have enacted various laws which place restrictions on the employment of child labour like the Child Labour (Prohibition and Regulation) Act, 1986, Minimum Wages Act, Contract Labour (Abolition and Prevention) Act, Migrant Labour Act, Employment Guarantee Schemes, Children Pledging of Labour Act, Employment of Children Act, etc.[51]

More recently, the Commission for Protection of Child Rights Act, 2005 has been passed to provide for the constitution of a National and State Commission for Protection of child rights and Children's Courts for providing speedy trial of offences against children or of violation of child rights. The Right to Education Act, 2008 has been passed to provide free and compulsory education to children between 6-14 years of age with the main intent to curb down the menace of child labour.

Despite, a plethora of legislation, constitutional provisions, and international instruments either prohibiting or regulating child labour, child labour still continues to thrive in our country. 'Poverty' though is often cited as the main cause for the continuance and growth of child labour in our country, the converse fact that child labour aids and abets in the perpetuation

---

49. S. Pandiaraj, 'Elimination of Child Labour in India: Towards a Glorious Illusion', 46 IJIL 84 (2006).
50. Pawan Sharma, 'Child Labour: A Socio-Legal Study", 36 JILI 193 (1994).
51. *Ibid.*

of poverty, cannot be discounted. The higher judiciary has often been sympathetic to the issue of child labour.[52]

In the celebrated case of *People's Union for Democratic Rights v. Union of India,*[53] (popularly known as the *Asiad case*) P.N. Bhagwati, J., equating child labour with forced labour under Aricle 23 observed that there is no reason why the word 'forced' should be read in a narrow and restricted manner so as to be confined only to physical or legal force particularly when the national charter, its fundamental document has promised to build a new socialist republic where there will be socio-economic justice for all and everyone. Constitutional prohibition for employment of a child below 14 years of age is provided under Article 24.

The Court opined in *Bandhua Mukti Morcha v. Union of India,*[54] that various welfare enactments made by Parliament and the appropriate State legislatures are only on paper and illusory unless they are effectively promoted and the right to life of the child driven to labour is made a reality. Pragmatic, realistic and constructive steps and actions are required to be taken to enable children belonging to weaker sections of society to enjoy their childhood and develop their personality. Child labour, therefore, must be eradicated through well planned and focused poverty alleviation, programmes and through imposition of trade sanctions in employment of children, etc. Total banishment of employment may drive children into destitution and other mischievous environments, making them vagrants, hardened criminals and prone to social risks, etc. Therefore, while exploitation of the child must be progressively banned, other simultaneous alternatives to the child should be evolved including providing education, health care, nutritious food, shelter and other means of livelihood with self-respect and dignity. Immediate ban of child labour would be both unrealistic and counterproductive. Ban of employment of children must begin from the most hazardous and intolerable activities like slavery, bonded labour, trafficking, prostitution, pornography, dangerous forms of labour and the like.

Education has always been stressed upon by the Court and

52. Thomas Paul, 'Social Security and Labour Welfare Legislation', Annual Survey of India, Vol. XL, 2004 at 447.
53. AIR 1982 SC 1473.
54. (1997) 10 SCC 549.

in the advent of child labour it becomes more viable and important. In this context *Mohini Jain v. State of Karnataka,*[55] is a landmark judgment where the Supreme Court held 'right to education' to be another unenumerated right being basic and compulsory for each and every child especially between 6-14 years of age.

In *Ajay Goswami v. Union of India & others,*[56] while deciding the issue relating to education Lakshmanan, J., held the right to education as a basic right for awakening of the child. The Court further added that India has been accepted on the Rights of Child which has accepted the concluded by the UN General Assembly on 20-11-1989. This Convention affirms that children's rights require special protection and it aims, not only to provide such protection but also to insure the continuous improvement in the situation of children all over the world, as well as their development and education in conditions of peace and security. Thus, the Convention not only protects the child's civil and political rights but also extends protection to child's economic, social, cultural and humanitarian rights.

Recently, the Supreme Court Bench comprising of K.G. Balakrishnan, C.J., and B.S. Chauhan, J., opined that "only if the Right To Education Act is implemented in letter and spirit, then the ugly face of child labour can be wiped out from the country. Then there will be no child at work but in school, the place where he/she ought to be."[57]

In the landmark judgment in *M.C. Mehta v. State of Tamil Nadu,*[58] (known as *Child Labour Abolition Case*), a three-judge Bench held that Children below the age of 14 years cannot be employed in any hazardous industry or mines or other work. Taking up the suffering of children of Sivakasi Cracker Factories the bench completely condemned such violation of rights of person of tender age and issued various directions to the Government so as to take steps to abolish child labour.

The Court directed for setting up of Child Labour Rehabilitation Welfare Fund and asked the offender to pay compensation of Rs. 20,000 for each child; (2) the Government must ensure the job of any adult member from such child's

55. (1992) 3 SCC 66.
56. (2007) 1 SCC 143.
57. *The Times of India*, Kolkata (ed.), 8 January 2010.
58. (1996) 6 SCC 756.

family; (3) penal provision contained in the 1986 Act will be used where employment of a child labour prohibited by the Act, is found; etc.[59]

*Narendra Malav v. State of Gujarat*[60] is a PIL which brought to notice to the Apex Court the issue of child labour in the salt mines of Gujarat. The Court requested the *amicus curiae* and a NGO to enquire and investigate for the purpose of ascertaining the measure taken by various agencies for the welfare of salt workers and their families and to suggest ways and means to improve their conditions. The Court also directed the state government through the Assistant Labour Commissioner to provide all the assistance for this purpose.

The Constitution of India imposes primary responsibility on the State to ensure that all the needs of children are met and their basic human rights are fully protected. The State is required to direct its policy towards securing children opportunities and facilities to develop in a healthy manner and in conditions of freedom and dignity and that childhood and youth are protected against exploitation and moral and material abandonment.[61]

The Parliament of India, in order to fulfil its obligation under the Constitution, has enacted the Juvenile Justice (Care and Protection of Children) Act, 2000. It specifically deals with the problems of juveniles in conflict with law and children in need of care and protection. The Act provides for proper care, protection and treatment by catering development needs of children, for adjudication and disposition of matters, by adopting child-friendly approach.

The Child Labour (Prohibition and Regulation) Act, 1986 repealed the Employment of Children Act, 1938; and the (Amendment) Act, 2006 amends the Schedule (Part A) to add to the list of occupation in which employment of children is prohibited. This amendment prohibits the employment of children as domestic workers or servants and employment in restaurants, hotels/motels, tea shops, resorts or other recreational centres. This comes into force on 10/10/2006.[62]

---

59. *Ibid.*
60. (2004) 10 SCALE 12, as in 'Annual Survey of Indian Law', Vol. XL, 2004 at 447.
61. U. Chandra, 'Human Rights', Allahabad Law Agency Publications, (Seventh edn.), 2008 at 282.
62. www.loksabha.nic.in visited on 23/11/2009.

Although, like most of the promises been made, not much is done even still for complete eradication of child labour. Some basic lacunae are still in existence like, India has agreed to 'progressively implement' Article 32 of CRC which prohibits any kind of child economic exploitation and prohibition in hazardous or harmful employment. This means that we will not implement it immediately, but will do so as and when our social conditions permit. Nothing has moved in this direction so far, although the Committee in the rights of the child has recommended that the Government of India must give full scope to the rights of the child. Secondly, the child labour though restricts it but not completely since it goes for restricted regulation but not complete prohibition as employment in non-hazardous place is provided by the Act itself.

Thus, we may conclude that the labour sector has seen a lot of ups and down. A lot has been provided by the Government in order to run their governance for maximum period and also because, now the judiciary plays very important role of provider and the guardian of human rights. Not only this even the International instruments have done a lot for raising the living standards of all people including the labour sector and after the advent of globalization and increased economic empowerment our judiciary has to increase its ambit by wide interpretation of Constitutional provisions so as to attain the basic goals set out in our Preamble, for the welfare of "We, the people."

## CONCLUSION

It is clear from the above discussion that the corporations in today's world are involved in many different perspectives of human rights violations. Though many steps have taken on both national and international front to bring the abusers behind bars but the ground.reality is totally the other side of the coin. The big business enterprises violates human rights and easily escape the liability or even if penalty is imposed that is too mere for such corporations, which they make good in few months through their new ventures. Even there is no uniformity in the national and international provisions which provide an easy escape for the multinational corporations. At such an advent judiciary plays a very significant role but has again the long and costly procedure benefits the enterprises.

Situation may be pathetic but is not uncontrollable. Such enterprises could be made more responsible towards human rights if there are certain stringent penal punishments having strict application. Most importantly we have observed that though there are plethora of cases and laws but there is no specific direct legislation been applicable on the corporate human rights violators. Thus, there is an urgent need of enacting a statute in consonance with the *Guiding Principles* of the UN to make such corporations liable for the human rights violations, imposing of strict penal punishments, quick redressal and to establish a neutral investigating committee to look into such matters.

Such suggestions when applied in consonance with the basic constitutional provisions and the responsible aware citizens are the only hope of restricting such human rights violations by the enterprise so as to compel them to protect and respect the human rights of the individuals.

# PART V

# MONEY AND THE CORPORATE LAW

CHAPTER 11

# Money Laundering and Banks

*Dr. Ravinder Kumar*

## INTRODUCTION

In simple words, money laundering is a process that criminals use to erase the connection between the crime and money by concealing the original source of funds. It is a process by which the proceeds of a crime and their true ownership is concealed or made opaque, so that they appear to come from a legitimate source.[1]

The literal meaning of laundering or launder as stated in the Webster's Dictionary is to undergo washing or cleaning.[2] Drawing from these definitions, it becomes evident that money laundering is a process by which criminals make their 'dirty' money appear 'clean' or legitimate.[3]

---

1. Anabil Bhattacharya, "An overview of the Prevention of Money Laundering Act, 2002", *Insurance Times*, 26(11), 2006, at 21.
2. The New International Webster's Comprehensive Dictionary of the English Language (Encyclopaedic Edition, Florida: Trident Press International, 1998) at 721.
3. *Supra* note 1, at 21. Since the term originated in the United States of America, legal dictionaries refer to the federal crimes definition. Thus, the Black's Law Dictionary defines money laundering as the federal crime of transferring illegally obtained money through legitimate persons or accounts so that its original source cannot be traced. [Black's Law Dictionary (Bryan A. Garner, ed., 7th edn., St. Paul Minn West Group, 1999) at 889]. For this reason, money laundering is defined as investment or other transfer of money flowing from racketeering, drug transactions and other illegal sources into legitimate channels, so that its original source may not be traced. See also Akash Choubey and Sarvesh

Money Laundering[4] refers to the conversion or "Laundering" of money which is illegally obtained, so as to make it appear to originate from a legitimate source[5]. Money Laundering is being employed by launderers worldwide to conceal criminal activity associated with it such as drug/arms trafficking, terrorism and extortion[6]

Money Laundering can be defined as the change of unlawfully obtained cash/currency into lawful funds. Money Laundering can be traced back to the Hawala Mechanism, which facilitated the conversion of money from black into white. "Hawala" is an Arabic word connoting the transfer of money or information involving two persons using a third person. Such funds are used to prop up drug trafficking, terrorism and arms deals, which observably pose a hazard to Banks and other Financial Institutions, which become part of this not deliberately but not without cost. As per an estimate of the International Monetary Fund the amount of money laundered globally could be between $800 billion to $2 trillion each year contributing to 5% of world's GDP.[7] Although money laundering is impossible to measure with precision, it is estimated that US $300 billion to US $500 billion in proceeds from serious crime (not tax evasion) is laundered each year[8] The catastrophic events that happened in the United States on 11 September 2001 and other terrorist

Singh, "Money Laundering: The Growing Menace", *Company Law Journal*, 02 (02), 2003, at 22.

4. Section 2(1) of Prevention of Money Laundering Act, 2002, defines "Money Laundering" has the meaning assigned to it in section 3. Section 3 provides for offence of money laundering—whosoever directly or indirectly attempts to indulge or knowingly assists or knowingly is a party or is actually involved in any process or activity connected with the proceeds of crime and projecting it as untainted property shall be guilty of offence of money laundering.
5. Popularly this is known as making black money white.
6. S. Ganesh, Money Laundering, article available at http://www.rbi.org.in/scripts/btcdisplay.aspx?pg=btcmoneylaunder.htm (Last visited on December 12, 2008)
7. RBI for new Reporting System for Banks, PTI, posted online on 22nd October, 2005.
8. Scott, David (1995), "Money Laundering and International Efforts to Fight it: Public Policy of the Private Sector," Public Policy for the private Sector, Note No. 48, The World Bank available at: http:www.imf.org/pubs/ft/fandd/1997/03/pdf/quirks.pdf.

attacks that are being carried out with alarming promptness across the world, are a bleak aide memoire of the power of organised crime. In the stir of the terrorist attacks, a number of governments have called for a swift and coordinated endeavor to perceive and put off the misuse of the world fiscal system by terrorists. Banks and financial institutions are susceptible from the Money Laundering point of view since criminal earnings can enter banks in the form of large cash deposits. Bank officials therefore need to put into effect unvarying watchfulness in opening of accounts with large cash deposits and in checking doubtful transactions.

Throughout the world, banks have become a chief end of Money Laundering operations and monetary crime because they are endowed with a range of services and instruments that can be used to cover up the source of money. With their refined, coherent and beguiling behaviour, Money Launderers attempt to make bankers lesser their guard so as to accomplish their purpose.

With increasing complexity in the use of know-how for transportation of funds and given the fact that there has been substantial liberalization and progressive taking apart of controls in the regulatory framework in India, banks in India need to be in a state of high alert so that they can maneuver clear of Money Laundering. It is imperative to bear in mind that bank and financial institutions are both transmitters of money and regulators of the flow of money.

In India, we by now have assured far-sighted banking practices which check the propagation of Money Laundering activities in the country. The Reserve Bank of India has asked banks to put in place a suitable policy framework on the 'Know Your Customer' guidelines and `Anti-Money Laundering' measures with the endorsement of their boards, within the next three months. In this regard RBI had issued a circular dated August 16, 2005 on Know Your Customers guidelines on Anti-Money Laundering. The RBI has highlighted that banks can successfully control and decrease their perils only if they have an perceptive of the standard and realistic activity of the customer so that they have the ways of identifying transactions that fall outside the usual outline of activity. However, the degree of supervision would depend on the risk sensitivity of the account. Every bank should set key pointers for accounts, taking note of the milieu of the customer, such as the country of origin, sources of funds, the type of transactions involved and other risk factors. Banks should put in place a scheme of periodical assessment of risk tagging of accounts.

Money Laundering is a grave, exceedingly chic and inclusive criminal activity. The extent of organisation exhibited in Money Laundering is a foremost reason for alarm of banks and bank supervisors. Banks and other financial institutions can defend themselves against Money Laundering by putting into practice an effective KYC Policy, knowing their customers, checking the source of funds, keeping an eye on the behavior of accounts, and by learning to recognize disbelieving/ lopsided dealings.

## HISTORICAL BACKGROUND

The term 'Money Laundering' is one of fairly recent origin. The original sighting was in the newspapers reporting the 'Watergate Scandal' in the United States in 1973[9]. In judicial or legal context the expression first appeared in America in the case of *US v. $4,255,625.39*[10]. The term 'money laundering' is said to originate from Mafia ownership of *Laundromats*[11] in the United States. Gangsters in US were earning huge sums in cash from extortion, prostitution, gambling and bootleg liquor. They needed to show a legitimate source for these earnings. One of the ways in which they were able to do this was by purchasing outwardly legitimate businesses and to mix their illicit earnings with the legitimate earnings they received from these businesses. *Laundromats* were chosen by these gangsters because they were cash businesses and this was an undoubted advantage to people

9. The action of the US President Richard Nixon's "Committee to reelect the President" that moved illegal campaign contributions to Mexico, and then brought the money back through a company in Miami. It was Britain's newspaper 'Guardian' that coined the term, referring to the process as "laundering".
10. (1982) 551 F. Sup. 314, quoted in Gururaj, B.N., Commentaries on FEMA, Money Laundering Act and COFEPOSA, Nagpur: Wadhwa, Ed. 2005, p. 729.
11. A service mark used for a commercial establishment equipped with washing machines and dryers, usually coin-operated and self-service. Excerpted from The American Heritage Dictionary of English Language, Third Edition.

like A1 Capone who purchased them.[12] A1 Capone was prosecuted, though not for money laundering but for tax evasion. However, the conviction of A1 Capone may have triggered the money laundering business off the ground. But other historians differ from this in as much as they are of the view that money laundering is called so, because it perfectly describes what takes place illegal or dirty money is put through a cycle of transactions, or washed, so that it comes out at the other end as legal or clean money. In other words, the source of illegally obtained funds is obscured through a succession of transfers and deals, in order that those same funds can eventually be made to appear as legitimately earned income.[13]

Another important mode of doing money laundering was with Swiss Bank. Many persons involved in illegal activities used the number of Swiss Bank accounts to his illegal money. They used the "loan-back" concept, which meant that the hitherto illegal money could now be disguised as 'loans' provide by compliant foreign banks, which could be declared as their 'revenue' if necessary, and a tax-deduction obtained in the bargain.

Money Laundering as a crime attracted the interest in the 1980s, within a drug trafficking context.[14] It was from an increasing awareness of the huge profits generated from this criminal activity and a concern at the massive drug abuse problem in western society which created the impetus for governments to act against the drug dealers by creating legislation that would deprive them of their illicit gains.[15]

### (A) Money Laundering: Stages

The most organised crime activities are found in economic field. Here the goal of the criminal is to use the proceeds of crime

12. Gururaj, B.N., Commentaries on FEMA, Money Laundering Act and COFEPOSA, Nagpur: Wadhwa, Ed. 2005, p. 729.
13. Alagiri, Dhandapani, Ed., "Money Laundering: Issues and Perspective", Hyderabad: ICFAI University Press, 2006, p. 729.
14. When under UN Convention against the Illicit Traffic in Narcotic Drugs and Psychotropic Substances, criminalization of the proceeds of drug-related offences was provided. However, later many other crimes were included in the purview of 'predicate offences' to find out a money laundering activity.
15. See www.laundryman.u-net.com/ for historical materials on money-laundering (last accessed on November 10, 2008).

in the same manner as legal earnings, and this is possible as long as the source of the funds remains concealed. The task of the money launderer, therefore, is to make the proceeds of crime appear to be of legal origin, or of sufficiently obscure origin that any attempt to link those assets to criminal behaviour would be futile. In the context of developed states, it is generally understood that this task is accomplished through three basic steps: placement, layering and integration.

*Placement*

"Placement" refers to the physical disposal of bulk cash proceeds derived from illegal activities (i.e. such as drug sales or prostitution). This is the first step of the money-laundering process and the ultimate aim of this phase is to remove the cash from the location of acquisition so as to avoid detection from the authorities. This is achieved by investing criminal money into the legal financial system by opening up a bank account in the name of unknown individuals or organizations and depositing the money in the account.[16] In the familiar context of the drug trade, this will typically involve depositing or otherwise converting amounts of cash that would be unusually large by normal commercial standards. As placement of large sums of cash may trigger formal reporting mechanisms in many jurisdictions, elaborate means may be employed at this stage to avoid detection. These may include the use of 'front' businesses such as bars, restaurants, or casinos that may reasonably claim to do business in cash. They may also involve the use of 'surfing' techniques—numerous deposits of amounts small enough to avoid raising suspicion or triggering reporting mechanisms. Once the cash has been placed, it may then be moved with greater ease and less suspicion through the economy or if necessary offshore.

16. While counter measures to all three components of money laundering are important, laundered money is generally most vulnerable to detection at the placement stage. As a consequence, international regulatory and law enforcement efforts have concentrated especially on developing methods to make it difficult to place illicit funds without detection by developing measures such as mandatory record-keeping and even reporting of large requirements, and cross-border monetary declaration requirements.

*Layering*

"Layering" refers to the separation of illicit proceeds from their source by creating complex layers of financial transactions. Once the money derived from criminal activity has been converted to a bank account balance or a financial instrument, the next step in laundering the funds is to 'layer' the money.[17] The launderer seeks to insert layers of transactions between the original criminal activity and the seemingly legitimate re-emergence of the funds into the legal economy. This may be accomplished several ways, but the goal remains the same: to render the path of the funds and their ownership as opaque as possible. The most common means used here are well known. Money launderers favour jurisdictions whose financial institutions provide legally protected anonymous banking and/or who provide 'off-the-shelf' shell companies under conditions of anonymity. Other methods include the importing or exporting of on existent products, the use of casinos or lotteries, and the purchase and resale of fixed assets or real estate. It is in this phase that the crime of laundering money becomes particularly transnational, as multiple jurisdictions are often used in further efforts to cloud the audit trail.

*Integration*

"Integration" refers to the re-injection of the laundered proceeds back into the economy in such a way that they re-enter the financial system as normal business funds. The goal of the placement and layering phases is to make it impossible to trace the funds to their original source. Once this condition has been achieved, the criminal assets may then be integrated into the legal economy. This may occur under the auspices of a company domiciled in the criminal's own jurisdiction, which conducts 'business' with offshore shell companies used in the layering process, or via returns on 'investments' in those companies. It may also take the form of loans with highly favourable or negligible terms of repayment, real estate investments, or other transactions, which will be unremarkable once the criminal has constructed a plausible legal commercial and business identity.

17. A process sometimes referred to as 'structuring'.

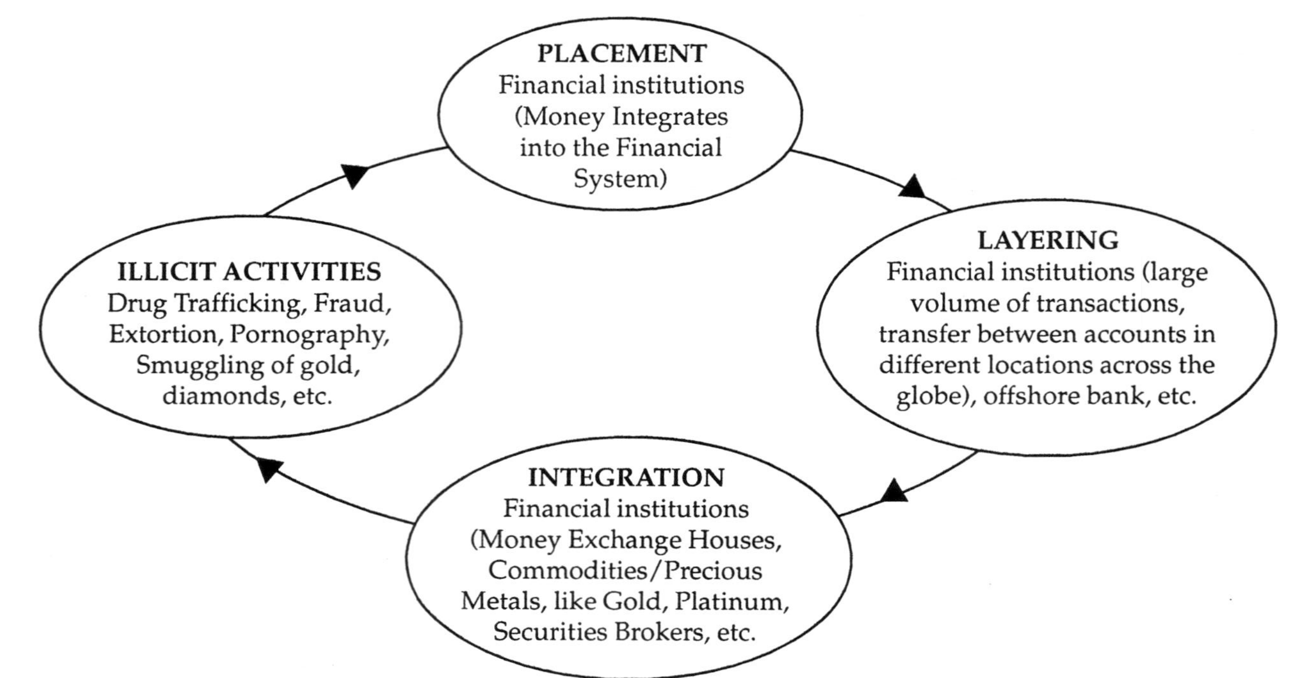
PLACEMENT
Financial institutions (Money Integrates into the Financial System)
LAYERING
Financial institutions (large volume of transactions, transfer between accounts in different locations across the globe), offshore bank, etc.
INTEGRATION
Financial institutions (Money Exchange Houses, Commodities/Precious Metals, like Gold, Platinum, Securities Brokers, etc.
ILLICIT ACTIVITIES
Drug Trafficking, Fraud, Extortion, Pornography, Smuggling of gold, diamonds, etc.

**How Money Laundering Works: Stages**

<table>
<tr><td colspan="10" align="center">DIRTY MONEY</td></tr>
<tr><td rowspan="2">Step 1<br>Placement</td><td colspan="9" align="center">BANKS</td></tr>
<tr><td colspan="3">Offshore Account</td><td colspan="5">Offshore Account</td><td>Offshore Account</td></tr>
<tr><td>Step 2<br>Layering</td><td>Boat</td><td colspan="2">Offshore Account</td><td colspan="2">Offshore Account</td><td colspan="2">Europe Account</td><td>US Account</td><td>US Account</td></tr>
<tr><td>Step 3<br>Integration</td><td>US Account</td><td>US Account</td><td>Business Investment</td><td>Business Investment</td><td>US Account</td><td>Business Investment</td><td>Shell Companies</td><td>Shell Companies</td><td>Shell Companies</td></tr>
<tr><td colspan="10" align="center">CLEAN MONEY</td></tr>
</table>

*Source:* http://money.howstuffworks.com/money-laundering.htm

*Economic Crimes: An Overview*

A table listing various economic offences, the relevant legislation and the enforcing authorities in India is given below:

| *Sl. No.* | *Economic Crimes* | *Acts of Legislation* | *Enforcement Authorities* |
|---|---|---|---|
| 1. | Tax Evasion | Income Tax Act | Central Board of Direct Taxes |
| 2. | Illicit Trafficking in contraband Goods (smuggling) | Customs Act, 1962 COFEPOSA, 1974 | Collectors of Customs |
| 3. | Evasion of Excise Duty | Central Excise and Salt Act, 1944 | Collectors of Central Excise |
| 4. | Cultural Object's Theft | Antiquity and Art Treasures Act, 1972 | Police/CBI |
| 5. | Money Laundering | Foreign Exchange Regulations Act, 1973 | Directorate of Enforcement |
| 6. | Foreign Contribution Manipulations | Foreign Contribution (Regulation) Act, 1976 | Police/CBI |
| 7. | Land Hijacking/Real Estate Fraud | IPC | Police/CBI |
| 8. | Trade in Human Body parts | Transplantations of Human Organs | Police/CBI |
| 9. | Illicit Drug Trafficking | Narcotics Drugs and Psychotropic Substances Act, 1985 and NDPS Act, 1988 | NCB[2]/Police/CBI |
| 10. | Fraudulent Bankruptcy | Banking Regulation Act, 1949 | CBI |
| 11. | Corruption and Bribery of Public Servants | Prevention of Corruption Act, 1988 | State/Anti-Corruption Bureaux/Vigilance Bureaux/CBI |
| 12. | Bank Fraud | IPC | Police/CBI |
| 13. | Insurance Fraud | IPC | Police/CBI |
| 14. | Racketeering in Employment | IPC | Police/CBI |
| 15. | Illegal Foreign Trade | Import & Export (Control) Act, 1947 | Directorate General of Foreign Trade/ CBI |
| 16. | Racketeering in False Travel Documents | Passport Act, 1920/IPC | Police/CBI |
| 17. | Credit Card Fraud | IPC | Police/CBI |
| 18. | Terrorists Activities | POTA, 2002 | Police/CBI |
| 19. | Illicit Trafficking in Arms | Arms Act, 1959 | Police/CBI |

| | | | |
|---|---|---|---|
| 20. | Illicit Trafficking in Explosives | Explosives Act, 1884 and Explosive Substance Act, 1908 | Police/CBI |
| 21. | Theft of Intellectual Property | Copyright Act, 1957 (Amendment, 1984 & 1994 | Police/CBI |
| 22. | Computer Crime/Software Piracy/Cyber Law | Copyright Act, 1957/I.T. Act, 2000 | Police/CBI |
| 23. | Stock Market Manipulations | IPC | Police/CBI |
| 24. | Company Fraud (Contraband) | Companies Act, 1956/IPC MRTP Act, 1968 | Police/CBI |

### (B) India and Money Laundering

In India, Money Laundering is to be seen from two different perspectives, i.e., Money laundering on international forum and Money laundering within the country. As far as the cross-border money-laundering is concerned India's strict foreign-exchange laws[18] and reporting norms have contributed to a great extent to control money-laundering on international forum[19]. However, there is threat from informal transactions like 'Hawala'.

The Reserve Bank of India (RBI), India's central bank, estimates that remittances to India sent through legal, formal channels in 2006-07 amounted to U.S. $28.2 billion. Due to large number of expatriate Indians in different parts of world, India continues to retain its position as the leading recipient of remittances in the world, followed by China and Mexico[20].

The Money Laundering Act was a much-needed piece of legislation to place India on an equal footing with other

---

18. Foreign Exchange Regulation Act with 1973. The law was very strict. It was relaxed by FEMA 1999 with the coming of liberalization. FERA though criticized by many for its strictness was successful in controlling cross-border money-laundering in the nascent stage of Indian economy.
19. India's strict foreign-exchange laws and transaction reporting requirements, combined with the banking industry's due diligence policy, make it increasingly difficult for criminals to use formal channels like banks and money transfer companies to launder money. However, large portions of illegal proceeds are often laundered through "hawala" or "hundi" networks or other informal money transfer systems.
20. International Narcotics Control Strategy Report dated February 29, 2008, available at http://www.state.gov./documents/organisation/102588.pdf (last visited 28th January, 2009).

countries, which have enacted comprehensive legislation on this subject. However it was criticized on the ground that an excessively strict legislation such as the Prevention of the Money Laundering Act may hinder the advent of international banks and institutions in India. Such an argument is completely unfounded, since most of these international banks operate under similar regimes in other countries and have suitable legal assistance at their disposal to help them comply with anti-money laundering laws.

It is axiomatic to say that an anti-money laundering legislation was much required in India for a long time.[21] The Indian Anti-Money Laundering Act has been enacted[22] with the twin objective of preventing money laundering by making it a criminal offence and providing for confiscation of property representing proceeds of crime.[23]

Since profit motive is the main incentive behind most crimes today, taking this incentive out is perhaps the best strategy for deterrence. Thus, several methods are now adopted by the law to expand its reach and cut down on the profits earned by

---

21. Impact of money laundering:
    (1) Tarnishes reputation of banks and thus harmful for business.
    (2) Erodes the economy by changing the demand for cash, making interest and exchange rates more volatile and by causing high inflation in countries where criminals are doing business.
    (3) Volatility in exchange and interest rates due to unanticipated transfer of funds.
    (4) Threat of monetary instability due to unsound asset structures.
    (5) Measurement errors in national account statistics.
    (6) Effects on tax collection and public expenditure allocation due to misreporting of income.
    (7) It empowers corruption and organised crime.
    (8) Sudden collapse of economy if money is suddenly withdrawn.
    Sourced from B.N. Gururaj, Commentaries on FEMA, Money Laundering Act and COFEPOSA (1st ed., Nagpur: Wadhwa and Co., 2005) at 728, 729.
22. Although the Act was passed in the 2002, the Government did not frame any rules until 2005, when a series of rules were notified. The Act is now applicable to all financial institutions, including insurance companies as per the rules. C.L. Bharadwaj, "New anti-money laundering guidelines by IRDA", 02(06), Corporate Law Cases, 2006, at 297.
23. K.K. Ramani, "Money Laundering", *SEBI and Corporate Laws*, 65 (06), 2006, at 319.

criminals. This is sufficiently achieved in most procedures adopted under the Prevention of Money Laundering Act, i.e. confiscation, attachment and imprisonment.[24]

For the purpose of a comprehensive legislation for preventing money laundering and connected activities, confiscation of proceeds of crime, setting up of agencies and mechanisms for coordinating measures for combating money laundering etc., the Prevention of Money Laundering Bill was introduced in the Lok Sabha in August, 1998, which ultimately passed on 17th January 2003. However, that can be implemented only in 2005[25]. The time when the Act of 2002 came to be enforced it was to old to cater to the current needs of the anti-money-laundering law. To bring the necessary changes in light of the liberalization of economy and securities market in India, there was a need to have more comprehensive anti-money-laundering law and that is how the Prevention of Money Laundering (Amendment) Act, 2008 came into existence.

The PML Act was enacted to prevent money-laundering and to provide for confiscation of property derived from, or involved in, money-laundering[26]. Offence of money-laundering means the projection of tainted money (proceeds of the crime) as untainted either directly or indirectly or assisting in such act knowingly or knowingly is a party or is actually involved in such process or activity[27].

If the Director has reason to believe that a person is in possession of property involved in money-laundering or he is dealing in such property, the Director is empowered to attach the property. Further, the attachment by the Director is provisional in nature for a period of 150 days[28] and needs to be confirmed by the Adjudicating Authority under Section 8 of PMLA 02.

---

24. Jyoti Trehan, Crime and Money Laundering: The Indian Perspective (London: Kluwer Law International, 2003) at 216.
25. 1st July, 2005.
26. Preamble of the said Act also refers to the Political Declaration and Global Programme of Action annexed to the resolution S-17/2 of General Assembly of the United Nations at its Seventeenth special session on 23rd February 1990, as well as the Sessions on 8th, 9th and 10th June 1998 which calls upon the Member States to adopt national money-laundering (rather it should be anti-money-laundering) legislation and programme.
27. Section 4 of PMLA-02
28. By PML (Amendment) Act, 2008, it is increased to 150 days.

Every banking company, financial institution and intermediary is under an obligation to maintain a record and furnish information to the Director within such time as prescribed of all transactions, the nature and value of which may be prescribed, whether such transactions comprise of a single transaction or a series of transactions integrally connected to each other and where such series of transactions take place within a month. The said records have to be maintained for a period of 10 years from the date of transactions[29] between the clients and the banking company or financial institution or intermediary, as the case may be. Further, aforesaid entities have to maintain the records of the identity of all its clients for a period of 10 years from the date of cessation of the transactions between the clients and them[30].

The Act provides for a comprehensive mechanism for survey, search and seizure. The authorities under the Act have power to enter any place for survey when the said authority has a reason to believe on the basis of material in his possession that any offence of money-laundering has been committed and the person in-charge of such place have to facilitate in the survey of such authority[31] .

Failure in the reporting requirements mentioned above leads to a punishment not less than 10 thousand rupees which may exceed to one lakh rupees for each failure. The Act provides for a reverse Burden of Proof as far as a criminal case is concerned. However, under the Act, the person charged of an offence of money laundering has to prove his innocence by showing that the property in dispute or money in dispute is untainted[32]. Moreover, there is a presumption as to records or property

29. Prior to the amendment (PML Act, 2008) was from the date of cessation of the transaction between the clients and the respective entities.
30. Section 13 of PMLA 02.
31. See Section 16—Power of Survey. This procedure is not arbitrary as it has to be according to the procedure established by law under Art. 21 of the Constitution and must be fair and reasonable, for example the reason to believe has to be put down in writing and the proceeds of the survey has to be transferred to the Adjudicating Authority in a sealed envelope as soon as possible.
32. See Section 24 of PMLA 02. Even otherwise, in tax matters, the courts and tribunals have generally adopted the view that in matters of illegal and clandestine transactions, the facts would be within the special knowledge of the accused and prosecution of revenue is not expected to prove such special facts by leading in evidence.

seized from a person that such record or property belonged to that person unless rebutted by him[33]. The offences under the Act are cognizable and non-bailable[34]. The cognizance of an offence under the Act can only be taken by Special Court when a complaint in writing is made by the Director or any officer authorized by Central Government in writing.

In the midst of mounting erudition in the use of technology for relocation of funds and given the fact that there has been substantial liberalization and progressive dismantling of controls in the regulatory framework in India, banks in India need to be in a state of high alert so that they can steer clear of Money Laundering. The banks and financial institutions are both transmitters of money and regulators of the surge of money. In India, we by now have certain cautious banking practices which check the propagation of Money Laundering tricks in the country.[35]

Springs of information on laundering activities in this vast region of the world are rather in short supply. However, the foremost factors observed in earlier typologies exercises are still in attendance. In India money laundering is still connected with drug trafficking and is without a doubt facilitated by the equivalent remittance systems known as 'hawala' and 'hundi'. In Asian countries launderers use legal 'underground banking' because it leaves no paper trail. Money never crosses the threshold the recognized banking system but is instead put out through alternative banking systems in India and Pakistan. These parallel banking systems are based on family or gang alliances and reinforced with an unspoken covenant of retributive violence. It is in this context the provisions of IPC have been included in the schedule of crime. This coordination by and large engages depositing money in one country in exchange for a "chit" or "chop" (seal), and the remittance of this money in another country on production of the chit.

There's legal skeleton existing in our country to curb Money Laundering. In India, until the introduction and implementation of The Prevention of Money Laundering Act, there were certain

33. See Section 22 of PMLA 02.
34. See Section 45 of the PMLA 02.
35. RBI Publication, *Bank Supervision: Challenges Ahead* by Kishori J. Udeshi on occasion of the Nani Phalkiwala Memorial Oration, dated October 18, 2004.

statutes existing which incidentally sought to address the problem:

(1) The Conservation of Foreign Exchange and Prevention of Smuggling Activities Act, 1974.
(2) The Income Tax Act, 1961.
(3) The Benami Transactions (Prohibition) Act, 1988.
(4) The Indian Penal Code and Code of Criminal Procedure, 1973.
(5) The Narcotic Drugs and Psychotropic Substances Act, 1985.
(6) The Prevention of Illicit Traffic in Narcotic Drugs and Psychotropic Substances Act, 1988.
(7) The Prevention of Terrorism Act (POTA), 2002, seeks to deal with types of heinous crimes like subversion, insurgency and terrorism in place of the existing criminal justice system, which is not designed to deal with such horrific crimes.
(8) The Bankers Books Evidence Act, 1891.
(9) The Banking Companies (Preservation of Records) Rules, 1985.

In proportion to the comprehensive concern over the abuse of the financial system for money laundering, drug trafficking and funding of terrorist activity, the Reserve Bank of India (RBI) has ordered Indian banks to put in place a strict Know Your Customer (KYC) guiding principle and build a database of customer contours. Banks were to complete this by 31st December 2005, at least in case of accounts activated through a power of attorney, or when they spot curious activity. KYC guidelines are meant to thwart banks from being used, deliberately or otherwise, for money laundering. Finance Minister P. Chidambaram has already affirmed that large cash transactions running into crores of rupees at quite a few banks are a clear pointer of exploitation.[36]

*India's International Position*

The General Assembly of United Nations adopted in February 1990 the political declaration and a global programme

36. "RBI recommends KYC", *The Financial Express*, Monday, June 13, 2005.

of action to prevent money laundering and to provide for confiscation of property derived from money laundering. The UN further called upon its member-states in June 1998 to adopt national money laundering legislation and programmes.

In continuation of this international effort, a Financial Action Task Force (FATF) on Money Laundering was formed as an inter-governmental body whose purpose is the development and promotion of policies to combat money laundering. Twenty-six countries are members of this including almost all the Western nations, Japan, Singapore, Hong Kong, and others. India is not a member of the FATF. Some of the recommendations by the FATF relating to the financial system are relevant as the present cases in India involve the commercial banks. They are as follows:

Identification of the customer and his representatives should have been made by a public register or document, or from another customer, or both. The elements of information to be identified are the name, legal form, address, director and the provision regulating his power to bind the entity. Identification should be made at the time of opening the account or safe deposit boxes and entering into large cash transactions.

The Financial Institutions (FIs) should pay special attention to all complex, unusually-large transactions, and all unusual patterns of transactions which have no apparent economic or visible and lawful purpose, or if they suspect that funds are from a criminal activity. They are required to report the same to the authorities concerned.

The FIs should develop programmes against money laundering in the form of internal policies, procedures and controls, besides training the officers and putting in place the adequate audit functions. Banks and other financial institutions and intermediaries should report all domestic and international transactions above a fixed amount to a national central agency.

The untold truth about global money laundering is that money laundering is a growing problem in India, though largely confined to domestic activities that are not only drug-related—fraud, corruption and smuggling are the obvious crimes in India.

Now a brief description of cases where hawala or hawala-like techniques were used to launder proceeds derived from various predicate offenses

*Narcotics Trafficking*

In mid-1997, several people were convicted of conspiracy to launder as well as laundering the proceeds of the sale of Pakistani heroin and opium. This case involved a legitimate foreign exchange business, Frankfurt-based MGM Marwex Geldwechsel, its U.S. branch, MGM Marwex International and a hawala network spanning several countries.

Further in another case, the investigation of a Delhi-based hashish trafficking organization revealed that the traffickers had established several false corporate identities. Under the cover of these identities, machinery was shipped to Germany, the United Kingdom, the Netherlands and Australia. Hashish was concealed in this machinery. Hawala was used to repatriate the proceeds of the hashish sales back to the Indian traffickers.

*Terrorism*

The investigation into the assassination of an important Indian politician revealed that the assassins were, in fact, terrorists. These terrorists used hawala to transfer the proceeds of the sale of narcotics to arms dealers for the purchase of military hardware.

*Alien Smuggling*

A worldwide alien smuggling network is suspected of using hawala banking techniques to move money between North America and South Asia to pay the alien smuggling 'fee' and additional payments (e.g. for lawyers) are also made.

*Insider Trading*

A citizen of a South Asian country, who was an investment banker in a major U.S. financial center, is accused of giving 'tips' to various friends and relatives. After some illegal trades took place, the banker resigned and apparently fled the United States for his homeland. At the same time, several of his associates also traveled to this same country as well as several European financial centers. An analysis of seized bank records indicates that money was wired to persons apparently of the same nationality in at least one of these financial centers. It is possible that these wire transfers were the first part of hawala-like transfers of the proceeds from the illicit trades to the investment banker's home country.

*Customs and Tax Violations (1)*

A Pakistani living in the Washington, D.C. metropolitan area was doing hawala transfers for other expatriates. Large cash transactions at the bank used by some of the defendants were brought to the attention of customs and tax authorities. Their subsequent investigation uncovered a scheme in which surgical instruments manufactured in Pakistan were being imported at inflated prices (over-invoicing) to facilitate the transfer of money from the United States to Pakistan, in apparent violation of Pakistani law. Convictions were obtained for customs violations, making false statements and tax fraud.

*Gambling*

Hawala has been used not only as an alternative remittance system but as an alternative banking system in a South Asian gambling operation. Currency control laws made it nearly impossible for citizens of one country to take money to gamble in another, and there are similar problems with bringing gambling winnings back into the country. The gambling operators have engaged hawaladars to accept money 'on deposit' from gamblers, and pay winnings through them as well. This is something of a testimony to the reliability of hawala. During a conversation with one of the authors of this paper, one of the principals in this gambling operation reported that this had been going on for nearly twenty years without any significant difficulties.

*Causes of Increase in Money Laundering and Inability to Control*[37]

There are various causes for increase in Money Laundering and the few of them can be enlisted as follows which is popularly known as 'Feature of an Ideal Financial Heaven':

- No deals for sharing tax information with other countries.
- Availability of instant corporations.
- Corporate Secrecy Laws—as the corporate law of certain countries enables launderers to hide behind shell companies.
- Excellent Electronic Communication.
- Tight Bank Secrecy Laws.

37. For detail discussion refers to www.undoc.org./undoc/money_laundering_haven_features.html.

- A Government that is Relatively Invulnerable to Outside Pressures.
- A high degree of Economic Dependence on the Financial Services Sector.
- A Geographical Location that Facilitates Business Travel to and from rich neighbours.
- Increase in sophistication and employment of professional people for doing the task[38].

*Harmful Effects of Money Laundering*

Briggate Unger[39] in there detail study were able to identify 25 different harmful effects of money laundering. Unger classifies the effects of money laundering on the basis of its gestation period within which it surfaces, under two broad heads, i.e. short-term effects of money laundering[40] and long-term effects of money laundering. The short-term effects usually happens within one or two years and includes losses to the victim and gains to the perpetrator of crime; distortion of consumption and saving; distortion of investment; artificial increase in prices; unfair competition; changes in imports and exports; effects on output, income and employment; lower or higher revenues for the public sector; changes in the demand for money, exchange rates, and interest rates; increase in the volatility of interest and exchange rates; greater availability of credit; higher capital inflows; distortion of economic statistics. The long-term effects usually happens within four years and these threatens privatisation; changes in foreign direct investment; risk for the

38. In 1996, Harvard educated economist Franklin Jurado went to prison for cleaning $36 million for Colombian drug Lord Jose Santa Cruz, London. People with a whole lot of dirty money typically hire financial experts to handle the laundering process. Its complex by necessity: The whole idea is to make it impossible for authorities to trace the dirty money while it's cleaned.
39. Brigitte Unger, The Scale and Impacts of Money Laundering, UK: Edward Elgar Publishing, 2007, p. 16
40. This usually happens within four years and these threatens privitisation; changes in foreign direct investment; risk for the financial sector, solvability, liquidity; profits for the financial sector; reputation of the financial sector; illegal business contaminates legal business; corruption and bribe; negative or positive effect on growth rates; undermines political institutions; undermines foreign policy goals; increase crime; and increase terrorism.

financial sector, solvability, liquidity; profits for the financial sector; reputation of the financial sector; illegal business contaminates legal business; corruption and bribe; negative or positive effect on growth rates; undermines political institutions; undermines foreign policy goals; increase crime; and increase terrorism.

Money Laundering threatens national governments and international relations between them through corruption of officials and legal systems. It undermines free enterprises and threatens financial stability by crowding out the private sector, because legitimate businesses cannot compete with the lower prices for goods and services that businesses using laundered funds can offers[41].

**(C) Banks and Money Laundering**

The insinuations of Money Laundering for banks are devastating. Launderers make use of currency deposits, fake businesses and cash being bred through justifiable businesses. Generally, banks and financial institutions are liable for action if their employees become caught up in Money Laundering tricks. At the same time, customs for record-keeping, coverage, account opening and deal monitoring are being pioneered by central banks across the globe for checking the frequency of Money Laundering. Employees of banks are also being trained to recognize suspicious transactions. The dilemma of the banker in the context of Money Laundering is to filter the transactions in lieu of legitimate business and banking activity from the irregular/suspicious transactions.

Bank's responsibility in avoiding money laundering commences with Know Your Customer (KYC) and to watch activities not consistent with customer's dealings. Banks operating staff must scrutinize doubtful activities/transactions like hefty deposits straight away followed by wire transfers, large cash transactions, varying currency to higher value notes, etc. It must be born in mind that illegal money can be moved by all manners of means. Criminal groups may deposit heavy cash by

41. Reena Roy, KYC: Anti-Money Laundering Act and Banks, See Alagiri, Dhandapani, Ed. Money Laundering: Issues and Perspectives, Hyderabad: ICFAI University Press, 2006, p. iii.

cheque in some account and take out it by debit cards or wire transfers.[42]

There is much world-weariness with suspect transaction being accounted. It is easier said than done to tell apart between objectively suspect transactions or those that short of the doorsill are merely suspected. Usual transactions may provide critical linkage. It is basically tailing the customer. Banks will have to do it, if they were to smoke out all such criminals.[43]

The more programmed the banking and financial system turns out to be, not as much of face-to-face contact flanked by clients and employees and greater the holes in the discovery unless client information is electronically looked into for uncharacteristic prototypes and associations. Criminal investigation is permissible in banking transactions in India. For example, the Income Tax Department can require information linking customer's accounts and transactions. A straying account can be frozen. This addresses the Basle Principle on Compliance with legislation and law enforcement agencies.[44]

The list below provides examples of some of the basic ways in which money can be laundered. Banks need to be wary of such transactions:

(1) *Crooked/Doubtful Transactions related to Money Laundering:* Customers depositing cash through a large number of cash deposit slips into the similar account or customers having plentiful accounts into which large cash deposits are made. Each deposit is such that the quantity thereof is not noteworthy but the collective of all credits is ample. This is known as "smurfing".

(2) A considerable boost in earnings in a sleeping account or large cash withdrawals from a formerly sleeping or immobile account, or from an account that has received an unforeseen large credit from abroad

(3) *Receipt or payment of big sums of cash, which have no clear rationale or connection to the account holder and / or his business*

(4) *Disinclination to offer standard information when opening an account or providing negligible or untrue information.*

42. http://www.samachar.com/features/220302-fpj.html
43. *Ibid.*
44. *Ibid.*

(5) Depositing high value third party cheques authorized in favour of the customer or other transactions on behalf of non-account holders.
(6) Abrupt amplification in cash deposits of an entity with no explanation.
(7) Employees leading sumptuous ways of life that do not match their known sources of income.

Although the above list is only pinpointing of the probable incidence of Money laundering, the call for punctual acknowledgment of suspicious/irregular transactions is emphasized.

## INTERNATIONAL PERSPECTIVE

Money Laundering is a truly global phenomenon. Action at the international level to combat money laundering began in 1988 with two important initiatives: The Basel Committee on Banking Regulations and Supervisory Practices and the United Nations convention against Illicit Traffic in narcotic drugs and Psychotropic substances[45].

### The Basle Statement of Principles[46]

The Committee on Banking Regulations and Supervisory Practices of the G-10 at a meeting in Basle in Switzerland, in December 1988, developed a set of principles to deal with the dangers posed by Money Launderers. The committee was fashioned by the Central Bank Governors of Belgium, Canada, France, Germany, Italy, Japan, Netherlands, Sweden, Switzerland and United States. These principles, which are now known as the Basle Principles, deal with the deterrence of criminal use of the banking system for the use of Money Laundering. Suggestions for banks and other financial institutions have been set out in the Basle Principles so that these institutions can look after themselves against Money Laundering. The Basle Statement of Principles covers all aspects of laundering through the banking system. The Basle Principles puts forward course of action and measures in four areas to rein in Money Laundering as given below:

45. There are 183 parties to this convention and 87 signatories. India accede to this treaty on March 1990, See www.un.org.treaty_adherence_convention_1988.pdf.
46. http://www.samachar.com/features/220302-fpj.html

(1) *Customer Identification:* This re-emphasizes the wise saying "Know Your Customer" (KYC). KYC necessitates that banks should make sensible pains to settle on the customer's true identity, and must set-up successful measures for verifying the *bona fides* of new customers.

(2) *Compliance with Laws*: The rules and regulations pertaining to financial transactions as performed in different Banking-related statutes, must be experimented. Banks should not tender services or make available dynamic aid in case of transactions where they have superior reason to assume that these are linked with Money Laundering activities.

(3) *Co-operation with Law Enforcement:* Authorities—Banks should combine forces fully with national law enforcement authorities to the degree permitted by precise local regulations regarding customer privacy.

(4) *Adherence to the Statement:* Holding fast to the Statement entails that banks need to adopt policies that are unswerving with the Statement and guarantee that all staff members are well versed of the banks policy in this regard. Some chief factors in supporting loyalty to the Statement of Principles are staff training and putting into practice definite procedures for customer identification and keeping hold of in-house records of transactions.[47]

## UN Convention against Illicit Traffic in Narcotic Drugs and Psychotropic Substance[48]

It was one of the historic conventions inasmuch as the parties to the Convention recognized the links between illicit drug traffic and other related organized criminal activities which undermine the legitimate economies and threaten the stability, security and sovereignty of States and that illicit drug trafficking is an international criminal activity that generates large profits and wealth, enabling transnational, criminal organizations to

47. Report on the Committee on Banking Regulations and Supervisory Practices of the G 10 at a meeting in Basle in Switzerland, in December 1988.

48. The Vienna Convention, 19th December 1988. A Delegation of 106 States participated in the Convention. Mr. Guillermo Bedregal Gutierrez (Bolivia) was elected President of the Convention. As of 24 March 2003, there were 167 parties and 87 signatories to this convention. See http://untreaty.un.org./english/treatyevent2003/treaty_7.htm.

penetrate, contaminate and corrupt the structures of government, legitimate commercial and financial businesses and society at all levels. The treaty required the signatories to criminalize the laundering of drug money, and to confiscate it where found. Based on the convention many countries have framed their national legislations. Council of Europe Convention on Laundering is motivated by this convention as well as this convention gave a framework for FATF to work.

**GPML (Global Programme against Money Laundering)**

The GPML was established in 1997 in response to the mandate given to UNODC by the 1988 UN Convention against Illicit Traffic in Narcotic Drugs and Psychotropic Substances. GPML mandate was strengthened in 1998 by the United Nations General Assembly Special Session (UNGASS) Political Declaration and Action Plan against Monet Laundering which broadened its remit beyond drug offences to all serious crime[49].

Thereafter some other Conventions have been adopted for AML/CFT-related crimes:

- International Convention for the Suppression of the financing of Terrorism (1999).
- UN Convention against Transnational Organized Crime (2000).
- UN Convention against corruption (2003).

**The Financial Action Task Force (FATF)**

In rejoinder to escalating apprehension over money laundering, the Financial Action Task Force on Money Laundering (FATF) was set-up by the G-7 Summit that was held in Paris in 1989. This inter-governmental body smoothed the progress of the expansion and promotion of policies, both at national and international levels, to combat Money Laundering. While reviewing Money Laundering techniques and counter-measures, the FATF monitors members' progress in implementing anti-money laundering measures. The FATF also join forces with other global bodies involved in skirmishing money laundering. Forty Recommendations, which provide a

49. UN Security Council Resolution 1267 (1999), 1373 (2001), 1540 (2004), 1566 (2004), and 1624 (2005) call on UN Member States to combat terrorism, including financing of terrorism.

comprehensive outline of the action needed to fight money laundering, have been described by the FATF. These forty recommendations are being put into practice by many banks worldwide.[50]

**Council of Europe Convention on Laundering, Search, Seizure and Confiscation of the Proceeds of Crime**

Popularly known as Strasbourg Convention[51] was intended to extend the provisions of international organized criminality in general beyond the area of drug trafficking.[52]

**Other Organisations and Initiatives against Anti-Money-Laundering (AML)**

Money Laundering is an increasingly ramified, complex phenomenon that must be tackled in an integrated and interdisplinary fashion[53]. For this reason there are many organizations throughout the world working coordinately:

*(a) International Money Laundering Information Network (IMoLIN)*[54]

IMoLIN is an Internet-based network assisting governments, organizations and individuals in the fight against money laundering and the financing of terrorism administered by UN office on Drugs and Crime.

*(b) Wolfsberg AML Principles*[55]

This gives eleven principles as an important step in the fight against money laundering, corruption and other related serious crimes[56]. Transparency International (TI), a Berlin-based NGO in collaboration with 11 International Private Banks[57] under the

50. www.fatf.org.in
51. http://conventions.coe.int/Treaties/Html/141.htm
52. UK was the first country to ratify this treaty in 1992.
53. Ernesto Savona, Responding to Money Laundering: International Perspectives, Harwood Academic Publishers, 1997, p. 1.
54. http://www.imolin.org/imloin/index.html
55. http://www.wolfsberg-principles.com (original principles were made public on October 30, 2000 in Zurich, Switzerland.
56. Global Anti-Money Laundering Guidelines for Private Banking, available art http://wolfsberg-principles.com(Last visited on December 22, 2008).
57. ABN AMRO Bank N.Y., Bank of Tokyo-Mitsubishi Ltd., Barclays Bank, Citigroup, Credit Suisse Group, Deutsche Bank AG, Goldman Sachs,

expert participation of Stanley Morris and Prof. Mark Pieth came out with these principles as important global guidance for sound business conduct in international private banking. The important of these principles is due to the fact that it comes from initiative by private sector. The Wolfsberg Principles are a non-binding set of best practice guidelines governing the establishment and maintenance of relationships between private bankers and clients[58].

*(c) Asia-Pacific Group on Money Laundering (APG)*[59]

The Asia/Pacific Group on Money Laundering (APG) is an international organizations consisting of 38 member countries/ jurisdictions[60] and a number of international and regional observers including the United Nations, IMF and World Bank. The APG is closely affiliated with the FATF based in the OCED Headquarters at Paris, France.

**Role of RBI**

The RBI issued the Know Your Customers (KYC) Guidelines —Anti-Money Laundering Standards on 16th August 2005. Remembering the requirements of PML Act, 2002, which all the banks in India have to take up by December 31, 2005 (conformity to AML standards). The Government has also established a Financial Intelligence Unit-India (FIU-IND), in rank with FATF recommendations. The FIU would be given the Suspicious Activity Reports from all FIs and would study them before passing them to the Enforcement Directorate for investigation and prosecution.[61] The RBI has asked all the banks to put the policy with the sanction of their boards, within the next three months. The RBI has stressed that banks can successfully control and decrease their risks only if they have an understanding of the normal and practical activity of the customer so that they have

---

HSBC, J.P. Morgan Private Bank, Santander Central Hispano, Societe Generale, and UBS AG.

58. Kris Hinterseer, "The Wolfsberg Anti-Money Laundering Principles," *Journal of Money Laundering Control*, Vol. 5(1), 2001, pp. 25-41
59. http://www.apgml.org/
60. India is also member of APG.
61. Report of the ITA-TCS Joint Seminar on Anti-Money Laundering held on 22 January, 2005 at Mumbai.

the means of spotting transactions that fall outside the standard model of activity.

**Financial Intelligence Unit-India (FIU-IND)**

Financial Intelligence Unit-India (FIU-IND) was set-up by the Government of India[62] as the central national agency responsible for receiving, processing, analyzing and disseminating information relating to suspect financial transactions. It is also responsible for coordination and strengthening efforts of national and international intelligence, investigation and enforcement agencies in pursuing the global efforts against money laundering and related crimes. FIU-IND is an independent body reporting directly to the Economic Intelligence Council (EIC) headed by the Finance Minister[63]. It mandate a series of reporting requirements as outlined below:

- Cash Transaction Reports.
- Suspicious Transaction Report.
- Counterfeit Currency Report.

*Internet Banking and Money Laundering*

The banks offering Internet banking service can open accounts simply following proper physical introduction and substantiation. This is first and foremost for the intention of appropriate recognition of the customer and also to avoid benami accounts as also money laundering activities that might be embarked upon by the customer. Administrators globally, look forward to the Internet banks also to pursue the practice of 'know your customer'. One of the foremost apprehensions connected with Internet Banking has been that the Internet banking transactions may become undetectable and are extremely mobile and may with no trouble be unnamed and may not leave a customary audit trail by permitting direct transfer of funds. It is relevant to note that money laundering transactions are cash transactions leaving no paper trail. Such an anxiety will be more in the case of use of electronic money or e-cash. In the case of Internet Banking the transactions are kicked off and completed between chosen accounts. The online banking system has to keep a record of all the transactions or series of

62. Vide O.M. dated 18 November 2004.
63. http://fiuindia.gov.in/about-overview.htm

transactions taking place within a month, the character and worth of which may be set by the Central Government. This will sufficiently guard in opposition to any abuse of the Internet banking services for the intention of money laundering. Further the condition of the banking companies to conserve specified ledgers, registers and other records for a period of 5 to 8 years, as per the Banking Companies (Period of Preservation of Records) Rules, 1985 promulgated by the Central Government also passably takes care of this worry.[64]

*Banking Crusade Against Money Laundering vis-à-vis "Know Your Customers" Guidelines*

RBI has issued "Know Your Customer" Guidelines [(RBI 2004-05/284) (DBOD.NO.AML.BC.58/14.01.001/2004-05) dated August 16, 2004] to embark upon the crisis of money laundering. These guidelines have been revisited in the context of the Recommendations made by the Financial Action Task Force (FATF) on Anti-Money Laundering (AML) standards and on Combating Financing of Terrorism (CFT) which have become the worldwide yardstick and have to be forcibly pursued by all the regulatory authorities. Acquiescence with these standards both by the banks/financial institutions and the country has become essential for international monetary relationships. Thorough guidelines based on the Recommendations of the Financial Action Task Force and the paper issued on Customer Due Diligence (CDD) for banks by the Basel Committee on Banking Supervision, with problem-solving suggestions wherever measured essential are together with this. Banks are recommended to make certain that a proper policy framework on Know Your Customer guidelines and Anti-Money Laundering measures is formulated and put in place with the approval of the Board within three months of the date of this circular. It may also be guaranteed that banks are fully accommodating with the provisions of this circular before December 31, 2005 with the say-so of their boards. These guidelines are issued under Section 35A of the Banking Regulation Act, 1949 and any flouting of or rebelliousness with the same may draw punishment under the relevant provisions of the Act.[65]

64. FATF Report of the Working Group on Internet Banking prepared by FATF Asia Secretariat and the Interpol, Hong Kong, 1996.
65. www.rbi.org.in

### *'Know Your Customer' Standards*

1. The purpose of KYC guidelines is to avert banks from being used, deliberately or by accident, by criminal elements for money laundering activities. KYC guidelines also allow banks to be familiar with/understand their customers and their monetary dealings better which in turn help them administer their menaces carefully. Banks must outline their KYC policies slotting in the following four key fundamentals:[66]

(1) Customer Acceptance Policy;
(2) Customer Identification Procedures;
(3) Monitoring of Transactions; and
(4) Risk management.

***For the purpose of KYC policy, a Customer may be defined as:***[67]

(1) Person/entity who maintains an account and/or has a business relationship with bank;

(2) One on whose behalf the account is maintained (i.e. the beneficial owner);

(3) Beneficiaries of transactions conducted by professional intermediaries, such as Stock Brokers, Chartered Accountants, Solicitors, etc. as permitted under the law, and

(4) Any person or entity connected with a financial transaction which can pose significant reputational or other risks to the bank, say, a wire transfer or issue of a high value demand draft as a single transaction.

### Customer Acceptance Policy (CAP)[68]

Banks should build up a clear Customer Acceptance Policy putting down clear conditions for getting of customers. The Customer Acceptance Policy should make sure that clear guidelines are in place on the following facets of customer relationship in the bank. No account is opened in nameless or fictitious/benami name(s).

RBI has also told banks to put in order an outline for new customers based on risk categorization like low risk, medium risk, high risk, etc. and may comprise those under high risk category for whom the supplies of funds are not apparent.

---

66. *Ibid.*
67. *Ibid.*
68. *Ibid.*

Strictures of risk awareness are evidently distinct in terms of the nature of business activity, location of customer and his clients, mode of payments, volume of turnover, social and financial status, etc. The bank should not to open an account or seal an existing account where the bank is powerless to apply fitting customer due diligence measures. Banks may affect improved due diligence measures based on the risk assessment, thereby necessitating concentrated due diligence for higher risk customers, particularly those for whom the sources of funds are not obvious such as non-resident customers, high net worth individuals, trust and charities, companies with close family shareholding or beneficial ownership, firms with sleeping partners, politically exposed person of foreign origin, non-face-to-face customers, those with dubious reputation as per available public information.

Essential checks previous to opening a new account so as to guarantee that the identity of the customer does not match with any person with branded criminal background or with banned units such as individual terrorists or terrorist organizations, etc. The customer profile will be a hush-hush file and particulars contained therein shall not be disclosed for cross-selling or any other purposes.[69]

**Customer Identification Procedure (CIP)**[70]

The policy permitted by the Board of banks should evidently explain in simple terms the Customer Identification Procedure to be carried out at singular stages, i.e. while instituting a banking relationship; carrying out a financial transaction or when the bank has a qualm about the validity/veracity or the satisfactoriness of the earlier obtained customer classification statistics. Customer Identification means identifying the customer and substantiating his/her identity by using dependable, self-determining source documents, data or information. Banks must get hold of plenty of information compulsory to institute, to their pleasure, the identity of each new customer, whether regular or occasional, and the idea of the intended nature of banking relationship.

69. www.rbi.org.in
70. http://www.domain-b.com/finance/banks/rbi/20041201_laundering.html

## Monitoring of Transactions[71]

Constant monitoring is a vital building block of valuable KYC procedures. Banks can successfully manage and lessen their risk only if they have an understanding of the standard and logical activity of the customer so that they have the means of spotting transactions that fall outside the expected model of activity. Nevertheless, the degree of monitoring will depend on the risk sensitivity of the account. Banks ought to pay unusual interest to all multifarious, oddly large transactions and all atypical patterns that have no evident economic or perceptible lawful intent. The bank may prescribe threshold limits for a particular category of accounts and pay particular attention to the transactions which exceed these limits. Transactions that entail large amounts of cash not in agreement with the usual and probable activity of the customer must chiefly draw the attention of the bank. Very high account turnover conflicting with the size of the balance upheld may point towards that funds are being 'washed' through the account. High-risk accounts have to be subjected to deep monitoring.

Bank is supposed to make certain that its branches have a reporting system for doubtful transactions of more than 10 lakhs to Financial Intelligence Unit (FIU) of India on a fortnightly basis. Banks should carry on to make sure that any transfer of funds by way of demand draft, mail telegraphic transfer or any other mode and issue of travelers cheques for value of Rs. 50000 and above is achieved by debit to the customer's account or against cheques and not against cash payment.[72]

## Risk Management[73]

The Board of Directors of the bank must make certain that a useful KYC guidelines is put in place by establishing suitable measures and ensuring their successful execution. It should envelop proper management oversight, systems and controls, isolation of duties, training and other related matters. Conscientiousness should be overtly allocated within the bank for making sure that the bank policies and procedures are put into operation effectively. Banks in-house audit and conformity functions have

71. *Ibid.*
72. RBI for new Reporting Systems for Banks, PTI, posted online, 22/10/2005.
73. www.rbi.org.in

a significant role in assessing and ensuring faithfulness to the KYC policies and procedures.

Banks should have an unending employee-training programme so that the members of the staff are sufficiently trained in KYC procedures. Training requirements should have diverse focuses for leading edge staff, compliance staff and staff dealing with new customers. It is decisive that all those concerned fully recognize the underlying principle behind the KYC policies and put into service them over and over again.

### Customer Education[74]

Accomplishment of KYC procedures necessitates banks to exact certain information from customers which may be of private nature or which has up till now never been called for. This can at times lead to a lot of questioning by the customer as to the aim and object of amassing such information. There is, as a result, a requirement for banks to plan definite literature/ pamphlets, etc. so as to edify the customer of the objectives of the KYC programme. The front desk staff needs to be in particular skilled to handle such circumstances while dealing with customers. Banks should pay extraordinary attention to any money laundering terrorization that may come up from new or developing technologies including internet banking that might favour mystery, and take actions, if wanted, to put a stop to their use in money laundering plans.

### KYC for the Existing Accounts[75]

RBI has solicited Banks to put into operation the new KYC norms recommended vide our circular to all the existing customers in a time bound method. While the revised guidelines will be relevant to all new customers, banks must apply the same to the existing customers on the basis of materiality and perils. Conversely, transactions in existing accounts should be endlessly scrutinized and any abnormal mold in the operation of the account should set-off an examination of the CDD procedures.

74. *Ibid.*
75. *Ibid.*

## CONCLUSION AND SUGGESTIONS

Combating money laundering is a dynamic process but no serious efforts were made to identify the genesis of the problem, the sources of tainted money, accumulation, modes of channelisation into a nation's financial system—yet India is perceived to be a major centre for "hawala" transactions, and needs to assess the threat not just to its economy, but its political system and sovereignty. The amendments to the Prevention of Money Laundering Act (PMLA), 2002, should be aimed at detecting and identifying money laundering and cross-border proceeds, with appropriate tools for deterrent and detection.

The international community has recognized the adverse consequences of cross-border money laundering movements as early as the 1980s and taken several initiatives such as the Vienna Convention (1988), dealing with drug trafficking money, and the Palermo Convention (2000) focusing on transnational crimes, none of which has been ratified by India. Recently India becomes a member of the Financial Action Task Force on Money Laundering (FATF), which seeks to improve national legal systems by introduction of international standards[76].

Currently, India has three separate laws dealing with money laundering. The Narcotics and Psychotropic Substances (NDPS) Act, 1985, applies to proceeds of drug offences in certain limited situations, the Unlawful Activities Act (UAPA), which under a 2004 amendment, provides for raising funds for terrorism being a predicated offence and PLMA, which came into effect only when the Rules were in place in 2005, and is intended to deal with all types of money laundering.

The NDPS Act, which applies only to drug offences, does not require a conviction for the predicate offence. PMLA requires a predicate offence conviction in order to take cognizance, and the schedules to the Act include corruption, prosecution of wildlife, drug and human trafficking, but virtually ignore capital and financial markets.

India has, however, taken initiatives in the accountability and supervisory roles of regulator in financial and capital markets, which are dealt by the Reserve Bank of India (RBI), the Securities and Exchange Board of India (SEBI) and Insurance

76. India becomes 34th member of FATF on 25th June, *Times of India*, 30th June, 2010 (Wednesday).

Regulatory and Development Authority (IRDA). The roles are well defined, and the RBI was the first to establish the customer due diligence guidelines while SEBI's vigilance in protecting capital markets does not need elaboration. SEBI promulgated its own guidelines on anti-money laundering measures even before the RBI.

Section 12 of PMLA requires all banks and intermediaries to maintain records of all transactions, according to nature and value and report to the director—currently under the rules this includes cash transactions involving more than one million rupees, or even less if connected integrally, involving forgery or counterfeit notes or instruments or any suspicious debits, credits, payments, loans, etc. In all fairness the PMLA rules pertaining to the maintenance of a verification of records for all the sectors have been in place since 2005. But the existing regimes encompassing PMLA, UAPA and NDPS have been virtually ineffective, with investigations far and few and even lesser prosecutions and convictions till date.

Powers of confiscation, freezing and forfeiture are also largely dependant on the law providing for the predicated offence. In fact, the PMLA provides for confiscation of proceeds of crime, but not of the instrumentalities used in an offence. International cooperation depends on bilateral arrangements and treaties where they exist, and letters of request in others. This is where FATF membership would provide a single window.

The proposed amendments seek to incorporate existing key provisions of the PMLA rules in recording and maintaining information and making reporting mandatory for all intermediaries, particularly for all foreign transactions. Casinos, money changers and transfer service providers, international credit card gateways are to be subjected to regulatory and reporting requirements. As of now, the latter are governed by the RBI regulations that mainly deal with their customer-related operations.

All offences pertaining to insider trading and market manipulation will also be brought into PMLA as well as smuggling of antiques, terrorism funding, human trafficking other than prostitution, and a wider range of environmental crimes.

Further, anti-money laundering law is essentially predicated on substantive laws. Thus, it is important to have adequate substantive laws for all serious crimes. For instance, substantive laws to deal with organized crime at the Central level are still a far-fetched dream in India. The next step would be to ensure that all these substantive laws are connected with the Money Laundering Act, which in turn should be properly conceived and enacted in the first instance. The Indian money laundering law is particularly flawed in this regard since it excludes violations under the Income Tax and Customs Act from the schedule of offences. Such lacunae need to be addressed at the earliest to make this law truly effective.[77]

Alongside substantive laws, procedural and evidentiary laws would need to be amended to tighten the money laundering effect. Procedural laws need to be simplified and aligned with laws of other countries, given the international dimensions of money laundering. These laws also need to take into consideration technological advancements and developments. Similarly, for evidentiary laws, the meaning of admissible evidence needs to be expanded. Adequate presumptions need to be put in place to deal with such crimes in particular. A robust witness protection programme also needs to be put in place.[78]

To effectively combat cross-border money laundering, India has to make its financial systems FATF compliant, provide for better tracking measures, and incorporate proper mechanism for investigation, prosecution, easier extradition processes, cross-border applicability in foreign jurisdictions, even when the predicated offence is committed in India.

77. *Supra* note 24, at 213-14.
78. *Ibid.*, at 214-15.

CHAPTER 12

# Plastic Money: How Safe are You?

*Dr. Lily Srivastava*

## INTRODUCTION

The world has now been draped in free market economy and with it comes free trade and commerce. The persons most affected by globalisation are the consumers who have now, access to a variety of goods and services which they did not have before. Globalisation leads to rapid growth and development in infrastructure and demands a proportionate maturity in the legal system.

We have seen the transition from *Caveat Emptor* to *Caveat Venditor* as the evolution of the legal system to suit the changing times. The banking sector in India too has seen vast and all encompassing changes in the past few decades with the advent of modern technology. The introduction of payment cards namely Credit, Debit, ATM cards, etc. which the urban youth of today might refer to as 'Plastic Money' is one such thing. The Indian consumer in recent times is faced with threats which were not foreseen till now. The level of protection provided to a similarly placed consumer in a developed country is far greater than what is provided to one in India.

The need of the hour is to recognise the void in the consumer protection laws pertaining to payment cards. There are many threats existing which put the consumer at a high risk of financial as well as identity loss. This begs the question just **'how safe are you?'**, when using Plastic Money.

## THREATS TO THE CONSUMER

The payment card holder is in a very vulnerable position. There are two factions of society that he needs to beware of, fraudsters and his own bank.

### Fraudsters—The Threat from Outsiders

**Skimming**[1] is a process whereby a person just creates a cloned version of the card. This clone can be created by either using leaked credit card information or by swiping the card on a device called a skimmer, which captures the data on the magnetic strip of the card. The data can then be transferred to expired or blank cards, which are easily available in the market. Developed countries, where the credit limits on cards are higher, are prone to skimming. There are now instances traced to smaller economies such as Indonesia, Malaysia, and India[2], etc.

**Phishing** is a form of spam in which the sender attempts to convince the user to reveal personal data such as banking details. The sender enhances the credibility of a phishing message by spoofing a convincing source address or using a deceptive domain name.[3] Basically, it is a computer fraud in which an unsuspecting user submits sensitive information to a malicious system impersonating a trustworthy one.[4] The Anti-Phishing laws are a recent development even in the United States. There is no federal legislation on the subject as of now but various states like California[5] and Washington[6] have taken the initiative to safeguard the consumers.

**Identity theft** is a criminal activity wherein the fraudster appropriates vital information such as name, birth date, account number among other details either by use of malicious programs

1. Lucy Lazarony, New study finds 1 in 10 Americans are victims of credit card fraud, Bankrate.com. 27-9-2000. URL: www.bankrate.com/brm/news/cc/20000927.asp retrieved on 26-12 2008.
2. Khyati Dharamsi, "Your credit card can be cloned", sify.com, 26 August 2008, URL: http://sify.com/finance/fullstory.php?id=14746556 retrieved on 26-12 2008.
3. Charles P. Pfleeger and Shari Lawrence Pfleeger, Security in Computing, Pearson Education Inc, 4th edn, 2008, p. 668.
4. *Ibid.*, p. 266.
5. Anti-Phishing Act of 2005 [u/s section 22948-22948. 3, California Codes (Business and Professions code)].
6. Anti-Phishing Consumer Protection Act of 2008.

such as Trojan horse or by masquerading himself as the employee of the bank. In the United States it is a federal offence.[7]

**Lost or stolen cards[8]:** Valid cards are at times lost or stolen from their holders. These have a high potential of being misused before the customer discovers it. Payment cards are sometimes stolen while in transit from the issuing bank to the prospective users. This gives an added advantage to the fraudster as the card is blank on the signature panel. In the United States the possession of stolen or counterfeit cards is punishable under the federal law.[9]

## The Banking Companies: The Threat from within

**Universal default clause[10]**: Banking companies have a set of standard form of contracts which remain ambiguous to the general public. At times this dangerous clause makes its way into these contracts. The credit card statements are filled with a number of items which include various rates of interests. It is important to note that the rates are floating.

Universal default is the term for a practice in the financial services industry for a particular lender to change the terms of a loan from the normal terms to the default terms when that lender is informed that their customer has defaulted with another lender, even though the customer has not defaulted with the first lender. This can include a default in payment on any periodical settlement.

**Grace period:** The customer at the point of issue of the credit card is informed that there shall be no finance charge on the debts for a certain period. It is called as the grace period during which the balances on credit card do not attract finance charges provided the credit card holder repays the entire outstanding amount with the monthly credit card bill.[11] The grace period

---

7. 18 U.S.C. §1028(a) (7), refer Debasis Nayak, Cyber Law: International Perspective, Asian School of Cyber Law, 2007, p. 70.
8. For further reading refer B.R. Sharma, Bank Frauds, Universal Law Publishing Co. Pvt Ltd, 2nd edn., p. 115.
9. 18 USC Part I chapter 47 § 1029.
10. Bill Burt, "'Universal default' rules explained", URL: http://www.bankrate.com/brm/news/credit-management/20040120a1.asp retrieved on 26-12 2008.
11. "The Fine Print", Frontline, URL:http://www.pbs.org/wgbh/pages/frontline/shows/credit/more/fineprint.html retrieved on 26-12 2008.

varies between each credit card and is usually between 20-60 days. It is also called the interest free period. If a credit card holder doesn't pay his bill before the due date his entire outstanding balance will attract interest rate and all new purchases on the credit card will also attract interest rate until the balances are repaid in full. Taking cash advances from the credit card also takes away any grace period.[12]

**No cap on rate of interest**[13]**:** Credit cards have become a vehicle for credit expansion at very attractive rates for card issuers. Unlike other debts, credit card arrears carry with them exorbitant amounts of interest. Law has been left wanting in this area, as these are treated as a mere payment mechanism. The law does not set any cap on the rate of interest that may be charged on amounts due to card companies and they have the leverage to act as they please, thus, leaving the consumer in a no win situation. The outcome of this is that the card holder gets trapped in a vicious circle of debt with the banks acting as money lenders who exploit the vulnerable customer.

**Other Problems**[14]: The most frequent consumer complaint is with regard to the billing problems of credit cards. Statements are not delivered on time, unauthorised payment of bills are made, charging an unimaginable rate of up to 150% per month on late payments. These are just some of the problems faced by card holders on a regular basis. Besides these the consumer also has to endure the harassing calls they get from financial agencies when they are unable to pay their credit card bills on time.

### ATM-cum-Debit Cards

India is the second fastest growing market for the financial cards in the Asia Pacific region, with banks now offering ATM-cum-Debit cards for savings or salary account, there are now well

12. Neelima Shankar, "Credit card finance charges in India: A Premier", The Rupee Times, URL: http://www.rupeetimes.com/article/credit_cards/credit_card_finance_charges_in_india_a_premier_1329.html retrieved on 26-12-2008.
13. Rajeev D. Mathur and Abhishek Saxena, "Cap credit card interest rates?", *The Economic Times*, URL: http://economictimes.indiatimes.com/rssarticleshow/msid-3473126,flstry-1.cms retrieved on 26-12-2008.
14. ConsumerComplaints.in, URL: http://www.consumercomplaints.in/ retrieved on 26-12-2008.

over 100 million debit cards in India—three times the number of credit cards.[15]

Financial experts often recommend debit cards as a money management tool because it limits the spending capacity of an individual to his own bank balance. Most Indian debit card holders use their cards only to withdraw money from ATMs and relatively only a few are using them for retail purchases as the market is gaining familiarity with its usage only now. But it is because the debit cards can also be used for shopping that you need to be more careful.

Many people wrongly assume that debit cards are much safe than credit cards. It can actually be worse because when a debit card is stolen, or cloned and then misused, there's no grace period while you can contest the charges. Your cash has already been electronically debited from your bank account. Things could get even more ugly if there is an overdraft facility on the account.

There are basically two types of debit cards in the market—Maestro[16] and Visa Debit[17]. There is a vast difference in the authentication procedure of these cards. The transaction via Maestro card has a safety valve by means of a Personal Identification Number (PIN) which prevents any misuse. While Visa cards offer more convenience, as the process only involves a swap and signature the risk increases. The consumer can be prey to card skimmers and there can be no protection as in these cases the fraud goes undetected for a long time.

**Counterfeit Currency from ATMs:** On more than one occasion the ATMs of various banks have dispensed counterfeit currency. There has been a growth in this trend in the past couple of years. Even the Reserve Bank of India has shown its concern

---

15. Mohan Shivanand and Teri Cettina, "Avoid these Debit card Traps", *Readers Digest*, September 2008, p. 58.
16. "Maestro" is a multinational debit card service owned by MasterCard. In India Maestro Debit cards are provided by the State Bank of India, State Bank affiliate banks, Punjab National Bank, Oriental Bank of Commerce, Bank of Rajasthan, etc. Similarly, "Cirrus" is a worldwide interbank network operated by MasterCard.
17. Visa debit is a multinational debit card service owned by Visa Inc. Visa Electron is a sister card to Visa Debit, like ICICI, The Federal Bank, The Corporation Bank, etc. provide Visa Services on Debit card.

on the subject through various press releases.[18] Although there is a procedure for verifying whether notes are ATM worthy or not the system is still not fool proof. The consumer is faced with a high risk of being cheated by its very own bank as the redressal in this situation suffers from many procedural complexities.

**The card cycle: The way money changes hands:** The mechanism of payment cards works out on the intricate web of contracts existing between various parties. In technical jargon the whole process is known as *'the card cycle'*. There are four parties in the card cycle namely the Card Holder, the Issuing Bank, The Merchant Establishment and the Acquiring Bank.

**The card holder** is the person, whose name is embossed on the card and is legally entitled to posses and uses the same to buy goods and services. The bank which issues the card in the favour of the card holder is known as **Issuing Bank**. The card holder enters into an agreement with the issuer to pay for the goods and services bought on the credit card along with the various applicable charges and interest due on the card. This agreement, rather sophistically, is known as the *'card holder agreement'* and is ratified by the cardholder as soon as he receives his card and signs on it.

**Merchant Establishment** is the place of business which accepts the card offered by the card holder as a means of payment for the goods or services provided. Merchant Establishment can accept the card in two ways:

- **Card Holder Present:** This is the transaction that takes place in the presence of the card holder at the merchant establishment which may be a shop, a restaurant, an airport booking counter, etc. The same is carried out by the use of an Electronic Data Capture machine (EDCs) and the terminal is usually referred to as Point of Sale (POS). A charge slip is produced in triplicate and signed by the cardholder.
- **Card Holder Not Present:** This is the transaction that takes place online wherein the card holder is not physically present but provides the details required

18. "RBI issues alert over counterfeit notes at ATMs", *Times of India*, 9-1-2007, URL: http://timesofindia.indiatimes.com/NEWS/India/RBI_issues_alert_over_counterfeit_notes_at_ATMs/articleshow/1102002.cms retrieved on 26-12-2008.

through internet. Here the merchant establishment can be any website providing goods or services either through direct sale or by auctions.

The bank which enables the business of the merchant by licensing him to accept cards as a mode of payment and facilitates its payment is known as **Acquiring Bank**. The contract between the merchant and the acquiring bank is one in which the acquiring bank undertakes to credit the account of the merchant with the value of goods sold or services rendered after deducting a commission known as service fees.

The contract between the cardholder and the merchant establishment is one of sale; the only difference is no money changes hands between them. The merchant expects the bank to settle the debt.

The issuing bank is also under a contractual obligation to pay for the use of its card. The issuer pays the acquirer the amount after charging a commission. The rate of this commission is usually less than the merchant's commission.

The process of card cycle more or less applies to both credit and debit cards.

## INTERNATIONAL SCENARIO

Two species of legislations come in question while discussing the payment card sector. One is the statues that declare the rights and responsibilities of the card holders *vis-a-vis* other members of the card cycle. The other relates to the laws which revolve around the credit reporting agencies set up to keep a check on credit defaulters.

### Category one: The Rights and Liabilities

**United States of America**: A number of federal and state enactments govern the consumers and the corporations. A US consumer is endowed with a number of statutory rights that defend him from the clutches of fraudsters and multinational corporations.

*The Fair Credit and Charge Card Disclosure Act, 1988*[19]—The purpose of this enactment was to make sure that consumers received detailed and uniform disclosures of rates and other cost

19. 15 U.S.C. 1637(c)-(g).

information related to credit and charge card accounts. The details required to be furnished under the act are the annual percentage rate (APR), the periodic rate, the annual fee, the grace period, the finance charges and other fees liable to be charged.[20]

*Truth in Lending Act, 1968*[21]—The enactment was the forerunner of the abovementioned statue and was designed to protect consumers in credit transactions by requiring clear disclosure of key terms of the lending arrangement and all costs.

*Fair Credit Billing Act, 1986*[22]—Passed as an amendment to Truth in Lending Act, 1968 the enactment is based on the premise that "Don't Pay What You Don't Owe"[23]. The following are the rights guaranteed to the card holder under the act—

1. Stop payment on low quality merchandise or services.
2. Dispute billing errors on credit cards and department store charge accounts.
3. Protection from unfair or confusing billing procedures by card issuers. For example, the Act states that a card issuer must:
   - Provide a written explanation to all new cardholders regarding how to dispute billing errors.
   - Provide a statement for each billing period in which the card holder owes money or is eligible for a credit.
   - Send the card holders statement at least 14 days before the payment is due.
   - Credit all payments to the card holder's account on the date they are received.
   - Promptly credit or refund overpayments and send any refunds due within seven business days after the card issuer receives the card holder's written refund request.

20. "What Consumers Should Know about the Cost and Terms of Credit", Federal Reserve bank of San Francisco, URL: http://www.frbsf.org/publications/consumer/cards.html, retrieved on 26-12 2008.
21. 15 U.S.C. § 1601 *et seq*.
22. Passed as an amendment to the Truth in Lending Act 15 U.S.C. § 1601 *et seq*.
23. Susan Weber, "Don't Pay What You Don't Owe", URL: http://creditcards.lovetoknow.com/Fair_Credit_Billing_Act retrieved on 26-12 2008.

The Act also lays down the rights of the card holder in case of billing disputes. The card holder has the right to:

1. Question any charge he/she feels should not be on your credit card statement.
2. Not pay any disputed charge while the credit card issuer is investigating the charge and the maximum liability is limited to $ 50.[24]
3. Contest the results of the investigation.
4. Know the name of anyone to whom the card issuer reports any unpaid, disputed charge.
5. Have the card issuer report the disputed charge as either being "settled" or "in question".
6. Question any billing error including:
   - Unauthorized charges,
   - Charges that list the wrong date or amount,
   - Math errors,
   - Failure to post-payments and credits such as returns,
   - Failure to send statements to your current address,
   - Charges for which one asks for an explanation, a clarification or a written proof of purchase.

The act also gives the card holder certain rights in respect to receiving poor quality goods and services—

1. Not pay for the merchandise if it can be proved that the merchandise is unusable or if the service had no value. To qualify:
2. Documentation is to be submitted as required by the card issuer to explain the situation.
3. The purchase must be more than $50.
4. The item must be purchased in the card holder's home state or within 100 miles of his/her current mailing address.

*Fair Debt Collections Practices Act, 1978*[25]—Under this Act collection agency may not allow collectors to threaten customers or make false statements that might scare the customer into making payments.

---

24. *Supra* n. 16, p. 60.
25. 15 U.S.C. § 1692 *et seq*.

*The Electronic Fund Transfer Act, 1978*[26]—Considering the fact that electronic fund transfer is not a perfect system in itself and there is a high possibility of errors creeping in the EFT Act was passed to establish the rights and liabilities of consumers as well as the responsibilities of all participants in EFT activities. This law prohibits use, transport, sale, proceed, or supply of counterfeit, stolen, altered, lost, or fraudulently obtained debit instruments in interstate or foreign commerce.[27]

**United Kingdom:** Similar to the system in the United States the United Kingdom has also adopted various measures to protect the consumer in the form of an all encompassing statute which has been amended from time to meet the growing needs of consumer protection.

*Consumer Credit Act, 1974*[28]—Under this Act customers who have a claim against a supplier for breach of contract or misrepresentation will generally have an equal claim against the card issuer, i.e. they may choose to go against either the seller or the card issuer or both. The right of the card holder is contained in section 75. For section 75 to apply, certain conditions must be met. Most credit card purchases will be covered, but:

1. the cash price of the goods or services must be more than £100 and not more than £30,000; and
2. Purchases are not covered if they are made by debit cards or by charge cards (where the monthly bill has to be settled in full).

*Consumer Credit Act, 2006*[29]—The main provisions of the Act extend the scope of the Consumer Credit Act, 1974. The Act creates an Ombudsman Scheme and increases the power of the Office of Fair Trading in relation to consumer credit.

**Category two: the Credit Reporting Agencies**

There are entities that collect and disseminate information about consumers to be used for credit evaluation and for certain other purposes. These are consumer reporting agencies which hold a consumers credit report in their databases.

---

26. 15 USC §1693 *et seq*.
27. *Supra* n.4, p. 713.
28. 1974 c. 39.
29. 2006 c. 14.

**United States of America:** Under two statutes namely the Fair Credit Reporting Act and the Fair Debit Collection Practices Act the setting up of *Credit Reporting Agencies* is discussed. These agencies fulfil the following responsibilities under the Acts—

1. Provide a consumer with information about him or her in the agency's files and to take steps to verify the accuracy of information disputed by a consumer. Under the Fair and Accurate Credit Transactions Act (FACTA), an amendment to the Fair Credit Reporting Act (FCRA) passed in 2003, consumers are able to receive one free credit report a year.
2. If negative information is removed as a result of a consumer's dispute, it may not be reinserted without notifying the consumer within five days, in writing.
3. Credit Reporting Agencies may not retain negative information for an excessive period. The FCRA describes how long negative information, such as late payments, bankruptcies, tax liens or judgments may stay on a consumer's credit report—typically seven years from the date of the delinquency. The exceptions: bankruptcies (10 years) and tax liens (seven years from the time they are paid).

**United Kingdom**[30]**:** The system in the UK Credit rating system closely mirrors that followed in the USA. Most banks and other credit-granting organisations subscribe to one or more of these organisations to ensure the quality of their lending. Credit reference agencies are bound by the Data Protection Act, which requires that data relating to identifiable individuals must be accurate, relevant, held for a proper purpose and not out-of-date. Individuals have a legal right to access data held on them. The Credit Reference Agencies are governed by the provisions of the Consumer Credit Act of 1974.

**France**[31]**:** The French system of credit reporting is unique. France favours strict regulation of consumer data. Actually there are no specific Consumer Reporting Agencies. Instead, the

---

30. Nial Mckay, "Playing with Plastic: How it works in the Rest of the World", Frontline, URL: http://www.pbs.org/wgbh/pages/frontline/shows/credit/more/world.html retrieved on 26-12 2008.
31. *Ibid.*

*Banque de France* manages a list of those who default on their loans. Once the bill is paid, the name is removed from the list, and even if the bill is not paid, the debtors' names are removed after five years. Further, the list is industry-specific, so credit card companies only have access to names held in the banking and financial databases. There have been both proponents and critics of this system. The critics state that the system quells market competition but its advocates state that the French banks are doing fine with the limited data available.

## INDIAN SCENARIO

The Credit Information Bureau (India) Limited was set-up by the Government of India in conjunction with the RBI and is India's first Credit Information Bureau. This was set-up under the *Credit Information Companies (Registration) Act, 2005.*

The objectives of the act include[32]—

1. To provide regulation of credit information companies,
2. To facilitate efficient distribution of credit, and
3. To have smooth management and conduct of Credit Information Companies.

The information to CIBIL is provided by the banks themselves. In the recent times there have been instances of misreporting wherein the customer is wrongly reported as a defaulter even after settlement of all the dues.[33] This adversely affects all the future credit transactions with respect to credit cards, loans, etc.

There is no proper mechanism to get a name removed from the Bureau's *defaulters list.* A single default in debt settlement can lead to high interest rate in all future transactions and even prevent the banks to offer loans to consumers.[34]

32. "Salient Features of the Act for Regulation of Credit Information Company" URL: http://www.indiacorporateadvisor.com/stt/san/sanjeevreport.asp retrieved on 26-12 2008.
33. Greha Mataliya, "Paid Outstanding: Name still on CIBIL defaulters list", 22-10-2008. URL:http://www.apnapaisa.com/tags/cibil retrieved on 26-12 2008.
34. http://www.consumercomplaints.in

## RECOMMENDATIONS

### Legal Issues

The governance of credit card operations is done by a fair practice code[35] made by a conglomeration of banks known as Indian Banks' Association. The law-makers of the country should realise the importance of the subject matter and pass statutes protecting the rights of the consumer. The consumer in India has no special rights with respect to his payment card usage unlike the consumer in developed countries.

The following rights have to be recognised by the legislature:

*Rights of the Consumer*

(a) A right to be protected from the harassment of the banking companies which use unethical means for debt collection on the lines of the US Fair Debt Collections Practices Act 1978.[36]

(b) A right not to be made liable for the fraudulent and unauthorised transactions taking place on the credit card.[37]

(c) A sealing to the maximum liability in the event of misuse of payment cards on the lines of the fair credit billing act.[38]

(d) A clean chit should be given to the consumer with respect to his credit report once the debt is settled or otherwise, every five years as in the French system.[39]

(e) A right to challenge and retrieve the fraudulently charged amount from the debit cards within a certain period.

*Restrictions on the merchants and card issuers*

(a) An obligation on the banks to disclose all the policies which may give rise to liability on part of the consumer on the lines of the fair disclosure act.[40]

---

35. The complete practice code is available on the official website of the Indian Banks Association, URL: http://www.iba.org.in/fpc_credit.asp retrieved on 26-12 2008
36. *Supra* n. 26.
37. *Supra* n. 23.
38. *Ibid.*
39. *Supra* n. 32.
40. *Supra* n. 20.

(b) An obligation on all financial institutions to furnish the consumer with the data that they furnish to the consumer reporting agencies.
(c) A penalty on the merchants in case they overlook to check the photograph on the card and compare the signatures.
(d) The information possessed by Consumer Rating Agencies should be provided only to that sector of the market to which it concerns and not indiscriminately as is done now.

*Other measures*

(a) The Reserve Bank of India should take initiative to curtail the use of universal default clauses which are aimed at defrauding the consumers.
(b) A better mechanism should be established for consumer redressal on the issue of counterfeit currency dispensed by ATMs.
(c) Strict anti-phishing laws should be formulated and passed by the legislature.
(d) The possession of stolen or counterfeit instruments should be made an offence.[41]

**Security Issues**

**Introduction of new technology:** The use of magnetic strips on the cards is an obsolete technology and suffers from many inherent defects which make it unsafe for modern consumers. The technology needs to be upgraded to meet the present times. We recommend that—

(a) EMV[42] standard chips or Smart Cards should be introduced in the architecture of payment cards to prevent skimming.[43]
(b) Biometrics of a person may be stored on the cards to prevent identity theft.[44]

41. *Supra* n. 10.
42. EMV stands for Europay MasterCard Visa.
43. "Axis Bank guards card against skimming, counterfeiting", *The Hindu Business Line*, 6-3-2008 URL: http://www.thehindubusinessline.com/bline/2008/03/06/stories/2008030652760600.htm
44. *Supra* n. 4, pp. 249-50, 264-66.

**Other Issues**

(a) Prepaid cards should be encouraged for online transactions.
(b) All the transactions on payment cards should be reported immediately to the consumer via SMS and email at a bare minimum expense.
(c) Photographs should be made mandatory on all payment cards.

## FACILITIES FOR SETTLING DISPUTES/GRIEVANCES

Enacting laws alone cannot solve the customers' problems. Customers also need to be informed of these laws. Banks are bound legally to give necessary information to the customers in all their transactions. Relevant information helps in safeguarding the interests of their customers. Redressal is the natural follow-up of hearing of complaints and making a settlement in a manner that is acceptable to customers as well as the sellers. In order to handle the disputes/grievances of the cardholders, facilities available are customer grievance redressal cell in banks, banking ombudsman services provided by RBI and consumer courts.

### Customer Grievance Redressal Cell in Banks

If the cardholders have any complaints regarding fee/charges, mistakes, deficiency of services they can approach the customer grievance redressal cell in banks with adequate evidence for getting solutions. Most of the cases are settled internally by banking authorities on getting complaints from the customers.

### Banking Ombudsman Services

If the cardholder does not get redressal through customer grievance redressal cell in banks, they can approach banking ombudsman services provided by RBI. Banking Ombudsman an independent dispute resolution authority set-up by the Reserve Bank in 1995 to deal with disputes that individuals and small business have with their banks. The banking ombudsman is a quasi-judicial authority. The RBI's revised Banking Ombudsman Scheme now includes customer complaints on credit card, deficiencies in providing the promised services by banks, levying service charges without prior notice to the customer and non-adherence to the fair practices code as adopted by individual banks. Data published by RBI in 2006-07 states that most complaints with banking ombudsman are related to credit cards.

**Consumer Court**

Grievances related to card cases can be filed at the Consumer Redressal Forums against the banks on the grounds of 'deficiency in service'. For redressal of grievances under the Consumer Protection Act, a credit cardholder may approach a District Forum if the value of goods and services provided is less than Rs. 20 lakh; the State Commission its the value is more than Rs. 20 lakh but less than Rs. 1 crore. The major advantage of the Consumer Court is that it allows a card user to file a complaint with the Consumer Forum of the district in which he is a resident provided the cause of action is within the jurisdiction of that District Forum. The law also requires that a complaint be filed within two years from the date on which the cause of action incurred in a District Forum of appropriate jurisdiction after payment of a nominal fee. Consumer Court is the final authority for redressing grievances connected with deficiency of card services if a cardholder does not get his problem solved from banking ombudsman[45].

## LATEST UPDATE: RBI GUIDELINE TO CONTROL FRAUDS

Banks/NBFCs should set-up internal control systems to combat frauds and actively participate in fraud prevention committees/task forces which formulate laws to prevent frauds and take proactive fraud control and enforcement measures.

With a view to reducing the instances of misuse of lost/stolen cards, it is recommended to banks/NBFCs that they may consider issuing (i) cards with photographs of the cardholder, (ii) cards with PIN, and (iii) signature laminated cards or any other advanced methods that may evolve from time to time.

In terms of instructions contained in the circular RBI/ DPSS.No.1501/02.14.003/2008-09 dated February 18, 2009 and the amendments thereof, issued by Department of Payment and Settlement Systems, Reserve Bank of India on security issues and

45. Rajani, V., An Evaluation of Business Deals Using Plastic Money in Kerala, pp. 187-90.

risk mitigation measures relating to online card not present transactions using Credit/Debit cards, banks were advised to put in place a system of providing for additional authentication/validation based on information not visible on the cards for all on-line card not present transactions including IVR transactions, with effect from February 1, 2011. The same has been extended to Mail Order Transactions Order (MOTO) transactions, which are also a subset of the card—not present transactions, with effect from May 01, 2012 vide DPSS circular DPSS. PD.CO.No. 223/02.14.003/2011-12 dated August 04, 2011.

Further, in terms of circular no. DPSS.CO.PD.2224/02.14.003/2010-11 dated March 29, 2011 banks have been advised to take steps to put in place a system of online alerts for all types of transactions irrespective of the amount, involving the usage of cards at various channels. The measures were to be implemented latest by June 30, 2011.

Banks are advised to block a lost card immediately on being informed by the customer and formalities, if any, including lodging of FIR can follow within a reasonable period.

Banks may consider introducing, at the option of the customers, an insurance cover to take care of the liabilities arising out of lost cards. In other words, only those cardholders who are ready to bear the cost of the premium should be provided an appropriate insurance cover in respect of lost cards[46].

## CONCLUSION

Kofi Annan once said that "arguing against globalization is like arguing against the laws of gravity." One needs to understand that criticising the ills of globalisation is futile and is a problem in itself. The real cause of concern is that when a nation embraces globalisation, the whole domestic system should evolve to flow with the tide of global economy.

In India we have seen the banking sector readily and feverishly pick up the pace of the western economies but the law-makers and regulators still lag behind. The Reserve Bank of India holds the view that credit card are basically payment mechanisms and refuses to change its stand. The legislators do

46. Master Circular on Credit Card Operations of Banks, RBI/2012-13/71 DBOD. No. FSD.BC.23/24.01.011/2012-13, dated July 02, 2012, http://www.rbi.org.in/scripts/BS_ViewMasCirculardetails.aspx?id=7338

not concern themselves with the plight of the consumers on this matter. The banking corporations are hoodwinking the society and have taken the place of the unscrupulous money lenders of old. This unique sphere of the banking industry has somehow managed to go totally undetected. The Indian consumer needs to be elevated to the standard of protection offered by foreign laws at the earliest.

# PART VI
# CORPORATE GOVERNANCE

# CHAPTER 13

# Oppression and Mismanagement *vis-a-vis* Arbitration Agreement: An Inquiry

*Dr. Naveen Kumar*

## INTRODUCTION

Harmonizing the conflict of interest between the majority and minority shareholders of a Company is a problem which is to be dealt with great caution. A proper balance needs to be maintained between the freedom of management to take decisions and the protection of interest of the minority shareholders. The subject of arbitrability of dispute relating to operation and mismanagement gains significance in the light of recent decision rendered by the Company Law Board (CLB) in the matter of *Uninor Ltd. and Ors. v. Unitech Wireless Tamil Nadu (P) Limited,*[1] where Justice D.R. Deshmukh, Chairman Company Law Board has under Section 8 of the Arbitration and Conciliation Act, 1996 allowed company's application seeking to resolve its dispute with its joint venture partner, Telenor, a Norwegian Mobile Phone Company, through international arbitration in Singapore. The fact that the CLB is flooded with petitions under section 397/398 of Company's Act, 1956 since the minorities rights are infringed in many companies. If a comparison is made between the period prior to the year 2000 and later it emerges that there has been a tremendous increase in the filling of petitions under these sections and the reason can be suggested as awareness among the shareholders is on the rise and adequate relief is being provided by the Company Law

1. (2012) 107 CLA 547 (CLB).

Board within a reasonable time in safeguarding the interest of the minority shareholders.

In this paper an attempt has been made to examine the statutory powers of the Company Law Board to adjudicate the petitions relating to the sections 397 and 398 under Company Act, 1956 for oppression and mismanagement. Whether an arbitration agreement can overpower the authority of a judicial body is a matter of great concern. Can an arbitration agreement oust the Jurisdiction of CLB? It is pertinent to study the problem in the light of various decisions of the Supreme Court of India which gives primacy to arbitration over the adjudication by the Company Law Board. It has been suggested to the Company Law Board, how to handle situations related to the petitions filed for oppression and mismanagement and how to reach to circumvent an arbitration agreement. It is also highlighted the new proposed changes suggested in Companies Bill, 2012 passed by the Loka Sabha.

## MEANING OF OPPRESSION

*The Oxford English Dictionary*[2] defines oppression as an exercise of authority or power in a burdensome, harsh or wrongful manner, unjust or cruel treatment of objects, inferiors, etc., the imposition of unreasonable or unjust burdens. In *Stroud Judicial Dictionary of Words and Phrases*[3] the term oppressive is interpreted with reference to section 210 of English Companies Act, 1948 and having its ordinary meaning of burdensome, harsh or wrongful.[4] Quoting the decision in Re Five Minute Car Wash Service[5], it is further interpreted as to establish a case of oppression within the section 210 referred above and that it had to be shown that those were alleged to have acted enough to prove that they had been unwise, inefficient and careless. Even the other dictionaries such as the *Law Lexion the Encyclopedia Law Dictionary with Legal Maxim*[6], *Halsbhury's Laws of England*[7]and

2. Oxford English Dictionary, 2nd ed., 1989, Oxford, London, pp. 870-71.
3. Stroud Judicial Dictionary of Words and Phrases, 5th ed., 1986, Sweet and Maxwell, London, pp. 17-79.
4. *Elder v. Elder E. Watson*, 1952 SC 49, see also Re Harmer (R.H.) (1959) 1 W.L.R 62, *Scottish Co operative Wholesale SOC v. Meyer* (1959) A.C. 324.
5. 1966; 1, W.L.R. 745.
6. Compiled and edited by P. Ramanatha Aiyer, Wadhwa & Co., Nagpur, 1993, p. 915.

*Black's Law Dictionary*[8] also define the term oppression more or less in the same terms.

The meaning of the term 'oppression' as explained by Lord Cooper in the Scootish case of *Elder v. Elder*, and cited by Justice Wanchoo in *Santi Prasad Jain v. Kalinga Tubes Ltd.*,[9] as follows:

> "The essence of the matter seems to be that the conduct complained of should at the lowest involve a visible departure from the standards of fair dealing, and a violation of the conditions of fair play on which every shareholder who entrust his money to the company is entitled to reply".

Further, the complainant must need to prove that the act of majority shareholder is unjust, harsh and tyrannical. It is not enough to show that there is just and equitable cause for winding up the company though that must be shown as a preliminary to the application of section 397. It also need to be explained that the conduct of the majority shareholders was oppressive to the minority as members. There must be continuous acts on the part of the majority shareholders, showing that the affairs of the company were being conducted in a manner oppressive to some part of the members.

The definitions of the said terms stray far away from what would amount to contractual obligations. Further, the scope of the Provisions of Sections 397 and 398 of the Act are more *in rem* than in *personum*. The powers of the CLB are derived under Sections 402 and 403 of the Act.

It was maintained by the Courts earlier, that an isolated incident can not constitute an act of oppression and based on that incident one cannot maintain a petition under section 397/398 of the Companies Act, 1956. The Supreme Court of India, in *Shanti Prasad Jain v. Kalinga Tubes Ltd.*,[10] has held that "there must be continuous acts on the part of the majority shareholders, continuing up to the date of the

7. Edited by Lord Hailsham, Vol. 7, London, Butterworths, 4th edition, 1974, p. 605.
8. Eighth Edition.
9. AIR 1965 SC 1535, see also Avtar Singh, Company Law, Eastern Book Company, 14th ed, 2004, p. 476.
10. *Ibid.*

> petition, showing that the affair of the company were being conducted in a manner oppressive to some part of the members".

*Applicability of Res Sub Judice and Res Judicata for Petitions under Sections 397 and 398*

There are two legal concepts under the provisions of Civil Procedure Code 1908 viz., *Res subjudice* and *Res judicata*. The same dispute can be raised or adjudicated simultaneously before two forums and it is called *'Res subjudice'*. A concluded proceeding cannot again be decided except in an appeal available and it is called *'Res judicata'*. Sections 10 and 11 of Civil Procedure Code, 1908 deal with *'Res subjudice'* and *'Res judicata'*. Certain established concepts like *'Res subjudice'* and *'Res judicata'* are followed by all forums, but, these concepts are also very important to a proceeding under sections 397/398 of the Companies Act, 1956. On this issue, the High Court of Allahabad in *Jaypee Cement Limited, In re,*[11] has held that "the law is well settled that where the right sough to be enforced by the suit is not a pre-existing common law right but is a right created by statute which provides the remedy for breach of that right, the suit is "impliedly barred". The right of members of a company against oppression and mismanagement is not a pre-existing common law right but is a right created by statute, i.e., the Companies Act. Therefore, such suits were *prima facie* not maintainable. It would be contrary to public policy to hold that if the oppression or mismanagement affects 10 per cent or more members by numbers or shares, they can approach the Company Law Board under sections 397/398 read with section 399 of the Companies Act and if it affects less than that number they can institute suits. Further, even if the aggrieved members were less than the minimum limit required by section 399, they were not rendered remediless, as they could approach the Central Government, which could refer the case to the Company Law Board under section 401." Though there are several judgments on this issue, it is not necessary to look into all those judgments, but, the issues in this regard can be summed-up as follows:

- The Company Law Board will decide as to whether the principles of *'Res judicata'* and *'Res subjudice'* can be

11. (2004) 122 Comp Cas 855.

applied in a proceeding under sections 397/398 of the Companies Act, 1956 based on the facts of the case.

- If there is only an isolated incident which has been decided by a Court, the members cannot get a different finding from the CLB with the same facts.
- Irrespective of pendency of other suits or claims, the CLB can look into the issues raised under sections 397/398 of the Companies Act, 1956 and will take a decision in the interests of the Company and in order to put an end to the matters complained.

## DISPUTES RELATING TO OPPRESSION AND MISMANAGEMENT

The issue of 'arbitrability of disputes relating to oppression and mismanagement' is most complex and one cannot say 'yes' or 'no' to the issue. However, without looking at the precedents governing the issue of .'arbitrability of disputes relating to oppression and mismanagement', one can easily say that the jurisdiction of Company Law Board under sections 397/398 of Companies Act, 1956 cannot be ousted through an arbitration clause on the following simple reasons.

- The CLB is supposed to look at the public interest also under sections 397/398 of the Companies Act, 1956 and as such, we can assume that the Arbitrator may not be in a position to look at public interest as mandated.
- In any proceeding before an arbitrator, a claim petition can be filed and it is similar to a plaint in a Civil Suit. In response to the Claim Petition, opposite party is required to file a counter-statement with his defence and it can also contain a counter-claim. In both plaint in ordinary civil suits before Civil Court and in proceedings before the Arbitrator, the claim or the relief sought should be specific and both the Court and the Arbitrator may not be in a position to go beyond the pleadings in normal circumstances. But, the power of Company Law Board under sections 397/398 of the Companies Act, 1956 is different and the object under section 397 is to put an end to the matters complained of, public interest and the interests of the Company. The CLB may provide relief

> which is completely different from the relief sought by the petitioners under sections 397/398. As such, it is clear that the Arbitrator cannot exercise or may lack competence in dealing with the issues under section 397/398 of the Companies Act, 1956.

On the issue of arbitrability of 'disputes pertaining to oppression and mismanagement', the High Court of Delhi, in *S.K. Dhawan and another v. R. Vir and others,*[12] was pleased to observe that "the shareholders of a company have a right to file a petition under section 397 or section 398 of the Companies Act, 1956, for relief against mismanagement or oppression, if the provisions of section 399 are satisfied. Their right is a statutory right which, by section 9, cannot be ousted by a provision in the articles of association of the company. Any article providing that a difference between the company and its directors or between the directors themselves or between any members of the company or between the company and any person shall be referred to arbitration cannot debar the jurisdiction of the court in the matter of a petition under section 397 or 398. The court will not stay a petition under sections 397 and 398 on an application under section 34 of the Arbitration Act, 1940, based on the arbitration clause".

On the same lines, the High Court of Delhi, in *O.P. Gupta v. Shiv General Finance (P.) Ltd. and others,*[13] has held that "merely because there is an article in the articles of association of the company to the effect that any dispute between the company on the one hand and its members on the other will be referred to arbitration, the court will not stay a petition under sections 397 and 398 of the Companies Act, 1956, for relief against mismanagement or oppression in the affairs of a company. Such an article cannot be called into play for the purpose of staying proceedings under section 397 or section 398. The provisions of sections 397 and 398 and of section 434 give exclusive jurisdiction to the court and the matters dealt with thereby cannot be referred to arbitration. No arbitrator can possibly give relief to the petitioner under sections 397 and 398 or pass any order under section 402 or section 403". Again, on the same lines, it was reiterated by the Bombay High Court, in *Manavendra Chitnis and*

12. (1977) 47 Comp Cas 277.
13. (1977) 47 Comp Cas 279.

*another v. Leela Chitnis Studios P. Ltd. and others,*[14] that "merely because there is an arbitration clause or an arbitration proceeding, or for that matter an award, the court's jurisdiction under sections 397 and 398 of the Companies Act, 1956, cannot stand fettered. On the other hand, the matter which can form the subject-matter of a petition under sections 397 and 398 cannot be the subject-matter of arbitration, for an arbitrator can have no powers such as are conferred on the court by sections such as section 402."

Inspite of any concluded proceedings, pendency of proceedings, conclusion of arbitration proceedings on some issue or pendency of the arbitration proceedings between or among the shareholders of the Company, the CLB can always entertain a petition under sections 397/398 and will take an appropriate decision in the interests of the company, in the interests of the shareholders, in public interests, in order to put an end to the matters complained of and it all depends upon the facts of the case and no hard and fast rule can be laid in this regard.

## GROUNDS FOR DISPUTES[15]

The common acts which are complained of in cases under sections 397 and 398 are as follows:

1. Not following the principles of partnership. Especially when the company is in the form of quasi Partnership.
2. Changing composition of the Board of Directors by unilateral appointment of family members of respondents as directors to the exclusion of the petitioner/without taking them into confidence.
3. Allotment of further shares only to the respondent group at the exclusion of the petitioner group, so as to push the petitioner group into minority or to convert the petitioner group from majority to minority.
4. Removal of the petitioners as directors of the company under section 284 or section 283 (1)(g) or other ground.
5. Ousting the petitioner from day-to-day management of the company.
6. Giving humiliating treatment to the petitioners.

---

14. (1985) 58 Comp Cas 113.
15. For more details, see A. Ramaiya, Guide to the Company Act, Lexis Nexis, Butterworths, Wadhwa, Nagpur, 16th edition, 2008.

7. Not granting inspection of books and records.
8. Withholding salary, perquisites which were being paid to the petitioner.
9. Diversification of funds for more risky ventures.
10. Siphoning of money.
11. Depriving petitioner group from dividend but taking out money only by the Respondent group by taking out heavy salary.

**Test of Oppression**

It is now well settled that an action can be legal but still unfair. Minority often can raise objections on the decisions of the Majority which they feel oppressive even if they are otherwise legal.

The Supreme Court in *V.S. Krishnan v. Westfort Hi-Tech Hospital Ltd*[16], observed that: "The oppressive act complained of may be fully permissible under law but may yet be oppressive and, therefore, the test as to whether an action is oppressive or not is not based on whether it is legally permissible or not since even if legally permissible, if the action is otherwise against probity, good conduct or is burdensome, harsh or wrong or is mala fide or for a collateral purpose, it would amount to oppression under Sections 397 and 398."

The CLB, irrespective of whether oppression is proved or not —in the interest of the company, generally ask the petitioner about the sum he expects to leave the company. Because merely deciding whether oppression or mismanagement exists or not, does not take any party anywhere. At times differences are so acute that it is not possible for the parties to work together ever again. The CLB has powers to pass orders under section 402 of the Act even if no case is proved under sections 397-398 of the Act. There are many cases in which it has been held that the CLB may pass such order with a view to bringing to an end the matters complained of, as it thinks fit even though a case of oppression/mismanagement has not been made out or the allegations of oppression/mismanagement have not been established[17].

---

16. [2008] 142 Comp Cas 235 (SC).
17. *Bharamgouda Adgouda Patil v. Sanjay Founders Pvt Ltd.*, [2009] 92 CLA 165.

In *Needle Industries (India) Ltd. v. Needle Industries Newey (India) Holding Ltd.,*[18] it was observed by the apex court that even if the case of oppression was not proved, substantial justice must be done between the parties and the parties must be placed as nearly as may be in the same position in which they would have been, if the wrong doing had not taken place. Similar view was expressed in *Sangramsinh P. Gaekwad v. Shantadevi P. Gaekwad (Dead)* by LRs.[19]

Many times, instead of deciding the case on merits, compromise is also suggested in the cases before the CLB where the petitioner is ready to exit the company at the price decided by the court. This happens in most of the cases of the nature of Quasi Partnership. Once parting ways is looked as the only way out the focus then shifts on only one aspect.

## VALUATION OF SHARES OF THE COMPANY

Either *suo-motu* or at the request of the parties, the CLB may appoint an independent valuer to value the shares of the company. In such cases, the valuation of the shares is made binding on both the parties. When both the parties agree to go for valuation by way of a consent order, matters might appear to be simple, as long as both parties act upon their consent.[20]

In *Consulting Engineers Services (India) Ltd. v. Kaikhosrou K. Framji,*[21] the CLB passed an order with the consent of the parties directing one to purchase the shares of the other without raising any technical objections. The party directed to purchase was not allowed to avoid the carrying out of the solemn promise duly recorded by the CLB just only by raising hyper technical pleas.

In the case of *Bertrand Faure Sitztechnik Gmbh & Co. v. IFB Automotive and Seating Systems Ltd.,*[22] it was held that the CLB has power to order compliance of the consent orders. Under the consent terms approved by the CLB one party was to purchase shares held by the other party. The price was negotiated before the CLB. No party could claim thereafter that there was

18. AIR 1981 SC 1298; 1981 SCR (3) 698.
19. (2005) 123 Comp Cas 566 (SC).
20. See also, Palmer's Company Law, Sweet & Maxwell, London, 24th edition, 2008, p. 8249.
21. (2002) 4 Comp LJ 227 (Delhi).
22. (1999) 97 Comp Cas 690 (CLB-PB).

undervaluation or overvaluation of shares. Failure to discharge an obligation which was not a condition precedent to the enforcement of the consent terms could not be brought into account for avoiding compliance.

In *Sir J.P. Srivastva & Sons (Rampur) P. Ltd. v. Gwalior Sugar P. Ltd.*,[23] the parties agreed to a consent order under which the petitioner was to transfer his shares to the respondent. The valuation was made by a chartered accountant appointed by CLB. The parties were held bound by the order and there was no scope for bringing in the fulfilment of any other obligation which was not mentioned in the order. The rate per share was fixed on the basis of the valuation report. Even in cases which are decided on merits and where oppression has been established, the way forward for the company is that the petitioners/respondents exit the company and in such cases, courts appoint valuers to determine the value of the shares of the petitioner to exit the company. In cases of division of undertaking, valuation matters a lot.

When is valuation said to be 'fair'? The answer to this question, if asked to the parties in dispute, is always different. Admittedly valuation is an art and not a science. It is subjective. A professional valuer tries to bring maximum objectivity in the valuation process. It takes lots of efforts to make the parties agree to the given valuation. Either the respondents want the amount payable to the petitioner reduced by something which they allege is payable by the petitioner to the company; to which the petitioner does not agree. There have been number of cases where both sides do not agree to the valuation done by an independent Professional. It is then for the court to intervene and pass necessary orders to ensure completion of the transaction. Fair value may be expressed as a price as between a willing vendor and willing purchaser. Even after appointment of valuer, parties may have reservations about the method of valuation adopted, the factors that have been considered for valuation, whether the impact of the dispute on the value of the shares has been considered or simply that the valuation favours the other party more.

23. (1999) 21 SCL 142.

## ARBITRABILITY OF A DISPUTE

Understanding the importance of arbitrability, the Parliament has taken due care of the same under the Arbitration Act by specifically enacting section 2(3) while dealing with the scope of arbitration and making sections 5 and 8 subject to section 2(3). Therefore, where an Act specifically provides a dispute resolution mechanism to resolve the disputes arising under such Act, arbitrator cannot arbitrate upon it. For example, Industrial Disputes Act provides for Industrial Tribunal, labour court and conciliation officers as dispute resolution machineries and hence labour disputes cannot be resolved by arbitration. Further, IDA provides for arbitration mechanism for which elaborate procedure is prescribed and arbitral award is also subject to the jurisdiction of the Industrial Tribunal. In effect, arbitration under the Arbitration Act is ruled out.

But this does not apply to an arbitrator appointed by the parties, as an arbitrator is neither a court nor a tribunal. Therefore, the arbitrator will not have any powers to grant the reliefs contemplated under section 402 as such powers cannot be conferred on him by the parties. This makes the position of an arbitrator inferior to CLB in as much as he will not be able to achieve the objects contemplated under sections 397 and 398 of the Companies Act. To achieve the objects of sections 397 and 398, wide powers as contemplated under section 402 is a must and in this regard the arbitrator comes nowhere near the CLB.

## LACK OF AWARENESS

Lack of awareness about alternative dispute resolution methods is the main reason why these have not found the required acceptability. More awareness should be created among the public to encourage them to resort to alternative methods for solving their disputes. The Arbitration and Conciliation Act, 1996, enables the certified Tribunals to refer disputes to arbitration. However, many a times there are differences of opinion on selection of arbitrators and warrants the interference of High Courts to appoint an arbitrator. It points to a direction where a change in the attitude of the people is required. Alternative Dispute Resolution Centres have to be established in all potential areas and the courts and tribunals should give more stress on mediation and conciliation methods to create visibility of this system and encourage people to approach the court as only the last resort and only after they exhaust other alternative methods.

In the case of corporate disputes, the underlying legislations should provide for resolving disputes informally. Even the Memorandum and Articles of Association of companies should recognize the settlements reached through mediation, arbitration and conciliation among the members where public interest is not affected and the informal dispute resolution methods will be an effective remedy to the situation.

## STATUS OF AN ARBITRATOR

Now let us examine the legal status of arbitrator as to whether he is a court or tribunal. Arbitration could be either 'consentient' i.e. agreed by parties or 'statutory', i.e. prescribed in a statute. In the former parties to a contract agree to resolve the disputes through arbitration while in the latter a particular statute prescribes that disputes should be resolved through arbitrator named therein for example Registrar of Cooperative Societies is the arbitrator prescribed under the cooperative societies legislation to adjudicate certain disputes. Arbitration can be resorted to under the Industrial Disputes Act, 1947 also. We are specifically concerned with consentient arbitration in this article.

The Arbitration Act prescribes certain standard procedures of arbitration in default of any contrary provisions agreed to between the parties. Thus, basically the arbitrator is the choice of the parties, i.e. 'chosen judge' and derives his authority under the arbitration agreement and not from any specific statute. The parties are free to agree for the procedure to be adopted, method of proving documents, etc. Thus, arbitration is a private arrangement to resolve dispute without resorting to ordinary civil courts. This is because the Arbitration Act does not override the provisions of special enactments under which certain disputes are to be resolved by a specific authority constituted under such enactment.

The distinction between a court, tribunal and an arbitrator came up before the Supreme Court,[24] wherein the question was whether the decision of the arbitrator to whom industrial dispute

24. *Engineering Mazdoor Sabha v. Hind Cycles Ltd.*, AIR 1963 SC 874.

is voluntarily referred under section 10A of the Industrial Disputes Act, can be termed as a court. The Supreme Court had held as under:

> "The arbitrator acting under section 10A of the Industrial Disputes Act is neither a court nor a tribunal even though some of the trappings of the court are present. The arbitrator under section 10A of the Act is not in the same position as a private arbitrator. He lacks essential and fundamental requisites in that he is not invested with the .State's inherent judicial power. He is appointed by the parties and the power to decide the dispute between the parties who appointed him is derived by him from the agreement of the parties and from no other source. The mere fact that his appointment once made by the parties is recognised by section 10A of the Act and, thereafter, he is clothed with certain powers having the trappings of the court, does not mean that the power of adjudication which he is exercising is derived from the State."

The above position is squarely applicable to an arbitrator appointed by parties in the ordinary course, i.e. consentient arbitrator. In other words, an arbitrator is neither a court nor a tribunal.

Even after making the above observation the CLB refused to refer the parties to arbitration on other grounds. It is humbly submitted that the above observation appears to be erroneous. Even if an arbitration agreement is covered under section 7 of the Arbitration Act, it is still an ordinary basic agreement under the Indian Contract Act and is amply covered under the sweep of the term 'agreement' used in section 9 of the Companies Act and not a special agreement made pursuant to a special legislation, i.e. Arbitration Act. The main purpose of section 7 of the Arbitration Act is to define what an arbitration agreement is for the purpose of that Act and nothing more. Therefore, an arbitration agreement does not acquire any special statutory right so as to become a statutory instrument so that it can go out of the grip of section 9 of the Companies Act.

In the case of *Naveen Kedia & Ors. v. Chennai Power Generation Ltd. & Ors.,*[25] the CLB referred the disputes which arose between

---

25. (1999) 95 Comp Cas 640.

the parties out of two inter-linked agreements, to arbitration on the ground that as a judicial authority it is bound to refer the parties to arbitration and has no discretion under section 45 of the Arbitration Act as it involves international arbitration. The dispute was between two parties and the relief claimed was that one party be directed to provide funds to the company as envisaged in the agreements. The warring parties were joint venture parties with 50:50 share holdings.

The principal agreement provided that the respective rights of the parties in the company shall be governed by the terms of the agreement and the company and its shareholders agreed to this. The CLB was influenced by this clause and came to the conclusion that whatever the issues complained against is covered by the agreement, which contains an arbitration clause. There was no finding or any observation whether the issues complained of in the petition also touches the provisions of the Companies Act so as to confer concurrent jurisdiction on it so that as a judicial authority it can refer the dispute to arbitration.

In the case of *Escorts Finance Ltd v. G.R. Solvents and Allied Industries Ltd. & Ors.,*[26] the CLB referred the dispute, that arose out of sponsorship agreement, to arbitration holding that allegations such as failure to amend articles of association, failure to appoint nominee of the petitioners on the board of the company and the siphoning of funds, etc. directly arose from the sponsorship agreement and as such it has to be referred to arbitration and petitioners have failed to make allegations as to substantial acts or oppression or mismanagement. In other words, the CLB was of the opinion that allegations contained in the petition were not relating to sections 397 and 398 of the Companies Act.

The Delhi High Court in *Gurnir Singh's* case[27] referred the parties to arbitration even though it squarely fell under sections 397 and 398 of the Companies Act whereas the CLB referred the parties to arbitration in *Navin Kedia's* case without coming to a finding whether at all the allegations, *prima facie,* fell under sections 397 and 398 of the Companies Act so that it has jurisdiction to entertain the petition and in *Escorts's* case even though there were allegations of oppression and mismanagement

26. (1999) 96 Comp Cas 323.
27. (1987) 62 Comp Cas 197.

as it found it does not fell under sections 397 and 398 of the Companies Act. However, in both the cases as a judicial authority it exercised its powers to refer the dispute to arbitration. In the case of *Kare Pvt Ltd.*[28] the Delhi High Court has held that:

> "The shareholders' right to file a petition under sections 397 and 398 of the Companies Act, 1956 is a statutory right which, by section 9, cannot be ousted by a provision in the articles of association of the company. Any article providing that a difference between the company and its directors or between the directors themselves or between any members of the company or between the company and any person shall be referred to arbitration cannot debar the jurisdiction of the court in the matter of a petition under sections 397 and 398."

The Bombay High Court in the case of *Manavendra Chitnis & Anr. v. Leela Chitnis Studios P Ltd. & Ors.,*[29] had held as under:

> "Merely because there is an arbitration clause or an arbitration proceeding, or for that matter an award, the court's jurisdiction under sections 397 and 398 of the Companies Act,1956 cannot stand fettered. On the other hand, the matters which can form the subject matter of a petition under sections 397 and 398 cannot be the subject matter of arbitration, for an arbitrator can have no powers such as are conferred on the court by section 402."

In the case of *Das Lagerwey Wind Turbines Ltd. v. Cynosure Investments Pvt. Ltd.,*[30] it has been held that the allegations made in the petition were independent of the subscription agreement and as such the dispute cannot be referred to arbitration under the subscription agreement.

With the help of above mentioned cases discussed it can be said that CLB has not evolved specific criteria in referring or rejecting the dispute to the arbitrator, which is primarily in the domain of CLB to adjudicate upon and there are many cases in which CLB refused to refer the parties to arbitration on merely technical grounds.

---

28. (1977) 47 Comp Cas 276.
29. (1985) 58 Comp Cas 113.
30. (2004) 119 Comp Cas 411.

## UNCERTAINTY AS TO FORUM FOR ARBITRATION

Where two agreements for the same transaction, namely, joint venture agreement and share purchase agreement, provide for different arbitral tribunals, then, in the light of uncertainty regarding the contractual forum to which the parties are to be referred, the application is generally entertained by CLB and not referred for arbitration.[31] Dispute cannot be referred to arbitration as said in *Sudershan Chopra v. CLB*[32] on the mentioned reasoning.

The rationale of the CLB is legally sound because the Companies Act, 1956 is a special Act compared with the Arbitration and Conciliation Act, 1996 where the latter Act is general as far as arbitration is concerned and the former is special as far as violations of its provisions are concerned. Since the CLB is a special Tribunal specifically established to deal with and adjudicate on issues resulting in violations of the Act, the provisions of arbitration would have no application to determine such issues.

Further, when the acts of the oppressor infringe the rights of the oppressed, such infringement or violations cannot be adjudicated through the process of arbitration because violation of statutory rights is not the subject of arbitration agreement.

To the extent possible, difference between the shareholding groups in any Company is to be addressed and every effort is to be made to ensure that the Company functions smoothly rather resorting to winding-up. It is challenging for the CLB to deal with the applications under Section 8 of the Arbitration and Conciliation Act, especially keeping in mind simultaneously the complications involved in matters under Section 397/398, public policy, national interest, international trade policy, relations with foreign states and the principle of fair and equitable justice.

The decision of the Madras High Court in *Oomor Sait, H.G. v. Asiam Sait,*[33] wherein it was held that "Civil Court can refuse to refer matter to arbitration if complicated question of fact or law is involved or where allegation of fraud is made....Allegations regarding clandestine operation of business under some other name, issue of bogus bills, manipulation of accounts, carrying on similar business without consent of other partner are serious

31. *Bhatia International v. Bulk Trading* (2002) 2 SCR 411.
32. (2004) 64 CLA 214 (P&H)].
33. 2001 (3) CTC 269.

allegations of fraud, misrepresentations, etc., and therefore, application for reference to Arbitrator is liable to be rejected."

It is undoubtedly true that the Arbitration Act can help in speedy justice and decrease the load of litigation on Indian Judiciary considerably. But the biggest drawback of the Arbitration Act is that it is silent about the necessary qualifications that a person must possess to be appointed as an arbitrator. On the contrary, Section 402 of the Companies Act, 1956 gives specific power to the specialised CLB to dispose disputes arising under section 397/398. Such loopholes can lead to gross injustice to the parties in serious matters like oppression and mismanagement in a company. The existing statutory control that we see over disputes in key sectors like power & telecom is a clear indicator that the Indian legislature is not yet ready to do away the governmental/court's interference to control key sectors of growth in India.

The Supreme Court in *P. Anand Gajapathi Raju v. P.V.G. Raju,*[34] observed that the language of section 8 of Arbitration and Conciliation Act, 1996 is pre-emptory in nature. Therefore, in cases where there is an arbitration clause in the agreement, it is obligatory for the court to refer the parties to arbitration in terms of their arbitration agreement and nothing remains to be decided in the original action after such an application is made except to refer the dispute to an arbitrator.

The Supreme Court in the matter of *Sukanya Holdings (P) Limited v. Jayesh H. Pandya*[35] held that the language used in section 8 is in a matter which is the subject-matter of an arbitration agreement. Court is required to refer the parties to arbitration. Therefore, the suit should be in respect of a matter which the parties have agreed and which comes within the ambit of arbitration agreement. Where, however, a suit commences—"as to matter" which lies outside the arbitration agreement and is also between some of the parties who are not parties to an arbitration agreement, there is no question of application of section 8. The words 'a matter' indicate entire subject-matter of the suit should be subjection to arbitration.

In *Afcons Infrastructure Limited v. Cherian Varkey Construction Company (P) Limited, Kochi,*[36] the Supreme Court ruled that power

34. 2000 (4) SCC 539.
35. AIR 2003 SC 2252.
36. AIR 2007 (NOC) 233 (Ker.).

of court to refer parties for arbitration would and must necessarily include the power and jurisdiction to appoint arbitrator also.

It is an important rule of interpretation that a special law prevails over the general law. In case of oppression and mismanagement, the Companies Act, 1956 is a special enactment, which deals with corporate management and shareholders' rights, whereas Arbitration and Conciliation Act, 1996 is the general enactment dealing with resolution of commercial disputes.

The Arbitration and Conciliation Act does not prescribe qualifications and experience of arbitrators, whereas the Companies Act, prescribes the qualification, experience and powers of the members of CLB to adjudicate the disputes in a judicial manner. Provisions of Section 10E of the Companies Act, provides powers and functions to the CLB and states that every bench of the CLB to be considered a civil court and its proceeding a judicial proceeding.

Under the Arbitration and Conciliation Act, 1996, relief is provided to the claimant, whereas under sections 397 and 398 of the Companies Act, relief is provided to the company.

Recently in *Telenor Asia (P) Limited and Ors. v. Unitech Wireless (Tamil Nadu) (P) Limited and Ors.*,[37] the CLB ruled that where the share subscription agreement and shareholders' agreements are vitiated by fraud are complicated question of law and fact, and the same ought not to be tried by the CLB in a summary jurisdiction under section 397/398, but left to be adjudicated by the arbitral tribunal. A reference to arbitral tribunal in case of international arbitration between the parties is now mandatory in law by virtue of section 45 of Arbitration and Conciliation Act, if the ingredients of the section are present, that is, the contract provides for it, one of the parties makes the requisite application and the judicial form does not find that the arbitration agreement is null and void, inoperative or incapable of being performed.

The dispute pertained to international arbitration in which the Wireless (Tamil Nadu) (P) Limited, Applicants were Indian Strategic Partners (ISP) in the joint venture agreement with Telenor Asia (P) Limited of Singapore. The CLB distinguished

37. (2012) 107 CLA 547 (CLB).

the case law cited before it on facts and explained why reference to arbitration was denied in those cases. It also rejected other arguments against allowing application for reference to arbitration explaining the legal position under section 45 of the Arbitration and Conciliation Act, which has made it mandatory to make reference to arbitration in case of international reference when contract provides for it. The CLB disposed of the application by referring the parties to arbitration in accordance with the rules of the Singapore International Arbitration Centre as per the agreement.

In *GC Holdings (P) Limited v. Ramasamy Athappan,*[38] the parties first filed their contentions before the CLB, which dealt with and resolved the issues. The CLB subsequently modified its own earlier order, issuing various directions. The parties then approached the High Court and the Single judge allowed the injunction application restraining the appellants from referring the disputes to arbitrator under section 45 of the Arbitration and Conciliation Act.

The Division Bench of the High Court of Madras ruled that where on the facts and circumstances of the case and in view of the pitched battle of litigation between the parties the Single Judge has rightly held that there was a waiver by estoppels and that the arbitration clause in the joint venture agreement had become inoperative, there will be no ground for interference with the order of the Single Judge allowing injunction application restraining the appellant from proceeding with the arbitration under section 45 of the Arbitration and Conciliation Act. When the CLB has already resolved the same issues in the company petition, the appellants cannot contend that they are needed to be raised in the arbitration.

## LEGALITY V. FAIRNESS OR UNFAIRNESS

It is now settled beyond doubt that legality or illegality of an act has nothing to do with fairness or unfairness of the act and, therefore, what the CLB has to examine the facts in order to ascertain whether the act has resulted into oppressive of the minority by the use of legal right that taints the act as an abuse of the right or the power. For example, a resolution validly passed

38. (2012) 109 CLA 238 (Mad).

can nevertheless amount to oppression.[39] In this regard, the following observations of Bhagwati, J. in *Sheth Mohanlal Ganpatram v. Sayaji Jubilee Cotton and Jute Mills Co.*[40] are pertinent: He said:

> "It may be that a resolution may be passed by the Board of Directors which is perfectly legal in the sense that it does not contravene any provision of law, and yet it may be oppressive to the minority shareholders or prejudicial to the interests of the company. Such a resolution can certainly be struck down by the court under section 397 or 398. Equally a converse case can happen. A resolution may be passed by the Board of Directors which may in the passing contravene a provision of law, but it may be very much in "...strictly the allotment of shares to the second respondent is not illegal." Yet, in a petition under section 397, it is not the legality or illegality of an action (that) has to be examined. But, it is the probity and fairness towards the petitioners, in the matter of their proprietary rights as shareholders, with which the said decision is taken must be necessarily considered".

In *Chander Mohan Jain v. CRM Digital Synergies P Ltd.*,[41] Hon'ble Chairman of the CLB observed:

> "Every shareholder has the right to enforce the rights arising out of the articles and such rights have to be considered to be proprietary rights and the denial could be an act of oppression. Whether equitable consideration can be superimposed on proprietary rights would depend on the facts of a case."

To substantiate the argument of the existence of partnership sometimes the principles of 'legitimate expectation' is pressed into service and it is contended that the petitioner has had legitimate expectation that the company would be run as partnership and he/she had equitable rights arising out of it. No doubt, the principle legitimate expectation has been considered to be relevant in certain circumstances in a private company, but

39. [Re A Company (No. 005685 of 1988) [1989] BCLC 427 (Ch D)].
40. (1964) 34 Comp Cas 777 (Guj).
41. (2008) 3 Comp LJ 125.

it is not easy to win over the court by persuading it to accept and apply this principle.

## POWERS OF ARBITRATOR TO GRANT RELIEF

The sole and exclusive jurisdiction to decide matters covered under section 397/398 as Calcutta High Court in *Pradip Kumar Sarkar v. Laxmi Tea Co. Ltd.*,[42] has held that these sections do not oust the jurisdiction of the civil court to entertain suits on the same subject-matter. If it is so, then an arbitrator can also entertain such complaints as long as they arise out of or in connection with the arbitration agreement and grant appropriate relief.

In *Bhadresh Kantilal Shah v. AIA Magotteaux Limited*[43] the specific issue was raised that an arbitrator is incapable of granting the relief as provided for section 402 of the Companies Act. The court said:

> "No doubt, Company Law Board has vast powers under Section 402 of the Act, yet, granting of relief depends on facts of a particular case and if for granting the relief, determination of *bona fide* disputes is required and the same is covered by an arbitration agreement, then, it is for the arbitrator to decide these issues and not the Company Law Board".

In *Muddada Chayanna v. Karna Narayan*,[44] the Hon'ble Court held that:

> "Where the special tribunal, out of the ordinary course is appointed by an Act to determine questions as to rights which are the creation of that Act, then, except so far as is otherwise expressly provided or necessarily implied, that tribunal's jurisdiction to determine those questions is exclusive."

An analogy can also be drawn from numerous cases wherein different courts have held that wherever some special court or tribunal is provided then the matters should be referred to that particular judicial only.

42. (1990) 67 Comp Cas 491 (Cal).
43. (2002) 2 Comp LJ 323 (CLB).
44. AIR 1979 SC 1320.

In *Shnakar Lal Laxminarayan Rathi v. Udhey Singh Dinkar Rao Rajurkar,*[45] it was said that the jurisdiction of the Rent Controller under the Rent Control Order cannot be taken away by an arbitration agreement. In *Osprey Undertaking Agencies Limited v. ONGC,*[46] it has held that matters covered in an admiralty suit cannot be made subject matter of arbitration agreement. In *Gopi Rai v. Baij Nath Rai,*[47] it has been held that probate proceedings cannot be referred to arbitration and this has been reiterated by the Supreme Court in *Chiranjilal Shrilal Goenka Jasjit Singh*[48] that probate court alone has exclusive jurisdiction in probate matter and the same cannot be referred to arbitration.

Moreover, in *Surinder Kumar Dhawan v. R. Vir,*[49] it was held that the jurisdiction of the court under sections 397 and 398 of the Companies Act, 1956, is concerned with the management of the company in the special and is a statutory jurisdiction which cannot be ousted by arbitration clause.

Further, in *O.P. Gupta v. Shiv General Finance (P) Ltd. and others,*[50] it was categorically stated that the provisions of sections 397/398 and 434 give exclusive jurisdiction to the court and the matters dealt with thereby cannot be referred to arbitration. No arbitrator can possibly give relief to the petitioner under sections 397 and 398 or pass any order under section 402 or section 403. The parties have freedom to contract. They can include an arbitration clause in the contract to settle all differences and disputes arising between the parties out of or relating to their contract by arbitration in accordance with the law and procedure of their choice. However, the CLB alone is vested with statutory powers to deal with the cases of oppression and mismanagement.

## PROPOSED NEW PROVISION UNDER COMPANY BILL, 2012

The Company Bill, 2012 has clubbed the provision of oppression and mis-management under one section of the New

45. AIR 1976 Bom 237.
46. AIR 1976 Bom 137.
47. AIR 1930 All 840.
48. JT (1993) 2 SC 341.
49. (1974) 1 Comp LJ 168 (Del.).
50. (1975) 2 Comp LJ 217 (Del.).

Company Bill to accommodate various changes also brought in the English Company Law by the recommendation of Jenkinson's Committee Report. In India also it is mandatory for incorporating various changes in the existing Company Law to deal with the protection of minority shareholders. The provisions of class action suit will further enrich the proposed Bill to be more investor-friendly particularly for the minority shareholders. The Ministry of Company Affairs with the suggestion for incorporating the words, or in a manner prejudicial to the interest of the company for forming a ground for making an application to the Tribunal for relief, etc. in Clause 212(1)(a), the Committee expect that appropriate modification to this effect is made in the clause.[51] Further, one or more member or one or more creditor may file an application before the Tribunal on behalf of the members and creditors if they are of the opinion that the management or control of the affairs of company are being conducted in a manner prejudicial to the interests of the company or its members or creditors and to restrain the company from oppression and mismanagement.[52]

## CONCLUSION

In the light of the above discussion, by way of conclusion, it can be suggested that the Company Law Board cannot refer the dispute involving oppression and mismanagement under sections 397 and 398 of the Companies Act to an arbitrator for adjudication. The disputing parties themselves, who satisfy the eligibility criteria under section 399, also cannot settle the dispute involving issues of oppression and mismanagement under sections 397 and 398 of the Companies Act through arbitration. However, it appears that a disputing party who does not satisfy the eligibility criteria under section 399, can settle the dispute involving issues of oppression and mismanagement under sections 397 and 398 of the Companies Act by filing a suit before an ordinary civil court of appropriate jurisdiction. Even in such circumstances the dispute cannot be settled too by an arbitrator because he cannot provide the relief as specified under section 402 of the Companies Act. Thus, the issue of arbitration of a dispute relating to oppression and mismanagement seems

51. Standing Committee Report on Company Bill, 2009.
52. Section 216 of the Company Bill, 2012.

unfavourable to the arbitrator and favourable to the CLB or a civil court.

However, another situation also emerges out of the examination of the above mentioned provisions. It is clearly indicated that CLB is the appropriate forum to resolve disputes relating to oppression and mismanagement. However, they nowhere specify that arbitration is barred in such matters. Arbitration is also permitted (if we read Section 402 of the Companies Act along with Sections 8 and 45 of the Arbitration Act). Hence, we can safely conclude that arbitration is not barred in cases of oppression and mismanagement. However, a cautious study of Section 8 of the Arbitration Act seems to restrict litigation. In fact, it bars judiciary from interfering in the matters which are subject matter of arbitration. As a result, a sense of uncertainty continues in disputes relating to oppression and mismanagement.

CHAPTER 14

# Restructuring Corporate Governance in Fraudsters' Regime

*Sukanya Acharya*

## INTRODUCTION

The recent past decade has remarkably unfolded many sensationalized corporate chicanery and bamboozlements in the public domain initiating with the stunning collapse of Enron in the U.S. in the year 2001 and followed by the India's Enron, the Satyam Fraud fiasco in the year 2009 which had created ripples of deliberations among the corporate honchos and the big enchiladas in the corporate world, the corporate supervisors and regulators and the multitudinous domestic and foreign investors and stakeholders and the myriad population. Frustrations and infuriation abounded the public at large who witnessed the fall of the major corporations that were hell-bent on ruining the economic structure of the country. A confluence of debacles compelled the public eye to focus on the emerging phenomenon of corporate governance. The widely publicized scandals around the world like the Enron, WorldCom, Adelphia, Tyco, the Harshad Mehta Scam, the UTI Scam, the Satyam fiasco and the very recent 2G Spectrum Allocation Scam created an atmosphere of doubt and distrust among the investing entities. The confidences of the investors botched in the ability to make informed decisions along with millions of shareholders who were left impoverished. The vexed and apprehensive community grew anxious about the prospects of the corporate successes and failures, rising unemployment and the severe decline of their savings invested in the corporate stocks. Questions were raised as to whether the transgressions and misdemeanors were confined to the ranks of a few corporate renegades or the corporate indiscretion was intentional and systematic. All thoughts therefore converged into a single direction in terms of an assortment of recommendations from diverse committees, regulatory bodies, the media and the government and public opinions which voiced from all round the globe culminating into the process of restructuring the corporate governance framework in the fraudsters' regime.

In the prevailing quandary, corporate scandals, frauds and bamboozlements are not a new contrivance in the corporate world. Conventional wisdom explains a sudden concentration of corporate financial scandals as the consequence of a stock market bubble. When the bubble burst, scandals follow, and, eventually, new regulation. Historically, this has been true at least since the South Seas Bubble.[1] The first documented failure of governance in this world was the South Sea Bubble in the 1700s which led to some qualitative improvement in the corporate standards of business practices and laws in England. Similarly, much of the securities laws in USA were put in place after the capital market collapse in 1929. It is evident that the major business lapses and failures led to the metamorphosis of the corporate governance mechanism which process is continuing incessantly in the present economic scenario. The period from the end of the Second World War till the mid-1970s was a comparatively stable and peaceful period. The ostensible pressure for reforms in corporate governance has heightened in the last two decades. This change and the constant adaption to it have imparted a flexible characteristic making the corporate system resilient.[2] The upheaval witnessed since the 1980s in the reformation of the corporate governance system owing to the major corporate downfall and decadence which invariably involved swindles and debacles has however led to some changes in the corporate functioning and restraint in the fraudulent activities in the

1. A Theory of Corporate Scandals: Why the U.S. and Europe differ by John C. Coffee, 2005, The Center for Law and Economics, New York, available at http://www.law.columbia.edu/center_program/law_economics, last visited on 20-04-11.
2. A.K. Majumdar, Company Law and Practice, Taxman Publications, 13th edition, 2007, p. 542.

corporations which led to increased awareness of the motif of corporate governance and its importance in the corporatized world.

In the past few years, public attention has been directed to the continuing revelations by major corporations of accounting misreporting and frauds, mismanagement, bankruptcy and excessive executives' compensation. Most of these cases have been revealed in United States, whose capital markets, corporate governance rules and accounting systems have always been considered as an efficiency and effectiveness example. The wave of scandals began with the demise of Enron and Arthur Andersen. Later, the list of corporate irregularities and failures has grown every day: WorldCom, Kmart, Tyco, Global Crossing, Adelphia and many others. Some of these companies such as Enron, WorldCom and Tyco have destroyed billions and billions of dollars in shareholder value while moving toward bankruptcy. The number and the importance of American corporate scandals have raised questions about the quality of corporate governance in the United States. In fact, even if some of these scandals can be considered as a result of the market bubble burst in 2000, the broadness of corporate misconduct and misreporting also suggests a failure of the American corporate governance system. Furthermore, many scandals have also characterised the European scenario, showing that probably every corporate governance system in modern economies is far from preventing the fraud risk and the damages of misleading financial information. A common aspect characterising the main scandals is the relevance of corporate reporting failure, as shown by the willingness of corporate managers to inflate financial results, either by overstating revenues or by understating costs, or to divert company funds to private uses. Fraudulent "earning management" or "misreporting" are indeed a leit-motif of recent corporate scandals. Investors' confidence in the quality of corporate financial reporting has been seriously damaged. The ever-increasing process of overstated earnings, inflated asset values and understated liabilities, suggests the possible existence of deficiencies in the accounting standards and in corporate governance rules. Both issues play a primary role in financial information by public companies. Accounting frauds and financial shenanigans are an increasing phenomenon in the current competitive scenario, even if nature and consequences of frauds are far from being completely understood.[3]

The global financial crisis has led to an intense debate on the adequacy of corporate governance regulations and practices the world over. In developed markets such as US and UK, the tax payers' money has been used to bail out tainted corporations that were on the verge of extinction. In India, we faced a corporate governance challenge of a different nature in the aftermath of the Satyam episode—that of promoter-induced frauds. The question that has since kept cropping up is whether there are more skeletons in the closet. In the context of debating corporate governance failures and corporate frauds, a lot of questions have been raised about the effectiveness of independent directors and auditors. Regulators, particularly in the UK and US have responded to public pressure and pressure from shareholder activists by strengthening regulations. Some of these regulations have cast tremendous duties and responsibilities on the non-executive directors. The UK has even gone to the extent of prescribing a new governance code for leading audit firms. But it is also important to look at the role of promoters or executives in ensuring good governance and consider how the lines should be drawn in terms of the responsibilities of the board and that of management. *Corporate governance is an extension of the overall governance eco-system and hence cannot be viewed in isolation.* It is important to therefore look at the entire value chain comprising regulators, shareholders, employees, rating agencies and consumers and introspects where the improvement levers lie.[4]

The current article zooms into the topical cases of corporate swindles which eventually compelled the government as well as the securities market regulatory authorities of our country to plunge into action so as to ensure corrective measures in the form of best corporate governance norms for the corporate entities thereby provide bulwark and assurance to the large swarm of

---

3. The Relation between Accounting Frauds and Corporate Governance Systems: An Analysis of Recent Scandals by Riccardo Tiscini, Francesca di Donato, June 2006, available at http://papers.ssrn.com/sol3/papers.cfm?abstract_id=1086624, last visited on 20-04-11.

4. Enhancing Transparency and Accountability in Indian Corporate: A Report by KPMG, 2010, available at https://www.in.kpmg.com/Secure Data/aci/Files/Enhancing_Transparency.pdf, last visited on 20-04-2011.

investors, domestic and foreign which bring in capital flows into the securities market. It becomes imperative to investigate into the nature of the fraud, what factors can motivate and provide incentives to it, what factors influence the probability of fraud detection and what corporate governance mechanisms can be effective in discovering corporate fraudulent activities. The present discourse would highlight the recent infamous scandals and frauds in the corporate entities by attempting to define the concept of corporate fraud and signifying the elements that constitutes such a crime. The discourse concentrates on the regulatory and legal framework in the Indian context drawing upon the experiences of the United States and the United Kingdom which seeks to prevent the recurrence of fraud and hoax in the corporate bodies which enhances the corporate governance structure in the corporate entities. The disquisition analyses the adequacy and sufficiency of the recommendations of the various committees and the pensile Companies Bill, 2009 providing a bulwark to the interests of the large mass of investors and imposing the governance paradigm upon the executives of the company while discharging the corporate calling.

## CORPORATE FRAUD

The state-of-the-art of the Indian corporatized society in the past decade had revealed a legion of corporate swindles, some of them being unmasked and exposed while some others left cloaked and clouded. Sonorously, the activities of the multiple corporations leave an imprint on the lives of the multitudinous population as well as on the economy of the country. The commission of corporate frauds and embezzlements for a remarkable long time remained the trendsetting mien of large corporations who dodged the criminal liability from the clutches of law. The corporations cannot elude the criminal liability after having committed serious frauds and bamboozlements. Criminal liability refers to the culpability of the companies who have to face the trial for gross violations of the criminal law. The obvious reason besides others remained the inadequacies and leniencies facing the criminal laws and corporate laws of our country. The corporations ducked out the criminal liability owing to the reasons that firstly, the corporation being a separate legal entity cannot have the *mens rea* or the guilty mind to commit an offence and secondly, corporations cannot be imprisoned; the only other remedy left is to set a fine which converts the criminal aspect of the crime into a civil wrong.

**Nature of Corporate Fraud**

The financial felony and crimes of the corporations are once again topical. Since the collapse of the technology bubble in 2000 and the cataclysm of Satyam in 2009, the subsequent wave of bankruptcies and the allied exposure of systematic fraud in what were formerly deemed reputable corporations, the world's electronic and print media have been buzzing with talk. Documentaries, articles, video clips and blogs debate the causes and remedies of corporate fraud and criticise either the paucity of the enforcement or the over reaction of the government. Pundits lament the decline of business ethics while those accredited in law, criminology, accounting and business management establish think tanks, run ethics workshops and offer executive courses to businesses seeking to promote particular corporate social responsibility. Profiles on fallen corporate moguls like Kenneth Lay and Jeff Fastow of Enron, Bernie Ebbers of WorldCom, Conrad Black and David Radler of Hollinger Incorporated and Ramalinga Raju of Satyam in India abound. Legal experts and politicians, government and non-governmental standard setting bodies and professions like accountants, lawyers, investment brokers, etc. have sprung into action. In 2001-02, the United States which is still the world's dominant economic players, despite the growing competition from China and India, passed a number of laws to prevent, deter and punish corporate frauds. The most notable was Sarbanes Oxley Act, 2002, an ambitious bi-partisan statute covering a wide range of corporate fraud. And when the United States takes action to protect its stock exchanges all the other countries and companies wishing to trade or sell products in its markets are compelled to listen to it and accord compliance to it.[5]

Financial crime has been referred to as a ***White Collar Crime,*** a term which was first coined in the year 1939 by the criminologist and sociologist, Professor **Edwin H. Sutherland**

5. John Minkes and Leonardo Minkes, Corporate and White Collar Crime, 1st published 2008, Sage Publications India Pvt. Ltd., New Delhi, at p. 39.

which has become synonymous with the full range of frauds committed by companies and governments corporations as well.[6] The term 'white collar crimes' has been defined as being one *"committed by a person of respectability and high social status in the course of his occupation."* Sutherland also included crimes committed by corporations and other legal entities within his definition. Sutherland's study of white collar crime was prompted by the view that criminology had incorrectly focused on social and economic determinants of crime, such as family background and level of wealth. Sutherland was of a view that, crime is committed at every level of society and by persons of widely divergent socio-economic backgrounds. In particular, according to Sutherland, crime is often committed by persons operating through large and powerful organizations. White collar crime, as Sutherland concluded, has a greatly underestimated impact upon our society. However, it was not only Sutherland, but many others who preferred to define white collar crimes on the status basis. **Hartung** defines a white-collar offense as a violation of law regulating business, which is committed for a firm by the firm or its agents in the conduct of its business." **Cressey** seems implicitly to be using a wider concept in accordance with Sutherland's explicit definition—a concept broad enough to include also embezzlement. In 1970, U.S. Department of Justice official **Herbert Edlehertz** described white collar crime as "an illegal act or series of illegal acts committed by non-physical means and by concealment or guile, to obtain money or property, or to obtain business advantage."[7]

As characterized by scholars of criminal behaviour, corporate fraud is a type of white collar crime. **Edwin Sutherland** defined the term "white collar crime" in order to help explain crime commonly found among individuals associated with business or of an upper socio-economic class. Sutherland defined "white collar crime" as a "crime committed by a person of respectability and high social status in the course of his occupation." Following Sutherland's observations, sociologists have attempted to define corporate crime more clearly. According to sociologist **David Friedrichs** (1996), corporate crimes are "illegal and harmful acts

6. Nicholas Ryder, Financial Crime in the 21st Century, Law and Policy, 2011, Edward Elgar Publishing Ltd., UK, at p. 2.
7. White Collar Crime in India by Shelley, G.H., February 1st 2011, available at www.jurisonline.com, last visited on 22-04-2011.

committed by officers and employees of corporations to promote corporate and personal interests." Similarly, sociologist **David Simon** (2001) refers to corporate crime as "acts of economic domination." According to most definitions, corporate crimes victimize the general public, consumers, a corporation's employees, or a corporation's competitors. Offenses often include acts like corporate stealing, corruption, or fraud and have broad domestic or, in some cases, international implications.[8] Many argue that the term 'white-collar crime' insufficiently describes the wide range of offences committed by the 'powerful', be they wealthy individuals or corporations. Most accept a distinction between: 'classic' white-collar crime, which involves personal gain, at the expense of employers, 'the government', or clients (which can also be described as occupational crime) and offences which involve increased profits or the survival of the organization—often known as organizational or corporate crime. Others prefer to use the broader term **economic crime** (used in many European, particularly Scandinavian countries, where the term 'white-collar crime' is rarely used) wherein economic crime defined as 'crimes of profit which take place within the framework of commercial activity'.[9]

Many types of corporate crimes may not have violent consequences, but the price paid by its victims is catastrophic nevertheless. Corporate crimes generally impact a greater number of people. Fraud and anti-trust violations can impact on an entire organization, the economy, or possibly society as a whole. In 1991, corporate crime cost the American consumer $260.06 billion, six thousand times less than the amount taken in all bank robberies that same year and forty times more than the amount taken in all street crimes. Employees and consumers are forced to foot the costs of these activities through job loss and inflation. These statistics illustrate the seriousness of corporate crime and urgency with which it should be studied and

8. Controlling Corporate Crimes: An Analysis of Deterrence versus Compliance by Katherine Coleman, 1 Northwestern Interdisciplinary Law Review 185 (2008), available at www.cics.northwestern.edu/documents/nilr/v1n1Coleman, last visited on 22-04-2011.
9. Victims of White Collar and Corporate Crimes by Hazel Croall, available at http://www.uk.sagepub.com/stout/croall_white_collar%20-%20vics_crim_soc.pdf, last visited on 22-04-2011.

prevented.[10] Considering what Sutherland had put forward as the white collar crime, here we are to examine what are the contributing factors responsible for the development of white collar crime in the present society. It must be borne in mind that the nature of white collar crime, as propounded by Sutherland, is crimes committed by the elite class people during the pleasure of their office of profession. So, the nature of white collar crimes has evolved in the urban areas with the concentration of the industry and commercial activities in the urban areas. The changing socio-economic scenario of the society coupled with the increase of wealth and prosperity has furnished opportunities for such crimes. But still, one pertinent question that still remains is that where lies the necessity or compulsion behind commission of these white collar crimes. Here the persons indulging in these crimes are neither unemployed nor the oppressed or humiliated to such an extent that they would resort to such crimes that attack the base of the moral structure of the society. On the contrary, they are well-off, suave and well-educated masses of the society who are fortunate enough to live a well comfortable life in the society. Therefore, in trying to find out a tentative answer to this question it is often said that greed plays the dominant role behind the commission of these crimes. It has its root in competitive business community which tries to oust their rival competitors in order to earn maximum profits. The transnational encouragement of the hyper-mobility of capital, the never ending look for cheap foreign labour, the immobility of domestic labour, leads to the misuse and abuse of power by the corporate state. Globalization has lead to oligopolization and expansionism rather than genuine economic. However, the motives attributed behind the commission of white collar crimes are often not specific. Individuals change institutions and institutions change society. However, individuals acting on their own behalf are incidental to corporate deviance and white collar crimes. But from a general perception it can be said that an urge

10. Controlling Corporate Crimes: An Analysis of Deterrence versus Compliance by Katherine Coleman, 1 Northwestern Interdisciplinary Law Review 185 (2008), available at www.cics.northwestern.edu/documents/nilr/v1n1Coleman, last visited on 22-04-2011.

of making name and having more of a financial soundness are the contributing factors behind causation of white collar crimes.[11]

**Meaning and Elements of Corporate Fraud**

With greed increasingly informing the thought process and the actions of a large number of persons, fraud has a bigger presence in our lives than ever before. Fraud, an intentional deception made for personal gains or to damage another individual, is a significant factor worldwide in today's competitive world, and in entities irrespective of their size. Fraud is a major source of risk which can have disastrous effects on the finances of a company. It can cause irreversible and often irreparable damage to the image and reputation of a company. In recent times, with increase in awareness, companies have started focusing on pro-active risk management strategies. However, a lot remains to be done, especially having regard to the complexity of instruments and the speed of transactions. India has had its share of frauds and their incidence has often significantly impacted investor confidence. In an atmosphere of doubt and disbelief financial statements are often viewed with scepticism. This has also led to erosion of confidence and reduced trust among participants in the financial system. Today, the focus of white collar crimes has moved from the individual to the organization, where individuals alone or in collaboration with others commit acts that are criminal. One of such white collar crimes is the CORPORATE FRAUDS.

According to Oxford dictionary, a fraud is defined as, "the use of false representations to gain unjust advantage and criminal deception." Fraud is defined as: "any dishonesty through which one person intends to gain an advantage over another." It is committed by people exploiting processes with the intention of getting their greedy hands on assets, both tangible and intangible. A corporate fraud occurs when a company or organization deliberately changes or conceals the information in order to make it appear healthy. A company may commit fraud by manipulating accounting records, hiding debt, or failing to inform shareholders of loans and bonuses given to its executives. The falsification of financial information, including false

11. White Collar Crime in India by Shelley, G.H., February 1st 2011, available at www.jurisonline.com, last visited on 22-04-2011.

accounting entries, bogus trades designed to inflate profits or hide losses and false transactions will help the organization to attract funds from the lenders and investors. The motives of committing fraud by a company may be many, but the main motive is making money and creating a false soundness for the company in order to save its image in the market and to misguide the government departments to avoid the heavy tax burdens. In common parlance, the concept of corporate fraud implies the following:

(i) Violation of a person's fiduciary duties to the organization.
(ii) Committed in secret and concealed.
(iii) Committed for a direct or indirect benefit to the perpetrator.
(iv) Costs the organisation and the stakeholders its assets, revenues and other liabilities.[12]

In legal connotation, fraud is generally defined as an intentionally false representation about a material point, which causes a victim to suffer harm. High profile corporate failures in recent years have focussed significant public and regulatory interest on corporate fraud. The penalties for fraudulent financial reporting have significantly increased in response to society's view on this type of behaviour. For example, Bernard Ebbers, the former chairman of WorldCom was jailed for 25 years for orchestrating a $US11 billion financial statement fraud. Corporate fraud is a much more serious problem as it devastates the careers of many honest managers, puts jobs at risk, and undermines people's confidence in business. Corporate frauds can be prevented by secure processes and by ensuring that people with access to them are honest. This is easier said than done, failures will occur, so reactive plans are the safety net.[13] These recent well publicized frauds have affected the work of the external financial statement auditor. In Australia, the Auditing Standard ASA 240 as stated in "The Auditor's Responsibility to Consider Fraud in an Audit of a Financial Report" has increased the external auditor's responsibility in this area. It defines fraud

12. Tracy Coenen, Essentials of Corporate Fraud, 2008, John Wiley & Sons Inc., Hoboken, New Jersey, at p. 6.
13. Michael J. Comer, Investigating Corporate Fraud, 2003, Gower Publishing Ltd., Hants GU11 3HR, UK, at p. 4.

as "...an intentional act by one or more individuals among management, those charged with governance, employees, or third parties, involving the use of deception to obtain an unjust or illegal advantage." ASA 240 continues by stating that there are two types of intentional misstatements relevant to the auditor. First, there are misstatements that result from fraudulent financial reporting and second, there are misstatements that result from misappropriation of assets.[14] In the aftermath of corporate scandals and the passage of the Sarbanes-Oxley Act of 2002 (SOX), the audit committee is vested with greater authority to oversee financial reporting and the appropriation of assets. As a result, the audit committee is responsible for adequate supervision and reporting and for responding to: fraud in a financial statement audit; actual, perceived or potential conflicts of interest; anonymous tips and complaints; and through interaction with general counsel, compliance matters such as those that relate to the Foreign Corrupt Practices Act (FCPA). With different industry definitions and viewpoints, fraud can be a tough issue for audit committee members to grasp for oversight purposes. The Institute of Internal Auditors (IIA), the American Institute of Certified Public Accountants (AICPA) and the Association of Certified Fraud Examiners (ACFE) collaborated in 2008 on landmark guidance that defines fraud as *"fraud is any intentional act or omission designed to deceive others, resulting in the victim suffering a loss and/or the perpetrator achieving a gain"*. Separately, the IIA has defined fraud as: *"any illegal acts characterized by deceit, concealment or violation of trust. These acts are not dependent upon the application of threat of violence or of physical force. Frauds are perpetrated by individuals and organizations to obtain money, property or services; to avoid payment or loss of services; or to secure personal or business advantages"*.[15] Accounting and financial fraud is defined as "deliberate misstatement or omission of amounts or disclosures in financial statements to deceive

14. The Importance of Internal Audit in Fraud Detection by Paul Coram, available at http://aaahq.org/audit/midyear/07midyear/papers/coram_theimportanceofinternalaudit.pdf, last visited on 22-04-2011.
15. Managing Fraud Risk: The Audit Committee Perspective, The Audit Committee Guide Series, available at http://www.grantthornton.com/staticfiles/GTCom/Audit/Assurancepublications/Audit%20committee%20guides/ACH_Guides_Managing_Fraud_Risk_.pdf, last visited on 22-04-2011.

financial statement users, particularly investors and creditors". The concept of accounting fraud can also be expressed like manipulated earnings or accounting irregularities.[16]

In India, the Commission on 'Prevention of Corruption' in its report in 1964 observed, "the advancement of technological and scientific development is contributing to the emergence of mass society with a large rank in file and a small controlling elite, encouraging the growth of monopolies, the rise of a managerial class and intricate institutional mechanisms. Strict adherence to high standard of ethical behaviour is necessary for the even and honest functioning of the new social, political and economic processes. The inability of all sections of society to appreciate this need in full results in the emergence and growth of white collar and economic crimes renders enforcement of the laws, themselves not sufficiently deterrent, more difficult."

The three *elements* that are present in every corporate fraud which have come to be popularly known as the *'**fraud triangle**'* are:

(i) motivation,
(ii) opportunity, and
(iii) rationalization

Under the ***motivation*** component of fraud is the pressure or need that a person feels. It could be a true financial need or other real needs. Greed also plays a dominant factor motivating the person to commit fraud in the organisation. The motivation could also be a *perceived* financial need whereby a person strongly desires material goods but does not have the means to acquire it. Any pressure in one's business life may also conceivably motivate someone to commit corporate fraud. Motive often develops from financial pressure resulting from a fraudster's excessive life style, or from the gap between the financial remuneration earned and the responsibility held by the individual, or pressure to meet financial targets, or the

16. The Relation Between Accounting Frauds And Corporate Governance Systems: An Analysis Of The Recent Scandals, by Riccardo Tiscini, Francesca di Donato, available at http://ssrn.com/abstract=1086624, last visited on 22-04-2011.

superiority complexes of the individual or basic greed.[17]

Under the ***opportunity*** component of fraud, the opportunity to commit the fraud includes the access to assets, people, information and technology that enables the person not only to commit fraud but also to conceal it. Employees are given all sorts of access to assets and records in order to carry out their job and this access is one of the key components of fraud. Opportunity generally occurs through weaknesses in the internal controls and creates an atmosphere where fraudsters believe they are likely to be successful and undetected. Therefore, companies primarily focus their prevention efforts on this aspect of the fraud triangle by enforcing certain types of controls and by implementing effective fraud risk management policies. Trust, however, though important in business often becomes the door opener for fraudsters.[18]

The third and final piece of fraud triangle is ***rationalisation***. It is a process by which an employee determines that the fraudulent behaviour is 'okay' in his mind. For those with deficient moral codes, the process of rationalisation is easy. Rationalization is the fraudster's internal dialogue that provides the self-justification for his actions. The fraudster convinces himself that he is owed this remuneration by the employer. The management of a company has the most control over the opportunity portion of the fraud triangle as it can limit the access to assets and put controls over place that ensure monitoring of system and people. Motivation can be constrained by management as well although not to the degree that opportunity can be limited. The best way to reduce needs is by paying employees fairly in order to reduce perceived financial burdens and by creating performance systems that are reasonable. Rationalisation is probably the most dangerous piece of the fraud triangle because it is one that companies have the least control over. It is nearly impossible for the management to eliminate the rationalisation piece because they cannot control the minds of the employees. Management has no way of knowing what lies an

17. Profile of a Fraudster, Survey 2007, KPMG Holding, the Swiss member firm of KPMG International, available at www.kpmg.co.uk/pubs/ProfileofaFraudsterSurvey, last visited on 22-04-2011.
18. Profile of a Fraudster, Survey 2007, KPMG Holding, the Swiss member firm of KPMG International, available at www.kpmg.co.uk/pubs/ProfileofaFraudsterSurvey, last visited on 22-04-2011.

employee may tell himself in order to justify the fraud element in his mind, so there is virtually no way of counteracting the lies.[19]

The legal position in respect of frauds has three dimensions, viz., ***contractual, tortuous*** and ***criminal*** in the Indian context which is summarised as under:

(i) **Contractual dimension of fraud**: Fraud is defined in section 17 of the Indian Contract Act (unlike UK law, where fraud is not defined and is based on common law practice) for the purpose of a contract and in so far as the operation of the Contract Act is concerned. In such event the contract becomes voidable. The party suffering from the fraud may terminate the contract on his option. He may also like to continue with the contract. Law provides absolute option to the concerned party as a special additional right to neutralize the advantage or gain by the party committing fraud. The court may also compensate him if he suffers from any damage before terminating the contract. But he has a burden of proof to show to the court that he was defrauded by the other party intentionally according to the definitional conditions laid down by the Act, that (a) a party having the knowledge of fact essential to the contract did not disclose the fact which would have altered the decision of the other party; (b) or a material misstatement was made knowing that the statement was false; and (c) that the party intended to obtain a favourable decision from the other party by committing such an act.

(ii) **Tortuous dimension of fraud**: As a civil wrong with in the parameter of right *in rem* discourse, fraud covers any action or abstinence, statutory or otherwise, which may cause damages to other. Everyone has a right not to be defrauded in any situation. So if any fraud is caused on any person in any other situation other than the contractual situation whether it does or does not fall under any specified crime, the person can bring the matter to the notice of the district court for obtaining remedies. Thus, in any market situation, fraud is regarded as 'foul' play in the market game and as such,

19. Tracy Coenen, Essentials of Corporate Fraud, 2008, John Wiley & Sons, Inc., Hoboken, New Jersey, at p. 10.

the regulator may neutralize the impact of the act by (a) penalizing the player by giving him warning for minor foul so that he does not dare it repeat (like showing a green card in a soccer game); (b) suspend him from the game; (c) debar him from playing the game permanently; and (d) impose penal compensation to indemnify the person suffering from fraud.

(iii) **Criminal dimension of fraud**: Fraud as such, is not a criminal offence in India. If any fraud is committed in a bilateral contractual situation or otherwise whether involving personal fund or public fund, also an act of cheating or if such an act involves impersonation, criminal breach of trust or criminal conspiracy, or forgery, or falsification or destruction of documents for wrongful gain, or embezzlement of funds, then and only then, such fraud can be an offence. Big 'scams' that often take place in the secondary capital market by way of 'price rigging' or 'insider trading' are not offences. These are 'foul play' only. In the next chapter these activities are examined so as to see how much gap exists in the substantive criminal law.[20]

## CORPORATE GOVERNANCE

***Corporate Governance***, has never ever, since the *Satyam Episode*, become such a buzzword for all. The year 2009 turned out to be eventful for corporate governance in India. It was ushered in with the admission of a mammoth fraud by the chairman of Satyam Computers, which was in turn preceded by an attempt by the company to engage in certain related party transactions by embarking upon unrelated businesses. The event has often drawn parallels with the fraud at Enron. A confessional letter from Mr. Ramalinga Raju, founder Chairman of Satyam, divulged the accounting scam of the order of US $ 1.6 billion, and shook the whole country with tremors felt throughout the globe. Mr. Ramalinga Raju can be credited as the only corporate fraudster to have admitted his misdemeanours—fudging of accounts, inflated revenues, non-existing profits, and the fraudulent bank deposits and audaciously sustaining it for seven

20. The Report of the Expert Committee on Legal Aspects of Bank Fraud, 2001, available at www.rbi.org.in, last visited on 22-04-2011.

long years. The Mr. Ramalinga Raju's misdeeds, unfortunately had given negative publicity of India Inc so far a positive story. The fraud has undermined the trust in the government, companies, and markets alike. In India, nobody had ever imagined anything to go wrong at Satyam, one of India's best known IT companies, which ironically had received the Golden Peacock Award for Corporate Governance in 2008. This episode has led to debates in India, about inadequacies in the corporate governance norms.[21] The worst aspect of the recent corporate misconduct has been the collective failure of corporate governance mechanisms to detect financial misreporting and to prevent sudden and surprising corporate debacles. In fact, one of the most important issues of corporate governance systems is related to the mechanisms that provide shareholders with information about the corporate business, and the legal rules establishing responsibilities for managers and boards of directors.

In this world of corporate recklessness, it has become imperative for us rivet our attention on the efficacy and adequacy of the corporate governance norms to bridle the unbridled corrupt business personnel. The prevalence of financial scandals, the world over, highlights the increasing importance of corporate governance. The major facets of corporate governance are transparency and disclosure, control and accountability, and the appropriate form of board structure that may prevent such scandals. The relationship between corporate governance reforms and recession is cyclical, where corporate regulations and restructuring follow after corporate collapse during recession. Recent financial collapses like financial meltdown, European Crisis, etc. have highlighted the importance of corporate governance for effective risk management and the role

---

21. See "Post Satyam: Corporate governance structure in India" by Oishwarya Bhattacharya on May 12, 2010, available on http://jurisonline.in/, last visited on 22-04-2011. See also Letter from B. Ramalinga Raju, Chairman, Satyam Computer Services Ltd., to the Board of Directors, Satyam Computer Services Ltd. (Jan. 7, 2009), available at http://www.hindu.com/nic/satyam-chairman-statement.pdf., last visited on 22-04-2011 See also, Heather Timmons and Bettina Wassener, Satyam Chief Admits Huge Fraud, N.Y. TIMES, Jan. 8, 2009, http://www.nytimes.com/2009/01/08/business/worldbusiness/08satyam.html.

it should play in restoring the trust of shareholders. Shareholders have often ignored the excessive leverage for the sake of short-term gains and the regulators also fail to rein in the financial institutions who operate with too little capital, excessive leverage, liquidity risk and poor mortgage lending practices. In this regard, corporate governance needs strengthening for stability and soundness of corporate in specific and financial system in general.

Corporate Governance is looked upon as a distinctive brand and benchmark in the profile of Corporate Excellence. This is evident from the continuous updation of guidelines, rules and regulations by SEBI for ensuring transparency and accountability. In the process, SEBI had constituted a Committee on Corporate Governance under the Chairmanship of Shri Kumar Mangalam Birla. The Committee in its report observed that "the strong Corporate Governance is indispensable to resilient and vibrant capital markets and is an important instrument of investor protection. It is the blood that fills the veins of transparent corporate disclosure and high quality accounting practices. It is the muscle that moves a viable and accessible financial reporting structure."

**Meaning and Significance of Corporate Governance**

Corporate governance is a central and dynamic aspect of business. The term *'governance'* is derived from the Latin word *'gubernare'* meaning 'to steer' which implies that corporate governance involves the function of direction rather than control. The significance of corporate governance for corporate success and controlling corporate fraud cannot be overstated. Recent examples of massive corporate collapse resulting from weak system of corporate governance have highlighted the need to improve and reform corporate governance.[22]

Corporate governance is about commitment to values and voluntary ethical business code of companies. It is a synonym for sound management, transparency and disclosure. To quote the words of J. Wolfensohn, the former President of the World Bank, *"Corporate Governance is about promoting corporate fairness, transparency and accountability."* This includes the process of

22. D. Geeta Rani and R.K. Mishra, Corporate Governance, Theory and Practice, 1st edition, 2008, Excel Books, New Delhi at p. 1.

structuring, operating and controlling the company with specific aims of fulfilling its long-term strategic goals. Corporate governance system seeks to establish a control system and structure in an organisation, guides the decision-making process to ensure high degree of accountability to stakeholders and builds credibility by creating and maintaining an effective channel of information and disclosure. Corporate governance concerns the exercise of power in corporate entities and therefore the **OCED** provides for a functional definition of corporate governance as *"Corporate Governance is the system by which business corporations are directed and controlled"*.[23]

In a narrow sense, corporate governance involves a set of relationships amongst the Company's management, its board of directors, its shareholders, its auditors and other stakeholders which involve various rules and incentives, provide the structure through which the objectives of the company are set, and the means of attaining these objectives as well as monitoring performance are determined. Thus, the key aspects of good corporate governance include transparency of corporate structures and operations; the accountability of managers and the boards to shareholders; and corporate responsibility towards stakeholders. In a broader sense, however, corporate governance implies the extents to which companies are run in an open and honest manner which is important for the overall market confidence, the efficiency of capital allocation, the growth and development of countries' industrial bases, and ultimately the nations' overall wealth and welfare. It is important to note that in both the narrow as well as in the broad definitions, the concepts of disclosure and transparency occupy centre-stage. In the first instance, they create trust at the firm level among the suppliers of finance. In the second instance, they create overall confidence at the aggregate economy level. In both cases, they result in efficient allocation of capital.

The significance of corporate governance for the stability and equity of society is captured in the broader definition of the concept offered by **Adrian Cadbury (2004),** *"Corporate Governance is concerned with holding the balance between economic and social goals and between individual and communal goals. The governance*

23. Dr. Twinkle Prusty, Corporate Governance Compliance in Indian Industry, 2008, Regal Publications, New Delhi at p. 1.

*framework is therefore to encourage the efficient use of resources and equally to require accountability for the stewardship of those resources. The aim is to align the interests of individuals, corporations and society."* Therefore, corporate governance is a key element in improving the economic efficiency of a company which helps ensure that the corporations take into account the interests of the various constituencies and as such operate for the benefit for the society at large.[24] In the context of the challenges faced by the corporate terrene in the era of global convergence, a conscience for robust and efficacious corporate governance norms and standards has been developed which culminated in the form of various important reports and guidelines of the committees and regulatory authorities to ensure transparency, accuracy and reliability in the wake of shifting paradigm in the corporate fraudsters regime.

***International Committees on Corporate Governance***

The overview of some of the codes and regulations designed to improve corporate governance by the main committees in the US and UK has been discussed as follows:

*A. The Cadbury Committee on Corporate Governance*

It was the first committee to be constituted to report on the financial aspects of corporate governance, set-up under the chairmanship of Sir Adrian Cadbury. The stated objectives of the Cadbury Committee was "To help raise the standards of corporate governance and the level of confidence in financial reporting and auditing by setting out clearly what it sees as the respective responsibilities of those involved and what it believes his expected of them. The committee investigated the accountability of the board of directors to shareholders and to society. It submitted its report and associated "Code of Best Practices" in 1992 wherein it spelt out the methods of governance needed to achieve a balance between the essential power of the board of directors and their proper accountability. Its recommendations were not mandatory. The Cadbury code of best practices had 19 recommendations which stand in the nature of guidelines relating to the board of directors, non-executive

24. D. Geeta Rani and R.K. Mishra, Corporate Governance, Theory and Practice, 1st edition, 2008, Excel Books, New Delhi at p. 2.

directors, executive directors and those on reporting and control. The stress in the Cadbury committee report is on the crucial role of the board and the need for it to observe the Code of Best Practices. It is important recommendations include the setting up of an audit committee with independent members.[25]

*B. The Paul Ruthman Committee*

The committee was constituted later to deal with the said controversial point of Cadbury Report. It watered down the proposal on the grounds of practicality. It restricted the reporting requirement to internal financial controls only as against "the effectiveness of the company's system of internal control" as stipulated by the Code of Best Practices contained in the Cadbury Report. The final report submitted by the Committee chaired by Ron Hampel had some important and progressive elements, notably the extension of directors' responsibilities to "all relevant control objectives including business risk assessment and minimizing the risk of fraud".[26]

*C. The Greenbury Committee*

This committee was set-up in January 1995 to identify good practices by the Confederation of British Industry (CBI), in determining directors' remuneration and to prepare a code of such practices for use by public limited companies of United Kingdom. The committee aimed to provide an answer to the general concerns about the accountability by the proper allocation of responsibility for determining directors' remuneration, the proper reporting to shareholders and greater transparency in the process. The committee produced the Greenbury Code of Best Practice which was divided into the four sections: the Remuneration Committee, Disclosures and Approval Policy, Remuneration Policy and Service Contracts and Compensation Policy. The Greenbury Committee recommended that companies

25. The Cadbury Committee Report: A report by the committee on the financial aspects of corporate governance. The committee was chaired by Sir Adrian Cadbury and issued for comment on (27 May 1992). See D. Geeta Rani and R.K. Mishra, Corporate Governance, Theory and Practice, 1st edition, 2008, Excel Books, New Delhi at p. 61.
26. A.C. Fernando, Business Ethics and Corporate Governance: An Indian Perspective, 1st edition, 2009, Dorling Kindersley (India) Pvt. Ltd., New Delhi at p. 14.

in UK should implement the code as set out to the fullest extent practicable, that they should make annual compliance statements, and that investor institutions should use their power to ensure that the best practice is followed wherein the key concern should be to ensure, through the remuneration system, that directors share the interest of shareholders in making the company successful where performance-related remuneration can be highly effective in aligning interest in this way.[27]

*D. The Hampel Committee*

The Hampel committee was set-up in November 1995 to promote high standards on Corporate Governance both to protect investors and preserve and enhance the standing of companies listed on the London Stock Exchange. The committee developed further the Cadbury report which made the following recommendations as: (i) the auditors should report on internal control privately to the directors, (ii) the directors maintain and review all controls, (iii) companies should time to time review their need for internal audit function and control.

It also introduced the combined code that consolidated the recommendation of earlier corporate governance reports, i.e. the Cadbury Committee and Greenbury Committee.[28]

*E. The Turnbull Committee*

The Turnbull Committee was set-up by the Institute of Chartered Accountants in England and Wales (ICAEW) in 1999 to provide guidance to assist companies in implementing the requirements of the Combined Code relating to internal control. The committee provided guidance to assist companies in implementing the requirements of the Combined Code relating to internal control. It recommended that where companies do not have an internal audit function, the board should consider the need for carrying out an internal audit annually.

27. Greenbury Committee Report (1994) Investigating Board Members' Remuneration and Responsibilities, A.C. Fernando, Business Ethics and Corporate Governance: An Indian Perspective, 1st edition, 2009, Dorling Kindersley (India) Pvt. Ltd., New Delhi, at p. 14.
28. The committee report on corporate governance, The Hampel committee report (1998) cited in A.C. Fernando, Business Ethics and Corporate Governance: An Indian Perspective, 1st edition, 2009, Dorling Kindersley (India) Pvt. Ltd., New Delhi at p. 14.

The committee also recommended that board of directors confirm the existence of procedures for evaluation and managing key risks. Corporate Governance is constantly evolving to reflect the current corporate economic and legal environment. To be effective, corporate governance practices need to be tailor to particular needs, objectives and risk management structure of an organization.[29]

*F. The Higgs Report*

Although the Cadbury Report and the Hampel Report stimulated substantial improvements in corporate governance in the listed companies of UK, certain areas have been highlighted for further examination. The Higgs Report, 2003 dealt specifically with the role and effectiveness of non-executive directors, making recommendations for changes to the Combined Code which included a greater proportion of non-executive directors on boards and more apt remuneration for non-executive directors. One important recommendation of the Higgs Report was that one non-executive director should assume chief responsibility as a champion of the shareholders' interest.[30]

*G. The Smith Report*

The UK government in response to the Enron Scandal commissioned the Smith Committee in 2003 with the aim of examining the role of the audit committee in UK corporate governance. The main issue dealt within the report concerned the relationship between the external auditor and the companies they audit, as well as the role and responsibilities of companies' audit committees. The Committee preserved the UK tradition of a principle-based approach attempting not to create a 'once size fits all' set of rules for the listed companies which would be counter-productive as not all companies would be in a position to comply.[31]

---

29. The Combined Code of Best practices in Corporate Governance, The Turnbull Committee Report (1998), A.C. Fernando, Business Ethics and Corporate Governance: An Indian Perspective, 1st edition, 2009, Dorling Kindersley (India) Pvt. Ltd., New Delhi at p. 1.
30. D. Geeta Rani and R.K. Mishra, Corporate Governance, Theory and Practice, 1st edition, 2008, Excel Books, New Delhi at p. 70.
31. *Ibid.*

*H. World Bank on Corporate Governance*

The World Bank, involved in sustainable development was one of the earliest economic organization to study the issue of corporate governance and suggest certain guidelines. The World Bank report on corporate governance recognizes the complexity of the concept and focuses on the principles such as transparency, accountability, fairness and responsibility that are universal in their applications. Corporate governance is concerned with holding the balance between economic and social goals and between individual and communal goals. The governance framework is there to encourage the efficient use of resources and equally to require accountability for the stewardship of those resources. The aim is to align as nearly as possible, the interests of individuals, organizations and society. The foundation of any corporate governance is disclosure. Openness is the basis of public confidence in the corporate system and funds will flow to those centers of economic activity, which inspire trust. This report points the way to establishment of trust and the encouragement of enterprise. It marks an important milestone in the development of corporate governance.[32]

*I. OECD Principles*

Organization for Economic Co-operation and Development (OECD) was one of the earliest non-governmental organizations to work on and spell out principles and practices that should govern corporate in their goal to attain long-term shareholder value. The OECD was the trend setter as the Code of Best practices are associated with Cadbury report. The OECD principles in summary include the following elements:

(i) The rights of shareholders
(ii) Equitable treatment of shareholders
(iii) Role of stakeholders in corporate governance
(iv) Disclosure and Transparency
(v) Responsibilities of the board

The OECD guidelines are somewhat general and both the Anglo-American system and Continental European (or German) system would be quite consistent with it.[33]

32. *Ibid.*, p. 71.
33. Principles of Corporate Governance: A report by OECD Task Force on Corporate Governance (1999). See N. Balasubramanian, Corporate

*J. Sarbanes-Oxley Act, 2002*

The Sarbanes-Oxley Act (SOX) is a sincere attempt to address all the issues associated with corporate failure to achieve quality governance and to restore investor's confidence. The Act was formulated to protect investors by improving the accuracy and reliability of corporate disclosures, made precious to the securities laws and for other purposes. The Act contains a number of provisions that dramatically change the reporting and corporate director's governance obligations of public companies, the directors and officers. The most important aspect of SOX is that it makes it clear that company's senior officers are accountable and responsible for the corporate culture they create and must be faithful to the same rules they set out for other employees. The Act introduced sweeping corporate law changes relating to financial reporting, internal accounting controls, and personal loans from companies to their directors, whistle blowing and destruction of documents as a result of which some companies felt that the burden of compliance was too high in relation to the perceived benefits.[34]

**Indian Scenario on Corporate Governance**

There have been several major corporate governance initiatives launched in India since the mid-1990s. In 1996, the Confederation of Indian Industry (CII) took initiative for first institutional evaluation of corporate governance with an objective to develop a code for corporate governance. The 1999 Kumar Mangalam Birla Committee on Corporate Governance made recommendations delineating the responsibilities and obligations of boards and management for good governance and emphasizes the rights of shareholders. The 2000 Task Force on Corporate Excellence through Governance recommended the phased implementation of essential measures, depending upon the size and the capabilities of the companies and market requirements. The Advisory Group on Corporate Governance:

---

Governance and Stewardship, 2010, Tata McGraw Hill Education Private Limited, New Delhi at p. 602.

34. Sarbanes-Oxley Act of 2002 passed by the Congress of the United States of America on 23rd January, 2002. See D. Geeta Rani and R.K. Mishra, Corporate Governance, Theory and Practice, 1st edition, 2008, Excel Books, New Delhi at p. 72.

Standing Committee on International Financial Standards and Codes, 2001, gave special importance to audit committees and the appointment of truly independent directors to raise the quality of board deliberations and performance. In 2002, the Reserve Bank set-up the Consultative Group of Directors of banks and financial institutions recommended for making the role of the Board of Directors more effective with a view to minimizing risks and over-exposure. The Naresh Chandra Committee on Corporate Audit and Governance Committee in 2002 recommended for changes in the statutory auditor-company relationship, the procedure for appointment of auditors and determination of audit fees, independence of auditing functions. The SEBI Committee on Corporate Governance in 2003 discussed issues related to audit committees, audit reports, independent directors, related parties, risk management, directorships and director compensation, codes of conduct and financial disclosures. Finally, the Naresh Chandra Committee II on Regulation of Private Companies and Partnerships was constituted to suggest a scientific and rational regulatory environment. Clause 49 of the Listing Agreement, which deals with Corporate Governance norms that a listed entity should follow, was first introduced in the financial year 2000-01 based on recommendations of Kumar Mangalam Birla Committee. After these recommendations were in place for about two years, SEBI, in order to evaluate the adequacy of the existing practices and to further improve the existing practices set-up a committee under the Chairmanship of Mr. Narayana Murthy during 2002-03. The Murthy committee, after holding three meetings, had submitted the draft recommendations on corporate governance norms. After deliberations, SEBI accepted the recommendations in August 2003 and asked the Stock Exchanges to revise Clause 49 of the Listing Agreement based on Murthy committee recommendations. This led to widespread protests and representations from the Industry thereby forcing the Murthy committee to meet again to consider the objections. The committee, thereafter, considerably revised the earlier recommendations and the same was put up on SEBI website on 15th December 2003 for public comments. It was only on 29th October 2004 that SEBI finally announced revised Clause 49, which will have to be implemented by the end of financial year 2004-05. These revised recommendations have also considerably diluted the original

Murthy Committee recommendations. Areas where major changes were made include: (i) Independence of Directors to determine independence of a director, (ii) Whistle Blower policy, (iii) Performance evaluation of non-executive directors, (iv) Mandatory training of non-executive directors. Some important changes, which have been incorporated as five new clauses have been added to determine independence of a director. Two-third of the members of Audit committee shall be independent directors as against the present requirement of majority being independent. A new requirement has been provided for obtaining prior approval of shareholders for payment of fees/compensation to non-executive directors. The CEO/CFO Certification is a new requirement and is based on Sarbanes-Oxley Act of USA. The CEO or the Compliance officer can now sign the compliance report. The annual corporate governance report should disclose adoption or non-adoption of non-mandatory requirements. The revised Clause only requires CEO and CFO to certify to the Board the annual financial statements in the prescribed format.

*A. The CII Code*

CII pioneered the concept of corporate governance in India and is an internationally recognised name in this field. Its code, the Desirable Code of Corporate Governance, was the first of its kind and is recognised as one of the best in the world. Corporate India has started recognising the pivotal role that disclosures play in creating corporate value in the increasingly market-oriented environment since the time the Code was widely publicised. The objective of the CII was to develop and promote a code of corporate governance to be adopted and followed by the Indian companies. This initiative by the CII flowed from public concern regarding the protection of the investors' interest, especially the small investor, the promotion of transparency within business and industry; the need to move towards international standards in terms of disclosure of information by the corporate sector and through all of these to develop a high level of public confidence in business and industry.[35]

35. Confederation of Indian Industry (March 1998) Desirable Corporate Governance: A Code (Based on recommendations of the national task force on corporate governance, chaired by Shri Rahul Bajaj). See A.C. Fernando, Corporate Governance: Principles, Policies and Practice,

B. *The Kumar Mangalam Birla Committee Report and Clause 49 of the Listing Agreement*

While the CII code was well-received and some progressive companies adopted it, it was felt that under Indian conditions a statutory rather than a voluntary code would be more purposeful, and meaningful. Consequently, the second major corporate governance initiative in the country was undertaken by SEBI. In early 1999, it set-up a committee under the chairmanship of Sri Kumar Mangalam Birla to promote and raise the standards of good corporate governance. In early 2000, the SEBI board had accepted and ratified key recommendations of this committee, and these were incorporated into Clause 49 of the Listing Agreement of the Stock Exchanges. This report pointed out that the issue of corporate governance involves besides shareholders, all other stakeholders. The committee's recommendations have looked at corporate governance from the point of view of the stakeholders and in particular that of shareholders and investors. The control and reporting functions of boards, the roles of the various committees of the board, the role of management, all assume special significance when viewed from this perspective. At the heart of committee's report is the set of recommendations, which distinguish the responsibilities, and obligations of the boards and the management in instituting the systems for good Corporate Governance. Many of them are mandatory. These recommendations are expected to be enforced on listed companies for initial disclosures. This enables shareholders to know, where the companies are in which they have involved. The committee recognized that India had in place a basic system of corporate governance and that SEBI has already taken a number of initiatives towards raising the existing standards. The committee also recognized that the Confederation of Indian Industries (CII) had published a code entitled "Desirable code of corporate of Governance and was encouraged to note that some of the forward looking companies have already reviewed their annual report through complied with the code. Now to protect investors especially shareholders from any malpractices and injustice the Securities and Exchange Board of India appointed

---

2006, Dorling Kindersley (India) Pvt. Ltd., New Delhi, at p. 123. See also Subhash Chandra Das, Corporate Governance in India, An Evaluation, 2008, Prentice-Hall of India Ltd., Delhi.

committee on corporate governance on May 7, 1999 under chairmanship of Shri Kumar Managalam Birla, Member of SEBI Board to promote standard of Corporate Governance.[36]

*C. Naresh Chandra Committee Report*

The Naresh Chandra Committee was appointed in August 2002 by the Department of Company Affairs (DCA) under the Ministry of Finance and Company Affairs to examine various corporate governance issues. The Committee submitted its report in December 2002. It made recommendations in two key aspects of corporate governance: financial and non-financial disclosures and independent auditing and board oversight of management. The committee submitted its report on various aspects concerning corporate governance such as role, remuneration, and training, etc. of independent directors, audit committee, the auditors and then relationship with the company and how their roles can be regulated as improved. The committee stingily believes that "a good accounting system is a strong indication of the management commitment to governance. Good accounting means that it should ensure optimum disclosure and transparency, should be reliable and credible and should have comparability. According to the committee, the statutory auditor in a company is the "lead actor" in disclosure front and this has been amply recognized in sections 209 to 223 of the Companies Act, 1956.[37]

---

36. Department of Company Affairs (2000), Report of the taskforce on Corporate Excellence through Governance (on the basis of report submitted by a committee chaired by Dr. P.L. Sanjeeva Reddy and by Kumar Mangalam Birla Committee on Corporate Governance, Chartered Secretary (March 2000). See A.C. Fernando, Corporate Governance: Principles, Policies and Practice, 2006, Dorling Kindersley (India) Pvt. Ltd., New Delhi, at p. 123. See also D. Geeta Rani and R.K. Mishra, Corporate Governance, Theory and Practice, 1st edition, 2008, Excel Books, New Delhi. See also Subhash Chandra Das, Corporate Governance in India: An Evaluation, 2008, Prentice-Hall of India Ltd., Delhi.
37. Report on Corporate Governance by committee headed by Shri Naresh Chandra on regulation of private companies and partnership. See A.C. Fernando, Corporate Governance: Principles, Policies and Practice, 2006, Dorling Kindersley (India) Pvt. Ltd., New Delhi, at p. 123. See also D. Geeta Rani and R.K. Mishra, Corporate Governance, Theory and Practice, 1st edition, 2008, Excel Books, New Delhi. See also Subhash

*D. Narayana Murthy Committee Report on Corporate Governance*

The fourth initiative on corporate governance in India is in the form of the recommendations of the Narayana Murthy Committee. The Committee was set-up by SEBI, under the chairmanship of Mr. N.R. Narayana Murthy, to review Clause 49, and suggest measures to improve corporate governance standards. Some of the major recommendations of the committee primarily related to audit committees, audit reports, independent directors, related party transactions, risk management, directorships and director compensation, codes of conduct and financial disclosures. The committee recommended that in order to achieve the objectives of corporate governance and to realise the long-term shareholder value, the companies should agree to the terms and conditions such as: (i) in case of the appointment of a new director or reappointment of a director, the shareholders must be provided with a brief resume of the director, nature of his expertise in specific functional areas and names of the companies in which he holds the directorship and membership of committees of the board, (ii) information like quarterly result and presentation made by companies to analyst shall be put on company's website or shall be sent in such a form so as to enable the stock exchange on which the company is listed to put it on its own website, (iii) a board committee under the chairmanship of a non-executive director be formed to specifically look into the redressing of shareholder and investor complaints which shall be designated as Shareholders/Investors Grievances Committees, and (iv) to expedite the process of share transfer the board of directors shall delegate the power of share transfer to an officer or a committee or to the registrar and share transfer agents.[38]

---

Chandra Das, Corporate Governance in India, An Evaluation, 2008, Prentice-Hall of India Ltd., Delhi.

38. Securities and Exchange Board of India (2002) Report on SEBI Committee on Corporate Governance (under the chairmanship of Shri N.R. Narayanamurthy). A.C. Fernando, Corporate Governance: Principles, Policies and Practice, 2006, Dorling Kindersley (India) Pvt. Ltd., New Delhi, at p. 126. See also D. Geeta Rani and R.K. Mishra, Corporate Governance, Theory and Practice, 1st edition, 2008, Excel Books, New Delhi. See also Subhash Chandra Das, Corporate Governance in India, An Evaluation, 2008, Prentice-Hall of India Ltd., Delhi.

*E. Securities Exchange Board of India (SEBI) and Revised Clause 49 of Listing Agreement*

The SEBI was established in 1988 and became fully autonomous body in 1992 with defined responsibilities to cover both development and regulation of the market. It is the regulatory body for the investment market in India. The main function of the board is to maintain stable and efficient markets by creating and enforcing regulations in the market place. In accordance with the guidelines provided by the SEBI, the stock exchanges in India have modified the listing requirements by incorporating in the listing agreement a new clause 49 based on the recommendations of the Kumar Mangalam Birla Committee Report for proper disclosure of corporate governance compliance. As a part of its endeavour to improve the standards of corporate governance and in line with the needs of a dynamic market, constituted another committee under the chairmanship of Sri Narayana Murthy to review the progress of the corporate sector in meeting the norms of corporate governance which revised the clause 49 of the listing agreement to promote and raise the standards of corporate governance and required that the provisions of the revised clause 49 shall be implemented as per the schedule of implementation so determined. In accordance with the amendments made in the listing agreement of SEBI, the companies which are required to comply with the requirements of revised clause 49 shall submit a quarterly compliance report to the stock exchanges as per the prescribed guidelines. The Stock Exchanges shall ensure that all provisions of the revised clause 49 on corporate governance have been complied with.[39]

*F. Companies Bill, 2009*

It is observed that the scale and scope of economic reform and development in India over the past 20 years has been impressive. The country has opened up large parts of its economy and capital markets, and in the process has produced many highly regarded companies in sectors such as information technology, banking, autos, steel and textile manufacturing. These companies are now making their presence felt outside India through global mergers and acquisitions. Further reforms

39. Dr Twinkle Prusty, Corporate Governance Compliance in Indian Industries, 2008, Regal Publications, New Delhi, at p. 28.

have been made over the past decade to modernise both company law and securities regulations. The Companies Act, 1956 has been amended several times, in areas such as postal ballots and audit committees, while committees were appointed in 2002 and 2004 to recommend improvements. The Ministry of Corporate Affairs under the chairmanship of Dr. Jamshed J. Irani, on December 2004 established an Expert Committee on Company Law to review the existing corporate laws and regulations and focussed on the issue directly relevant to corporate governance where the recommendations of the report received consideration in the Companies Bill initially laid down before the Parliament in 2008 and reintroduced in August 2009. The Bill seeks to enable the corporate sector in India to operate in a regulatory environment of best international practices. It addresses various contemporary issues relating to corporate governance including the provisions relating to auditors and their relationship with the management of the company, independent directors with a view to improve corporate governance practices. The Bill is subject to greater flexibility and self-regulation by companies, better financial and non-financial disclosure, more efficient enforcement of law, process of appointment and qualification of auditors, prohibiting non-audit services by the auditors, compulsory rotation of auditors, remuneration of directors, etc.,[40] the provisions of the Bill are broadly considered to be suitable for addressing various contemporary issues relating to corporate governance including the discrepancies involved in the erstwhile Satyam swindle.

*G. CII Taskforce on Corporate Governance*

History tells us that even the best standards cannot prevent instances of major corporate misconduct. This has been true in the US—Enron, WorldCom, Tyco and, more recently gross miss-selling of collateralized debt obligations; in the UK; in France; in Germany; in Italy; in Japan; in South Korea; and many other OECD nations. The Satyam-Maytas Infra-Maytas Properties scandal that has rocked India since 16th December 2008 is another example of a massive fraud. Satyam is a one-off incident —especially considering the size of the malfeasance. The

40. Satyam Lessons and Corporate Governance Reforms by Pushkar Chandra, available at http://pushkarchandra.sulekha.com, last visited on 22-04-2011.

overwhelming majority of corporate India is well run, well regulated and does business in a sound and legal manner. However, the Satyam episode has prompted a relook at our corporate governance norms and how industry can go a step further through some voluntary measures. With this in mind, the CII set-up a Task Force under Mr. Naresh Chandra in February 2009 to recommend ways of further improving corporate governance standards and practices both in letter and spirit. The recommendations of the Naresh Chandra Task Force evolved over a series of meetings. The leitmotif of the report is to enunciate additional principles that can improve corporate governance in spirit and in practice. The report enumerates a set of voluntary recommendations with an objective to establish higher standards of probity and corporate governance in the country. The recommendations outlined in this report are aimed at listed companies and wholly owned subsidiaries of listed companies. According to the report, much of best-in-class corporate governance is voluntary of companies taking conscious decisions of going beyond the mere letter of law. The spirit of this Task Force Report is to encourage better practices through voluntary adoption-based on a firm conviction that good corporate governance not only comes from within but also generates significantly greater reputational and stakeholder value when perceived to go beyond the rubric of law.[41]

*H. Corporate Governance Voluntary Guidelines, 2009*

More recently, in December 2009, the Ministry of Corporate Affairs (MCA) published a new set of "Corporate Governance Voluntary Guidelines 2009", designed to encourage companies to adopt better practices in the running of boards and board committees, the appointment and rotation of external auditors, and creating a whistle blowing mechanism. The guidelines are divided into the following six parts: (i) Board of Directors, (ii) Responsibilities of the Board, (iii) Audit Committee of the Board, (iv) Auditors, (v) Secretarial Audit, (vi) Institution of mechanism for Whistle Blowing. These guidelines provide for a set of good practices which may be voluntarily adopted by the

41. Report of the CII Taskforce on Corporate Governance Chaired by Mr. Naresh Chandra (November 2009), available at http://www.mca.gov.in/Ministry/latestnews/Draft_Report_NareshChandra_CII.pdf, last visited on 22-04-2011.

Public companies. Private companies, particularly the bigger ones, may also like to adopt these guidelines. The guidelines are not intended to be a substitute for or addition to the existing laws but is recommendatory in nature. Despite these wide-ranging developments in regulation and policy, what becomes increasingly apparent in India is that the reform process has not addressed, or effectively addressed, a key challenge at the heart of the governance problem, namely, the accountability of promoters to other shareholders. Even though most listed companies have large controlling shareholders, typically a family, the regulation of related-party transactions in India is minimal. Promoters have considerable freedom of action in undertaking such transactions and are subject to only limited regulatory controls. They are also permitted to issue preferential warrants to themselves at an effective discount to the market price—something that would not be condoned in more developed markets. In this context, relying largely on independent directors (appointed by controlling shareholders), independent board committees and greater corporate disclosure as the primary mechanisms to check abuses of power by promoters and to safeguard the interests of minority shareholders is likely to prove weak and insufficient (as indeed it did in the Satyam case). Board reform is fundamentally important, and is a major issue of concern to institutional investors, but it needs to be complemented by other regulations that directly address the relationship between controlling and minority shareholders—in other words, a proper regime for the regulation of related-party transactions. While some leading Indian companies deserve credit for actively pursuing high standards of governance, including producing examples of world-class corporate disclosure, the strong growth of the economy and capital markets has fostered, in our view, a fair degree of complacency towards corporate governance and the rights of minority shareholders. As this paper shows, few listed companies in India are attuned to a major global trend of the past five years—the expansion of cross-border proxy voting—nor do they seem interested in voluntarily enhancing the transparency and fairness of their annual general meetings (e.g., by fully counting all votes through a "poll", rather than conducting voting by the old system of a show of hands). This complacency is also reflected in the ongoing difficulties that investors face in deciphering the financial statements of some listed companies, including even some large caps.[42]

## SUGGESTIONS

A corporation is a congregation of various stakeholders, namely, customers, employees, investors, vendor partners, government and society. A corporation should be fair and transparent to its stakeholders in all its transactions. This has become imperative in today's globalized business world where corporations need to access global pools of capital, need to attract and retain the best human capital from various parts of the world, need to partner with vendors on mega collaborations and need to live in harmony with the community. Unless a corporation embraces and demonstrates ethical conduct, it will not be able to succeed. As there is a saying 'As the Ruler, so the rule', it does not take much time for the wrongdoing to spread down the hierarchy. People who come to know of the wrongdoings of management or those who have themselves assisted the management in committing the fraud also tend to resort to fraud eventually.

Corporate governance is about ethical conduct in business. Ethics is concerned with the code of values and principles that enables a person to choose between right and wrong, and therefore, select from alternative courses of action. Good corporate governance is good business because it inspires investor confidence, which is so essential to attracting capital. All the confidence however, that the good companies build, and the good work that they do over time can be largely undone by a few unscrupulous businessmen, and fly-by-night operators. Such exceptions require to be handed out deterrent punishments. Though many Acts have been created for the security of the people's money, there could be no positive outcome from the owner's side. Their main goal is to earn as much as possible money from the public through inviting them to invest, and

42. Ministry of Corporate Affairs, Government of India. Corporate Governance Voluntary Guidelines, 2009 available at www.mca.gov.in, last visited on 22-04-2011. See India's Corporate Governance Voluntary Guidelines, 2009: Rhetoric Or Reality? by Umakanth Varottil, available at *papers.ssrn.com/sol3/papers.cfm?abstract_id=1634821, last visited on 22-04-2011.*

building their personal empires. It is the easiest way to earn mass money at a single attempt. Sometimes it seems that the efforts to build the business empires are just to attract the common public to invest in their companies and make themselves at the enjoying position. In India, there is a common phenomenon in every citizen that their own money means hard-earned money and public or others money is the easily-earned money. So, there shall be strict rules and punishments applied on the directors who gamble with the public money. Any relaxation towards the guilty will encourage the fraudsters to continue their fraudulent activities, affecting adversely not just the process of price formation on stock exchanges, but also the very basis of the functioning of the corporate world. Though complete prevention is impossible, prevention of frauds would be a desirable outcome for corporate governance programs. Implementing better corporate governance measures by the corporate entities themselves and application of laws strictly by the regulatory bodies by awarding stronger punishment to the fraud-makers can prevent these fraud practices. A better awareness is required among the public while investing in the corporate sector. Also, a corporate accountability should be developed in the companies since the money invested by the public is to be gainfully utilized and serve the interests of public at large. Thus, what is required is the good government based on effective representative democracy with a strong opposition drawing its substance from working people, which is well informed and does not confine itself only to rhetoric. This will reduce the instance so of corporate frauds to a substantial extent. Thus, white collar crimes can be avoided by the promotion of good corporate governance, with reasonable transparent processes within the corporation, to detect improper activities of its executives.[43]

The demise of many corporate superstructures due to corporate bamboozlements necessarily calls for the restructuring of the regulatory framework of corporate governance in the corporate terrene as well as bring about the required legislative changes in the important statute books which penalises corporate fraud and embezzlements. Since the late 1990's significant efforts have been taken by Indian regulators, as well as by Indian

43. Corporate Frauds in the World of Corporate Sector: A Critical Analysis, by Varsha Rajora, available at http://www.ssrn.com/, last visited on 22-04-2011.

industry representative and corporations, to achieve an overhaul of corporate governance in Indian firms. Not only were reform measures put into place prior to discovery of major corporate governance scandals, but both industry groups and government actors have sprung into action following the Satyam scandal. Despite these commendable efforts, the actual implementation and enforcement of corporate governance reforms remain challenging. Here are some important suggestions to redesign and reform the corporate governance framework so as to inhibit the recurrences of corporate frauds in the organisations.

## Suggestions for the Prevention of Corporate Frauds

### *A. Adoption of Fraud Prevention Policy*

An anti-fraud program enables an organization to address the concerns of its stakeholders. A comprehensive anti-fraud program provides a framework for a company to identify, mitigate and monitor the fraud risks impacting the business and report the occurrence of fraud, with the objective of building an effective anti-fraud culture over a period of time. Although an anti-fraud program cannot provide absolute assurance that frauds will not occur, it gives organizations the opportunity to 'legislate' a general sense of morality among their people. It also enables them to provide their employees with the necessary guidance so that they clearly understand what is expected of them and what constitutes unacceptable behaviour. Generally, many companies have an ethics policy, which set forth in detail, the expectations from the employees in the ethical climate of the company. Adoption of a written fraud policy is another important element of overall fraud prevention programs of a company or organization. It specifically spells out about the person, who is responsible and handles varying fraud matters in the conflicting situations. A fraud prevention policy is the first step towards effective fraud prevention program.

The fraud prevention process has four main elements which have been discussed below:

(i) Establishment of corporate governance.
(ii) Implementation of transaction-level control processes often referred to as the system of internal accounting controls.

(iii) Retrospective examination of governance and control processes through audit examinations.
(iv) Investigation and remediation of suspected or alleged problems.[44]

*1. Establishment of Corporate Governance*

Corporate governance is beyond the realm of law. It stems from the culture and mindset of management, and cannot be regulated by legislation alone. Corporate governance deals with conducting the affairs of the company such that there is fairness to all stakeholders. It is about openness, integrity and accountability. Corporate governance is about setting and monitoring objectives, policies, risk appetite, accountability and performance. An appropriate system of governance should be born with the company itself, and grow in complexity and reach as the company grows. It should predict any possible opportunity for fraud. It further communicates that compliance with laws, ethical business practices, accounting principles, and corporate policies is expected, and that any attempted or actual fraud is expected to be disclosed by those who know or suspect that fraud has occurred. Prevention, therefore, offers a more realistic view. In short, corporate governance is an entire culture that sets and monitors behavioural expectations intended to find the fraudster. In order to execute effective governance, boards and management must effectively oversee a number of key business processes, including the following:

1. Strategy and operation planning.
2. Risk Management.
3. Ethics and Compliance.
4. Performance measurement and monitoring.
5. Mergers, acquisitions, and other transformational transactions.
6. Management evaluation, compensation, and succession planning.
7. Communication and reporting.
8. Governance Dynamics.

44. Thomas W. Golden, Steven L. Skalak, and Mona M. Clayton, "The Corporate Fraud Cycle: How to break the chain?" available at http://www.pricewatercoopers.com/, last visited on 22-04-2011.

*2. Transaction-Level Control*

They are accounting and financial controls designed to ensure that only valid, authorized, and legitimate transactions occur and to safeguard corporate assets from losses due to theft or other fraudulent activity. These procedures are preventive because they may actively block or prevent a fraudulent transaction occurring. Such systems, however, are not foolproof, and fraudsters frequently take advantage of loopholes, inconsistencies, or vulnerable employees.

*3. Retrospective Examination*

Retrospective procedures, such as those performed by auditors and forensic accounting investigators, do not prevent fraud in the same way that font-end transaction controls do, but they form a key link in communicating tolerance for fraud and discovering problems before they grew to a size that could threaten the welfare of the organization. Although auditing cannot truly prevent fraud before it happens, but helps in fraud prevention policy.

*4. Investigation and Remediation*

An investigation should also form the basis for remediating control procedure. Investigations should lead to actions commensurate with the size and seriousness of the impropriety or fraud, no matter whether it is found to be a minor infraction of corporate policy or a major scheme to create fraudulent financial statements or misappropriate significant assets.

*5. Regulatory Role in Fraud Prevention*

From the last two decades India too has seen several corporate fraud experiences involving thousands of crores of public money. These frauds hit the Indian industry as well as country's financial system so severely that it has no other go except to bring changes in the policies of regulatory authorities like RBI, SEBI, etc. To bring the drastic changes in the corporate sector and to formulate the corporate governance policy, the Indian government initiated three high-level committees. The Naresh Chandra Committee was appointed by the Union government to look into the role of audit committees focusing primarily on independent directors. The Kumara Mangalam Birla Committee and Narayana Murthy Committee were appointed by

SEBI to look into the various aspects of corporate governance. These committees concluded:

1. Appointment of independent Directors in the Audit committees of the listed companies.
2. Certification of CEOs and CFOs on the Annual Audit Accounts.
3. Setting up an independent quality review board to periodically examine and review the quality of audit, secretarial and cost accounting firms, and pass judgment and comments on the quality and sufficiency of systems, infrastructure and practices.
4. Setting up of a corporate serious fraud office (CSFO) in the Department of Company Affairs.
5. Strengthening of ROC offices to ensure better compliance.
6. Outsourcing of non-statutory work, and tightening the law regarding lapses in sectorial compliance, by inserting a section analogous to section 233A to allow the government to special compliance audits.
7. Inclusion of clause 49 in the listing Agreement between the companies and SEBI by giving emphasis on the disclose practices and inclusion of independent directors on the board of a listed company, who would be responsible for upholding the corporate ethical culture.

*B. Measures to Improve and Enhance Corporate Governance*

The corporate entities that overlook the corporate governance norms would eventually find themselves at a competitive disadvantage in attracting long-term investments and in sustaining its corporate identity. Thus, there is an imperative need to adhere to the best practices coupled with strict vigilance by the regulators and also the professionals involved which shall definitely go a long way in recuperating investors' confidence and contributing to the economic growth of the country. The following measures may be considered to begin about improvements in the corporate governance standards:

1. Stricter piece of legislations need to be passed so as to regulate and implement the internationally accepted principles of accounting, reinforcing the standards of

financial disclosure, conflict of interest disclosure, following the anti-trust laws, bankruptcy laws and prohibition of insider trading.

2. Public education efforts are needed to promote better understanding of essential corporate governance principles and their relationships to democratic development.
3. Companies need to undertake voluntary reforms by developing their codes of conduct and best practices guidelines.
4. Independent and non-executive directors with expertise and experience should be appointed to the corporate boards and the qualifications should be provided in crystal clear terms in the appropriate legislations.
5. There is a need for capacity building and leveraging of the state-of-the-art technology, e-governance and better management practices.
6. To provide for mandatory fraud risk management policies in the organisation of every company by way of inclusion in the appropriate legislations.
7. To provide for stringent action against the auditors and other professionals who violate the professional ethics and indulges in unethical businesses and also involved in corruption along with the government officials like the recent 2G Spectrum Allocation scam.
8. To provide for stricter penalties for the defaulting directors of the companies for engaging in unethical and corrupt business practices.
9. To provide mechanisms for rating on the basis of effective compliance with the corporate governance standards.
10. To bring about necessary changes in the boardroom dynamics of the corporate bodies by amending the existing Companies Act, 1956.
11. To provide for heavy penal provisions with pricey fines and rigorous imprisonment both for committing corporate frauds by violating the corporate governance norms as well as the requirements of the listing agreement.

12. To provide for more supervisory powers to SEBI by making it the sole regulator of all listed companies.
13. To strengthen and incorporate whistle blowing policies in the company's policies with adequate safeguards for the protection of the whistle blowers under the legislative framework.
14. To institutionalise the growing emerging trends towards corporate social responsibility, quality of information, harmonisation of accounting standards, shareholders' democracy and providing for a benchmark in secretarial practices.
15. To incorporate the global corporate governance standards to the fullest extent for enabling the Indian companies to compete with the foreign counterparts and enhancing their position in the global transparency index.[45]

*C. Measures taken up by the Ministry of Corporate Affairs*

To prevent any recurrence of Satyam-like frauds, regulators and the authorities like the Ministry of Corporate Affairs (MCA), the Securities and Exchange Board of India (SEBI), The Institute of Company Secretaries of India (ICSI), the Institute of Chartered Accountants of India (ICAI) and the Institute of Cost and Works Accountants of India (ICWA), have undertaken a number of corporate governance initiatives.

***1. New Initiatives by the Government of India***

The government is planning to set-up an independent regulatory body on the lines of the Public Company Accounting Oversight Board (PCAOB) in the US to oversee the work of auditors. Initially the proposal will be placed before the MCA, the administrative ministry governing accounting practices in the country. Presently, the functioning of auditors is overseen by the ICAI, a body established under a stature of Parliament. While the ICAI is against the idea of setting up an independent regulatory body, government officials are sceptical about the ICAI's effectiveness in regulating the work of auditors. The PCAOB was

45. Dr. Twinkle Prusty, Corporate Governance Compliance in Indian Industries, 2008, Regal Publications, New Delhi at p. 250.

set-up in US, in response to an ever-increasing number of accounting frauds by public companies during the 1990s; this was followed by a series of high-profile accounting scandals and record-setting bankruptcies by large public companies, notably those in 2002 involving WorldCom and Enron. Prior to the creation of the PCAOB, the functioning of auditing firms was self-regulated through the Public Oversight Board, a private organisation members were appointed by the auditing firms. PCAOB is a private, non-profit corporation created by the Sarbanes-Oxley Act, a 2002 United States federal law, to oversee the auditors of public companies. Its stated purpose is to 'protect the interests of investors and further the public interest in the preparation of informative, fair, and independent audit reports'.

### 2. *Market Research and Analysis Unit*

Recently, the government has decided to set-up a specialised Market Research and Analysis Unit (MRAU) to scrutinize media reports, corporate press releases and advertisements which can have a bearing on share prices of companies. One of the important tasks of the MRAU, to be set-up within the Serious Fraud Investigation Office (SFIO), would be to provide early signals of corporate wrong doings to the government. The new unit would work in close coordination with SEBI, the Enforcement Directorate, the Income Tax Department and the Reserve Bank of India. The objective behind setting up of MRAU is not to monitor frauds, but to set-up a risk management system to catch early signals and take preventive action.

### 3. *Introduction of Companies Bill, 2009*

The Companies Act, 1956 is set to be overhauled with the Ministry of Corporate Affairs (MCA) introducing the new Companies Bill, 2009, in the Lok Sabha. The Bill has been introduced in the last Lok Sabha, but had lapsed with the dissolution of the House. When enacted, this will bring about significant changes in the way business is done in India, make it easier to start and close businesses and protect shareholders. The main objective is to delink the procedural aspects (of company law regulations) from the substantive law and provide greater flexibility in rule-making to enable adaptation to the changing economic and technical environment. The new Bill would not have provisions in the older legislation that had become redundant. The Bill is based on the concept of self-regulation, recognises the chief executive officer, the chief financial officer and the company secretary as "key managerial personnel' for a single forum for mergers and acquisitions. The Bill is largely based on the recommendations made by the expert committee headed by J.J. Irani and is expected to be simplified and shorter version of the present Act and proposes to minimise government intervention in management of companies. The MCA has plans to make amendments including defining the accountability of independent directors, as part of the bill. Further, the government also seeks to make stringent norms for auditors and corporate governance in the bill.

***4. Roadmap for Switching to IFRS System of Accounting***

The Government will chalk out its roadmap on the transition to Financial Reporting Standards (IFRS) system of accounting by November 2009. The accounting system is adopted by the International Accounting Standards Board and over 100 countries have acknowledged its use. Initially, the Government is planning to bring only the top 150-200 companies into the IFRS ambit on the basis of their borrowing and turnover. It has been proposed that the new standards would initially be applicable to all those companies that have access to foreign capital, those that are listed overseas, companies with branches abroad and companies with joint ventures and subsidiaries abroad.

***5. Amendment to the Chartered Accountants Act, 1949***

The Ministry of Corporate Affairs (MCA) in consultation with the Institute of Chartered Accountants of India (ICAI) is planning to strengthen the accountability of chartered accountants (CAs) by changing the way they perform their duties. The ministry will initiate the process after it receives ICAI's report on the Satyam Computer Services scam. The ICAI is a statutory body established by an Act of Parliament, the Chartered Accountants Act, 1949—for regulating the profession in the country. Meanwhile, the MCA has initiated a comprehensive review of the legal provisions and regulations governing chartered accountants, particularly, the operation of surrogate firms in India by large foreign audit firms following the Satyam accounting fraud. The review is a joint exercise by the ministry and the industry and is based on feedback from various chartered accountants forums.[46]

## CONCLUSION

Enron, WorldCom, Bear Stearns, Fanny Mae, Freddie Mac, Countrywide, Washington Mutual, Lehman Bros, AIG and Wachovia, all in the United States; Northern Rock, Kuapthing, Fortis and ING in the United Kingdom; and the India's Satyam Computers—this partial list of the *who is who* in the corporate world all had one thing in common: all of them landed up in deep financial distress and some of them disappeared in the first decade of the 21st century. The 1990s in India saw a number of company failures and many instances of mismanagement, with some well known corporate leaders and executives being hauled up for non-performance and non-compliance with legal requirements. A scam of sever magnitude, comparable to a scaled-down version of Black Monday disaster of September 1987 on the New York Stock Exchange and other related markets, rocked the Indian stock markets in 1992-93, exposing the inadequacies of procedural and regulatory controls in the country. It is therefore impossible not to be struck by the enormity of these corporate disasters clocked up in the span of a short decade at the turn of the century, and the cost these have imposed on the public in terms of a burgeoning downturn or depression, unemployment, property value erosion leading to an unprecedented, of rescue and rehabilitation packages by the governments worth trillions of dollars.[47] The rich and complex governance system (of policy, laws, regulations, public institutions, self-regulated professional bodies, and managerial ethos) has evolved over centuries in developed market economies. In emerging markets, however, many elements of this mosaic are absent or countries are ill-equipped to address the

46. Reforming Corporate Governance available at http://www.epwrf.res.in/upload/MER/mer10903008.pdf, last visited on 22-04-2011.
47. N. Balasubramanian, Corporate Governance and Stewardship, 2010, Tata McGraw-Hill Education Private Limited, New Delhi, at p. 1.

corporate governance challenges they face. These challenges are all the more daunting because of the complexity of the ownership structure of the corporate sector, interlocking relationships with government and the financial sector, weak legal and judicial systems, absent or underdeveloped institutions, and scarce human resource capabilities. A concerted call for action is the normal societal response to the bewildering corporate scams and swindles, translating into a series of questions as to how the regulatory and monitoring agencies, the auditors, the board of directors of the concerned companies failed to prevent or detect such irregularities in time. This is also followed by some introspection as to what is right and equitable, and what is expected of those in charge of overseeing the orderly conduct of business and the protection of the rights of the aggrieved parties. The 'governance' mechanism itself then becomes the subject of critical scrutiny and evaluation.

Thus, there is a clarion call for all companies to piously follow and adhere to the corporate governance standards as it is imperative for achieving excellence in the corporatized regime. The embodiments of good corporate governance lies in transparency, accountability, investor and stakeholder protection, appropriate compliance with legislative rules and conventions and enforcing societal values. However, simply by confining to the adherence of rules and regulations without the creation of corporate conscience and consciousness, the culture of transparency, fair disclosure and corporate democracy, shall erode the corporate capabilities to sustain and remain vibrant in terms of benchmarking the best quality of governance in the world. The recurrence of corporate governance crises in highly developed, as well as developing, economies reminds us that the price of economic growth and opportunity is indeed eternal vigilance. Ultimately, the most effective and sustainable governance reforms will be those that simultaneously increase the costs of corporate frauds and decrease the benefits that individuals and corporations can derive from ignoring governance norms and laws. To recall an exhortation of Kumar Mangalam Birla Report on Corporate Governance, *"it (corporate governance) has to become a way of life"* and when it does, and only then, can corporations can take their rightful place in the world. Finally, it can be concluded by maintaining that a lot remains to resolve and realise not by letters alone but also by actions. An agog and vigilant public, the edifying media and the enlightening and analytical craftsmanship of the political, economic and social visionaries will go a long way in helping us realise the goals set forth.

CHAPTER 15

# Control Mechanism in Corporate Governance

*Dr. Dipak Das*

In the era of liberation and lesser bureaucratic controls combined with globalization of corporations and capital markets a number of new issues related to control mechanisms in corporate governance are being raised. For a clear understanding of these issues, however, it is necessary to recount the important features of a corporate body as a legal entity evolved over the last one and half century. This chapter is, therefore, arranged in three parts: The first part deals with the features of a corporate body or a company as it is commonly known. The second part examines the existing internal and external control mechanisms and the degree to which they are effective. Suggestions for revitalizing those control systems in the third part.

## FEATURES OF A CORPORATION

Commercial revolution, which followed the industrial revolution, was due to the creation of a new form of organization with features which were entirely different from those of a partnership firm or a sole proprietary concern. This corporate form of organization, which obtained legal sanction for the first time in 1844, revolutionized the concept of capital collections and of creating formal organizational structures. Over the years during the period of one and a half century modifications in the features of a corporate body have certainly been made, though the basic features have been remained more or less the same.[1]

**Important Features of a Corporate Body as a Legal Entity can be Enumerated as follows:**

1. A corporate body has its own identity and independent existence, which is not to be confused with the identity of a particular individual or of a family.
2. A corporate body, in principle, is not owned by any one. Under the law an incorporated company is a distinct entity even if all its shares are practically controlled by one person. The persons, who contribute its capital are not its owners, are the shareholders. The corporation itself is the owner of its assets and is bound by its liabilities. Neither the promoters/directors nor the share-holders have proprietary rights over the corporation.
3. Liability of the shareholders is limited. The advantage of limited liability coupled with free transferability of shares have made the aggregation of small sums into huge capital possible.
4. Shareholders enjoy the power to appoint the directors, decide their remuneration and, if necessary, to remove them; but they do not have the power to interfere in the legitimate intravenous decisions of the Board of Directors.
5. A Corporation can get the benefit of availing the services of professional managers by assuring them full freedom of decision-making as there is no human employer and the shareholders exercise only a formative control.

Though a corporation has its own identity established by law, in reality it has to operate through individuals. This is precisely the reason why the identity of a corporation is often mixed-up, albeit wrongly, with the identity of an individual or of a family to which the individuals associated with its governance belong.[2]

---

1. Narayan Murthy, N.R., Corporate Governance: The Key Issues, *Vikalpa*, Vol. 24, No. 4, pp. 3-6.
2. *Ibid.*

## CONTROL MECHANISM OVER CORPORATE GOVERNANCE

Considering the huge resources at the disposal of a corporation and also considering the fact that the promoters/directors enjoy the opportunity of trading with other peoples' concentration of power of corporate governance in their hands without any checks and balances may prove to be dangerous even while conceding the need for lesser bureaucratic controls and more freedom for professional managers, the need for external and internal control mechanism for ensuring efficient corporate performance cannot be ignored. These control systems ensure that the divergence between profit-oriented and sometimes selfish decisions of Management and socially optimal decisions is kept at minimal level.[3]

Active and positive contributions by the following agencies are expected to provide a framework for such balanced corporate governance.

**Market forces:** In a free market, firms that cannot supply products that consumer desire at competitive prices cannot survive. Thus, the resource allocation decisions are guided by what Adam Smith advocated Invisible hand. This is possible in small and regional markets as coordination of different activities of a large number of manufacturers, agents, traders and financiers can be easily achieved through easy and direct interaction and communication. No single functionary can influence the market independently.

However, when the markets become large and complex and are dominated by a few mega organizations, the market discipline acts too slowly to be effective as a control mechanism. By this time its effect is seen it is too late to save a non-competitive organization.

Growing powers of multinationals have also accelerated the decline of the power of invisible hand as the main mechanism of allocating resources and controlling the market within and also between the national economies. Coordination of large flows of materials through the process of production are decisions of a few corporations. These corporations employ highly trained

3. S.C. Das, Management Accountant, J.J. Irani Committee Report on Company Law Related to Corporate Governance, September 2005, pp. 719-32.

professional managers who take these resource allocation decisions. Thus, the visible hand of management takes over from the so-called invisible hand of the market as a control mechanism.

Inadequacy of the external market forces as the control mechanism over the corporate performance brings us to the internal forces.

**Shareholders:** Shareholders as the contributors of the capital of a corporation have the ultimate right to control its performance. They appoint the Board of Directors as their agent and entrust it with substantial autonomy and powers of management. As the number of shareholders is very large and they are scattered and ill-organized, in practice they do not exercise much control over the Board of Directors. Very few shareholders attend general meetings of companies either in persons or through proxies and as there is no provision for sending their votes by post, right to vote is never enjoyed by a very large majority of the shareholders.

The institutional investors also do not appear to play any significant and positive role in corporate governance. The general policy of the governance is not to disturb the pattern of management as far as possible, which is in tune with the current policy of non-interference. This policy is, however, stretched to such an extent that sometimes highly objectionable decisions are taken unanimously at general meeting of corporations in spite of the fact that government controlled financial institutions control 20 to 30 per cent votes. Their representatives either do not care to attend the general meetings or they vote in collusion with the Board of Directors. Recent instances of promoters allotting themselves shares at preferential rates and thus enriching themselves to the extent of Rs. 5000 crore at the cost of general investors are the glaring examples of the blow to corporate democracy and erosion of the shareholders' powers.

If the individual and institutional shareholders' go on abandoning their responsibility and do not try to influence corporate behavior, the professional managers' personal goals like higher remuneration, attractive perquisites, favorable contractual conditions, scope for empire building, etc. acquire priority over other goals.

**Board of Directors:** At the apex of the internal control system is the Board of Directors and thus it has the full responsibility of its performance. The Board of Directors appoints the Managing Director (MD) or the Chief Executive Officer (CEO) and provides broad guidelines for corporate governance. It is also expected that the BOD would review the performance of the MD/CEO continuously so that advance warning of impending crisis is received and the remedial actions are taken well in time. In practice, however, this does not seem to happen.

Though enough data about working of the Board of Directors are not readily available, scanty evidence obtained through published sources indicates that the Board of Directors are generally dominated by the MD/CEOs themselves.

The Board of Directors is often unwieldy with many insiders as their members. Opposition to the MD/CEOs is not welcomed and agreement with him is rewarded. Such a system results in autocracy rule where difficulties, instead of being dealt with self-correcting mechanism, are accumulated till they turn into crisis. In case of a serious crisis MD/CEO is removed after the crisis: an action taken too late to prevent the crisis situation.

As the policy of institutional investors is that of non-interference, the directors nominated by them also generally play a passive role, thereby allowing unrestrained freedom to the MD/CEO. Thus, it seems that just like shareholders, the Board of Directors also has abandoned its power of exercising control over corporate management.[4]

**Government:** Till recently, in India, government exercise considerable control over capital market as well as on management of corporations. The government control was directed at channelization of resources towards social justice. Agencies like Controller of Capital Issues and Company Law Board were created through which such control was exercised. Unfortunately, four decades of bureaucratic control resulted in the emergence of License Raj infested with corruption and malpractices. Bureaucratic delays and inefficiency created impediments in the management of corporations.

This picture is gradually changing over the last few years. With the liberalization of economy, government's role as a controlling force over corporate management has weakened to a great extent. Controls over the capital issues are no more in

4. S.N. Mahapatra and Sanjay Pandey, *Corporate Governance v. Corporate Crime, Management Accountant*, May 2004, pp. 387-90.

existence; controls over management of companies (approval of the Central Government for the appointment of MD and fixing his remuneration) are being relaxed and there are moves for simplification of procedures.

On the other hand, working of capital markets is also undergone a change. Mismanagement and lack of control over misbehaving agents in the capital markets had become very common in the past. It was not possible for a couple of stock exchanges even to submit a list of all members when the same was demanded by SEBI. So few brokers were dominating in the working of these exchanges and there was no protection to investors from unscrupulous dealers. With the establishment of SEBI the government is trying to monitor the working of capital markets but it seems to confront new problems every day. There seems to be a constant race between government acting through agencies like SEBI and Reserve Bank of India, making the rules and the experts employed by the capital market agencies trying to find loopholes in these rules.

During the days when the government control existed, at least formally in the form of rules and regulations, the companies would find the ways of remunerating their directors/promoter/ CEOs, etc. much in excess of the stipulated statutory limit. Thus, it can be said even under the conditions of controlled economy, the government controls were not meaningful. Now with the official government policy favoring decontrol, the role of the government as a controlling agency over corporate governance would become insignificant.[5]

The above stated facts indicated that both the internal as well as external control mechanisms have become ineffective, thereby resulting in unrestrained concentration of power of corporate governance in the hands of a few professional managers. Instances of misuse of such power, intentional as well as accidental, are not uncommon in developing as well as developed countries. Revitalising the control mechanism, therefore, becomes inevitable to ensure responsible corporate behavior. At the same time care

5. Dr. Sushama Bareja, Corporate Social Responsibility—A Key for Better Corporate Governance, *Management Accountant*, August 2004, pp. 635-37.

should be taken to ensure that the control mechanisms do not become stumbling blocks in quick and efficient decision-making.[6]

## REVITALISING THE CONTROL SYSTEM

A. Rethinking of the roles of different agencies in the corporate governance has become necessary. In addition to the stockholders exercising control over corporate governance, control by a number of stockholders is being accepted slowly, at least at conceptual level. Employees, creditors, consumers and suppliers are the direct stakeholders whereas society at large are an indirect stakeholders whose interests are affected by corporate decisions.

Employees are encouraged to become stakeholders of the company where they are working by giving them preferential allotment. This acts in two ways: they become more involved in the company's operations as they have a financial stake in its working: at the same time; they are also in a position to participate, though indirectly, in the corporate decision-making at the apex level. Their psychological value has become associated with the working of the company.

Convertibility clause in the agreement gives a right to the creditors to convert his loan into equity, getting a proprietary interest in the corporation.

Consumers are the king in the free market and through market mechanism they are in a position to exercise ultimate control over a corporation's existence. Consumer activists have successfully gained for the consumers a right of representation in the Board of Directors. Though it is done in a very few companies, it may be indicated as a trend in future.

Not to speak of a greater transparency in corporate affairs is expected by the society.

B. A system of checks and balances over the corporate management is provided for in the legal structure. Over the years there has been slackness in the implementation of the legal provisions in certain areas. Instead of

6. Vasudha Joshi, Institutional Investors and Corporate Governance, *Management Accountant*, November 2002, pp. 833-36.

introducing an entirely new system of checks and balances it is advisable to revitalized the old system and make it meaningful.

(i) Establishment of SEBI in 1992 was also a step in the right direction. If it is ensured that SEBI does not become another inefficient and effective bureaucratic organization and if a unified policy is adopted by SEBI and RBI, these institutions can play a vital role in providing a framework of controls and checks over corporate governance.

(ii) The role of the institutional investors should be given much attention. In countries like Germany and Japan institutional investors seem to have long-term view and they play an active role becoming active investors and playing meaningful role in corporate governance in our country can be explored. Considering the institutional investors can make worthwhile contribution of Board of Directors level. However, the existing legal system, government policy of these institutions themselves would need some restricting for the new role.

(iii) Possibility of the organizations like Chambers of Commerce or confederation of Industries acting as external auditors and exercising control, though indirect, over the activities as via-media between self-control (which may be absent sometimes) and bureaucratic control (which may prove to be an impediment in the organizational development.)

(iv) It needs a special thought to revitalize the Board of Directors with quality, efficient as well as effective personal so that the transparency in their operation can be observed.

(v) Lastly, introduction of the system of management audit—preferably by an outside agency—for a systematic and periodical appraisal of the performance of the board of directors can be thought about. Such an audit of the top management's performance has now become the necessary for survival in the competitive market.

CHAPTER 16

# Corporate e-Governance

*Rakesh Gupta*

## WHAT GOVERNANCE MEANS

In broadest sense governance refers to the range of institutions and practices by which authority is exercised to satisfy the interest of all the stakeholders including the society, and its meaning is shaped by the specific value systems prevalent in the society/country. Good governance should provide proper incentive for the authority (in case of companies the Board and the management) to pursue objectives that are in the interest of the country (read company) and the stakeholders (read shareholders). It should facilitate effective monitoring, thereby encouraging authorities (read companies) to use the resources effectively.

Good governance requires a mindset within the corporation, which integrates the corporate code of ethics into the day-to-day activities of its managers and workers. As sociologists note, companies must move from the "reactive and compliance mode" of corporate ethics, to the "integrity mode", where the functions of the entire organization are completely aligned with its value system.

## CONTEXT OF CORPORATE GOVERNANCE

Corporate Governance is often looked as a matter of regulatory compliance and not as a practice that could result in superior market valuation. Question is whether there exists a correlation between market valuations and the level of governance practiced by the companies. The studies have thoroughly established that market valuations certainly depend on the level of governance. The very definition of corporate governance stems from the organic with the entire gamut of activities having a direct or indirect influence on the financial health of corporate entities.

**Corporate Governance practices ensures that**

1. Board members act in the best interest of the shareholders;
2. The company acts in a lawful and ethical manner in their dealings with the stakeholders and their representatives;
3. All shareholders have the same right to participate in the governance of the company and receive fair treatment from the board and management, and all the rights of shareholders are clearly delineated and communicated;
4. The Board and its committees are structured to act independently from management, individuals or entities that have control over the management, and other non-shareholder groups;
5. Appropriate controls and procedures are in place covering management's activities in running the day-to-day operations of the company; and
6. The company's operational and financial activities as well as its governance activities are consistently reported to the shareholders in a fair, accurate, timely, reliable, complete and verifiable manner.

To improve corporate governance the legislature has very important role to play. Laws should be in place to protect shareholders' interest and ensure the enforcement of such laws and regulations. In case of firm's corporate governance practices having a positive effect on its market value the firms have incentives to improve their governance thereby increasing their market value and reducing the future cost of investments. Companies can expect a 10 to 12 per cent boost to their market valuation by going from worst to best on any single element of governance[1].

1. McKinsey survey.

IT Governance or ICT (Information & Communications Technology) Governance, is a subset discipline of Corporate Governance focused on information technology (IT) systems and their performance and risk management. The rising interest in IT governance is partly due to compliance initiatives.

A characteristic theme of IT governance discussions is that the IT capability can no longer be a black box. The traditional involvement of board-level executives in IT issues was to defer all key decisions to the company's IT professionals. IT governance implies a system in which all stakeholders, including the board, internal customers, and in particular departments such as finance, have the necessary input into the decision-making process. This prevents IT from independently making and later being held solely responsible for poor decisions. It also prevents critical users from later complaining that the system does not behave or perform as expected, as explained in the *Harvard Business Review* article by R. Nolan:

> "A board needs to understand the overall architecture of its company's IT applications portfolio... The board must ensure that management knows what information resources are out there, what condition they are in, and what role they play in generating revenue."

There are narrower and broader definitions of IT governance. "Specifying the decision rights and accountability framework to encourage desirable behaviour in the use of IT."[2]

In contrast, the definition to include foundational mechanisms: "... *the leadership and organisational structures and processes that ensure that the organisation's IT sustains and extends the organisation's strategies and objectives.*"[3]

While defines Corporate Governance of ICT as "*The system by which the current and future use of ICT is directed and controlled. It involves evaluating and directing the plans for the use of ICT to support the organisation and monitoring this use to achieve plans. It includes the strategy and policies for using ICT within an organisation.*"[4] The discipline of information technology governance derives from corporate governance and deals primarily with the connection between business focus and IT management of an

2. Weill and Ross.
3. IT Governance Institute.
4. AS8015, the Australian Standard for Corporate Governance of ICT.

organization. It highlights the importance of IT-related matters in contemporary organizations and states that strategic IT decisions should be owned by the corporate board, rather than by the chief information officer or other IT managers. The primary goals for information technology governance are to: (1) assure that the investments in IT generate business value, and (2) mitigate the risks that are associated with IT. This can be done by implementing an organizational structure with well-defined roles for the responsibility of information, business processes, applications, infrastructure, etc. "Decision rights are a key concern of IT governance"[5]. According to Weill and Ross, depending on the size, business scope, and IT maturity of an organization, either centralized, decentralized or federated models of responsibility for dealing with strategic IT matters are suggested. In this view, the well defined control of IT is the key to success. After the widely reported collapse of **Enron** in 2000, and the alleged problems within **Arthur Andersen** and **WorldCom**, the duties and responsibilities of the boards of directors for public and privately held corporations were questioned.

As a response to this, and to attempt to prevent similar problems from happening again in the US the **Sarbanes-Oxley Act** was written to stress the importance of business control and auditing. **Sarbanes-Oxley and Basel-II** in Europe have been catalysts for the development of the discipline of information technology governance since the early 2000s. However, the concerns of Sarbanes-Oxley (in particular Section 404) have less to do with IT decision rights[6], and more to do with operational control processes such as change management.

Following Corporate Collapses in Australia around the same time, working groups were established to develop standards for Corporate Governance. A series of Australian Standards for Corporate Governance were published in 2003, these were:

- Good Governance Principles (AS8000)
- Fraud and Corruption Control (AS8001)
- Organizational Codes of Conduct (AS8002)
- Corporate Social Responsibility (AS8003)
- Whistle Blower Protection Programs (AS8004)

5. *Supra*, 3.
6. *Ibid.*

**Corporate Governance under the Companies Act, 1956 As Notified In July, 2002**

The Companies Act, 1956, is always a step ahead of other corporate and economic legislations towards ensuring the good corporate governance in the liberalized global economy.

**Section 383A** was added by the Companies (Amendment) Act, 1974 with effect from 1/2/1975, providing for the appointment of qualified individual as company secretary and it has been rightly observed that "in view of the complexities of modern business, and the various Laws with which the managements of company are required to comply with, reliance upon qualified Company Secretaries is now a common feature of medium sized and big sized companies."

By the **Amendment Act, 1988** (w.e.f. 15-7-1988), the Company Secretary is brought within the meaning "officer in default" under section 5 of the Act.

With liberalized global economy of self-control, further changes were made towards these objectives of ensuring good corporate governance by the Companies (Amendment) Act, 2000 that the provisions are further liberalized that minimum paid-up capital requirement for compulsory appointment of Company Secretary is made flexible to enable revision from time to time. Accordingly, the paid up capital requirement Rs. 25 lakhs was increased to Rs. 50 lakhs.

To ensure compliance by companies below the capital limit requiring compulsory appointment of Secretary, a proviso was added in the section that such companies which do not require to employ whole time secretary and whose paid up share capital is Rs. 10 lakhs or more should obtain a compliance certificate from a practicing secretary to be annexed to directors' report and also to be filed to the Register of companies. Towards further liberalisation, the limit of Rs. 50 lakhs now, increased to Rs. 2 cores vide Notification No. 419(E) to be effective from 11/6/2002.

Thus, as per the Law at present,

(i) All companies with paid up capital of Rs. 10 lakhs or above but less than Rs. 2 crores need not employ a whole time company secretary and it would be sufficient to get a compliance certificate from a practicing Company Secretary once in a year, annex to the Directors' Report and file with the Registrar of Companies.

(ii) All companies with paid up less than Rs. 10 lakhs are neither required to appoint whole time secretary nor get a compliance certificate from practicing Secretary.

(iii) All companies with paid up capital to Rs. 2 crores and above should employ a whole time company secretary and need not file a compliance certificate either from the employed company secretary or from a practicing Company Secretary.

Further, with this liberalized provisions of increasing the limits to Rs. 2 crores, there may not be any valid reason to continue the proviso to **section 383(1A)** providing a defense for the non-appointment of company secretary.

To make the provision further effective ensuring the good corporate governance, it is suggested that:

1. To delete proviso to section 383(1A) providing defence for not appointing company secretary and amend section 383(1A) more stringent with severe punishment similar to section 58AA(9) as violating this section is the root cause for committing offences under various other sections of the Act
2. To amend provision to section 383A(1) omitting word 'and having a paid up share capital of ten lakh or more' to ensure the compliance of companies Act provisions which are applicable to small companies as well.
3. To provide for compliance report by the secretary in whole time employment of such companies with paid up share capital of Rs. 2 cores also or alternatively, such certificate from Secretary in practice may be prescribed as one cannot conduct audit and certify his own work.
4. To make sections 224 to 233A pertaining to Auditors applies to the company secretaries appointed as per proviso to section 383A(1) of Act by suitable amendment to the section 383A(1). Thus, **Companies Act, 1956** is always ahead of other Economic and Corporate Legislations towards ensuring the good corporate governance in this liberalized global economy.

## Amendments to Companies Act

Companies Bill builds tough amendments for investors' protection **The Companies (Amendment) Bill, 2003** proposed tough amendments to the **Companies Act, 1956** to improve corporate governance and reinforce investors' rights.

The Central Government can, for instance, attach the Bank accounts of persons associated with the securities market and their intermediaries for one month for violations of the Act.

The Bill proposes to cap circular trading by entities engaged in share-broking—as seen in the last stock scam—by introducing restrictions on inter-corporate loans to be made and received by share-broking companies.

**Law getting tougher to avoid fly by night operators because of followings:**

(a) Penalty for fraudulently including investors, including imprisonment.
(b) Reserves from revaluation of assets not to be used for issue of bonus shares.
(c) Interim dividends can't be revoked.
(d) Holding companies required preparing consolidated financial statements.
(e) Net worth threshold lowered to Rs. 5 crore for norms on board size and constitution of audit panel to apply.
(f) Promoters/directors must be identified at the time of incorporation.
(g) Number of investment firms an individual can float to be capped.
(h) Minimum holding to be prescribed to prevent proliferation of shell companies.
(i) To prevent recurrence of vanishing companies, the Bill mandates identification of promoters/directors at the time of incorporation.

The Bill has also introduced provision that would enable the Central Government to prescribe a cap on the number of investment companies an individual can float and minimum shareholding to prevent proliferation of shell companies.

An amendment to Section 372A of the Act proposes that a company should route all investments through a single investment company. To enable larger number of shareholders to attend AGMs, the Bill has said AGMs and other general meetings can be held on Sundays. Other provisions to protect investor interest include penalty for fraudulently inducing persons to investment money, including imprisonment. Such acts can fetch directors and officers of a company imprisonment for a term of six months to five years and a fine upto Rs. 1 lac. Similarly, penalties have been introduced to bar allotment of shares if a minimum subscription is not received. Promoters and officers of such companies can be fined up to Rs. 50,000 and even imprisoned for up to two years if application money is not refunded within six months.

**Companies Bill Limits Voting Rights to Sectoral Cap**

The Government is set to place restrictions on foreign investors seeking voting rights on preference shareholdings in lieu of dividend in case of companies where sectoral caps for foreign equity participation apply.

**Companies Amendment Bill, 2003**

The provision has been introduced to ensure that the preference share route is not used by foreigners to gain control of a corporate entity. The existing provisions of the **Companies Act, 1956** allow holders of cumulative preference shares to seek voting rights on all resolutions placed before the board of a company if they have not been paid dividend for two years. Similarly, the holders of non-cumulative preference shares are entitled to seek voting rights if the dividend remains unpaid for three years.

**Companies are not to be made Trojan Horses-Lifting of Corporate Veil**

Foreign investors in preference shares cannot vote if the Sectoral cap is topped. In all other cases differential voting will be allowed. Bill to let Government change rules to keep pace with FDI policy. Once the new provisions come into force, foreign investors in preference shares of Indian companies would be entitled to voting rights on par with their holding only if the voting rights so acquired are within the Sectoral cap level. In all other cases, the holders would be entitled to differential voting rights. More importantly, if the foreign equity participation is at the maximum permissible level in a Company the preference shareholder may not be allowed any voting rights. The amendment Bill will have provisions enabling the Government to place restrictions and make changes in accordance with changing

FDI policy. The issue of restricting voting rights on preference shares if it leads to breach of Sectoral cap has been under consideration for almost two years now, ever since foreign investors in BPL Telecom sought voting rights on their preference shares.

**2006 Amendment Statutory Provisions**

In the statement of Objects and Reasons to the **Companies (Amendment) Act, 2006:**

> "In the context of the rapid developments witnessed in technology, the Ministry of Company Affair decided to enable the operations carried out by the Ministry and its field offices to be performed more efficiently and effectively through the use of contemporary information Technology and computers. It was felt that the earlier efforts at computerization had not yielded the desired efficiency in operation of the system and operating system that took into account contemporary technology was necessary. Therefore, it was decided to implement a comprehensive e-Governance system and programme to achieve the above objective."
>
> "The Ministry of Company Affairs on the recommendations of Department of Information Technology is implementing an e-Governance initiative through the project named as "**MCA-21**". This project will provide the public, corporate entities and others as easy and secure online access to the corporate information, including filing of documents and public access to the information required to be in public domain under the statute, at any time and from anywhere. This would also result in efficiency in the statutory provision of corporate processes and efficient professional services under the Companies Act, 1956."
>
> "The filing and registration of documents is a statutory requirement under the Act. At present the Act lays down the procedure for filing various documents in physical form and processes associated therewith. While the broad enabling framework for such an initiative is available under the Information Technology Act, 2000 read with the Companies Act, 1956, enabling provisions would still be required to support certain online electronic processes

which have since become available due to technology advancement for various detailed procedural requirements under the Companies Act, 1956."

"It is therefore, proposed to insert new sections 610B, 610C, 610D and 610E in the Companies Act, 1956 so as to make provision for electronic filing systems and for payment of fee through electronic form under the said Act which are essential for the successful implementation of the **MCA-21 Project.** After the proposed amendments to the Companies Act, 1956 have been enacted, the documents in electronic form duly authenticated with digital signatures shall be accepted under the provisions of that Act. The proposed electronic system also provides for multiple modes of payment of statutory fees."

"The provisions of the Companies Act, 1956 allow an individual to be a director of upto fifteen companies and such companies can be located in the jurisdiction in any of the Registrar of Companies. There is a need for the individual identity of person(s) intending to be directors of companies to be established. This would also facilitate effective legal action against the directors of such companies under the law, keeping in view of the possibility of fraud by companies and the phenomenon of companies that raise funds from the public and vanish thereafter. It is therefore proposed to insert new sections 266A, 266B, 266C, 266D, 266E, 266F and 266G in the Companies Act, 1956 so as to *inter alia,* provide for allotment of a unique Director Identification Number to any individual, intending to be appointed as director in a company or to any existing director of a company, for the purpose of his identification as such, through electronic or other form and to provide for penalty for any violation in this regard."

**Amendments of Section 253**

The following proviso shall be inserted:

"Provided that no company shall appoint or re-appoint any individual as director of the company unless he has been allotted a Director Identification Number under section 266B."

**Insertion of new sections 266A, 266B, 266C, 266D, 266E, 266F, and 266G**

After section 266 of the Act, the following sections shall be inserted, namely:

"Director Identification Number" for the purpose of identification of the Director—

**266A.** Application for allotment of Director Identification Number in such form and manner (including electronic form).

**266B.** Allotment of Director Identification Number to be complied with by the Central Government within one month of receipt of the application.

**266C.** Prohibition to obtain more than one Director Identification Number.

**266D.** Obligation of the director to intimate Director Identification Number to the concerned company or companies within one month.

**266E.** Obligation of company to inform Director Identification Number to Registrar within one week.

**266F.** Obligation to indicate Director Identification Number.

**266G.** Penalty for contravention of provisions of section 266A or section 266C or section 266D or section 266E is punishable with a fine which may extent to five thousand rupees and where the contravention is a continuing one, with a further fine which may extend to five hundred rupees for every day during the contravention continues.

**Insertion of the new sections 610B, 610C, 610D, 610E**

**610B.** Provisions relating to the filing of applications, documents, inspection, etc., through electronic form.

**610C.** Power to modify Act in relation to electronic records (including the manner and form in which electronic records shall be filed).

**610D.** Providing of value added services through electronic form.

**610E.** Application of provisions of Act 21 of 2000—All the provisions of the Information Technology Act, 2000 relating to the electronic records (including the manner and format in which the electronic records shall be filed), in so far as they are not inconsistent with this Act, shall apply, or in relation, to the records in the electronic form under section 610B.

**Environment Friendly—Paperless Governance (operations)**

The **paperless office** is now considered to be a philosophy to work with minimal paper and convert all forms of documentation to a digital form. The ideal is driven by a number of motivators including productivity gains, costs savings, space saving, the need to share information and reduced environmental impact.

One key aspect of the paperless office philosophy is the conversion of paper documents, photos, engineering plans, microfiche and all the other paper-based systems to digital documents. The technologies that may be used include—

- scanners;
- high speed scanners—used for scanning very large volumes of paper;
- book copiers—that take photos of large books and manuscripts;
- wide format scanners—for scanning engineering drawings;
- photo scanners;
- negative scanners;
- microfiche scanner—used to convert microfiche to digital documents;
- digitization of postal mail—online access of scanned contents; and
- Fax to PDF conversion.

Each of the technologies uses software that converts the raster formats into other forms depending on need. Generally, they involve some form of image compression technology that produces smaller raster images or the use of Optical character recognition, or OCR, to convert the document to text. A combination of OCR and raster is used to enable search ability while maintaining the original form of the document.

## COPYRIGHT DIMENSION

An issue faced by those wishing to take the paperless philosophy to the limit has been copyright laws. These laws restrict the transfer of documents protected by copyright from one medium to another, such as converting books to electronic format.

An important step in the paper-to-digital conversion is the need to label and catalog the scanned documents. Such labeling allows the scanned documents to be searched. Some technologies have been developed to do this, but generally involves either human cataloging or automated indexing on the OCR document. However, scanners and software continue to improve, with small, portable scanners that are able to scan doubled-sided A4 documents at around 30-35 ppm to a raster format.

**Issue in Keeping Documents Digital**

**Business procedures and/or government regulations:** These often slow the adoption of exclusively electronic documents.

**The target readers' ability to receive and read the digital format:** The longevity of digital documents. Will they still be accessible to computer systems of the future?

**Comparison of paperless vs. traditional office philosophy:** A traditional office consisted of paper-based filing systems, which may have included filing cabinets, folders, shelves, compactuses, microfiche systems, and drawing cabinets, all of which take up considerable space, requiring maintenance and equipment. Meanwhile, a paperless office could simply consist of a desk, chair, computer (with a modest amount of local or network storage), scanner and printer, and the user could use and store all the information in digital form, including speech recognition and speech synthesis.

## CONCLUSION

Corporate governance is becoming complex with the advancing technologies and globalization. Incidentally all the various departments of the company are getting affected with any delay in the decisions and their communications. Even the interoffice memos and controlling the field staff which forms an integrated part of the governance is the issues which have to be tackled on "real time basis". With the advancements in the technology the internet and VPN (Virtual Private Networks, using the internet as the backbone) are the savior technologies which if not used can lead to not only heavy losses but also make the corporate structure crumble without any noise leading to evaporation of billions of dollars as capital vanish in the air. Recent episodes of Merrill Lynch and Lehman Brothers are good example of bad governance.

# Index